GW00566668

Saints and Rebels

Biography is didactic. Through biography a single individual's experiences with luck, challenge, failure, and accomplishment are thrust before us. Since we cannot escape our fate, we are keenly interested in the way others have faced their worlds, be they hostile or sympathetic, because the experiences and human responses that we read about and share with others give deeper meaning to our lives. In this sense biography shares common ground with poetry.

Martin Ridge
The Huntington Library

Saints and Rebels

Seven Nonconformists in Stuart England

Richard L. Greaves

 MERCER UNIVERSITY PRESS

ISBN 0-86554-136-1

Saints and Rebels
Copyright © 1985
Mercer University Press
All rights reserved
Printed in the United States of America

Library of Congress Cataloging in Publication Data
Greaves, Richard L.
    Saints and rebels.
    Includes bibliographical references and index.
    1. Dissenters, Religious—England—Biography.
2. England—Biography.   I. Title.
BX5206.G74   1985   285'.092'2 [B]   84-22799
ISBN 0-86554-136-1 (alk. paper)

Contents

To Richard B. Schlatter
and Leo F. Solt

List of Abbreviations ────────────────

Al. Cant.	*Alumni Cantabrigienses*, comp. J. Venn and J. A. Venn, 4 vols. (Cambridge, 1922-1927)
Al. Oxon.	*Alumni Oxonienses*, comp. J. Foster, 4 vols. (Oxford, 1891-1892)
Ath. Oxon.	*Athenae Oxonienses*, ed. P. Bliss, 4 vols. (London, 1813-1820)
BDBR	*Biographical Dictionary of British Radicals in the Seventeenth Century*, ed. Richard L. Greaves and Robert Zaller, 3 vols. (Brighton, 1982-1984)
BQ	*Baptist Quarterly*
Brown	Louise Fargo Brown, *The Political Activities of the Baptists and Fifth Monarchy Men in England During the Interregnum* (Washington DC, 1912)
Burton	*Diary of Thomas Burton, Esq.*, ed. John Towill Rutt, 4 vols. (London, 1828)
Calamy, *Cont.*	Edmund Calamy, *A Continuation of the Account of the Ministers, Lecturers, Masters and Fellows of Colleges, and Schoolmasters*, 2 vols. (London, 1727)
Calamy, *Life*	Edmund Calamy, *An Historical Account of My Own Life*, 2 vols. (2nd ed., London, 1830)
Calamy, *Non. Mem.*	Edmund Calamy, *The Nonconformist's Memorial*, rev. Samuel Palmer, 3 vols. (2nd. ed., London, 1802-1803)
Calamy Revised	*Calamy Revised*, ed. A. G. Matthews (Oxford, 1934)

Capp, FMM   B. S. Capp, *The Fifth Monarchy Men: A Study in Seventeenth-Century English Millenarianism* (London, 1972)

CJ   *Journals of the House of Commons* 1547-1714, 17 vols. (London, 1742ff.)

Clarke Papers   *The Clarke Papers*, ed. C. H. Firth, 4 vols. (Camden Society, n.s., 49, 54, 61-62; London, 1891, 1894, 1899, 1901)

CMHS   *Collections of the Massachusetts Historical Society*

Corr. of Owen   *The Correspondence of John Owen (1616-1683)*, ed. Peter Toon (Cambridge, 1970)

Cromwell, WS   *The Writings and Speeches of Oliver Cromwell*, ed. Wilbur Cortez Abbott, 4 vols. (Cambridge MA, 1937-1947)

Crosby   Thomas Crosby, *The History of the English Baptists, from the Reformation to the Beginning of the Reign of King George I*, 4 vols. (London, 1738-1740)

CSPD   *Calendar of State Papers, Domestic Series*

DNB   *Dictionary of National Biography*, ed. L. Stephen and S. Lee, 63 vols. (London, 1885-1900)

EHR   *English Historical Review*

Fasti Oxon.   *Fasti Oxonienses, ad cal. Athenae Oxonienses*, ed. P. Bliss (London, 1813-1820)

Firth & Davies   Charles H. Firth and Godfrey Davies, *The Regimental History of Cromwell's Army*, 2 vols. (Oxford, 1940)

Firth & Rait   Charles H. Firth and R. S. Rait, eds., *Acts and Ordinances of the Interregnum* 1642-1660, 3 vols. (London, 1911)

Gangraena   Thomas Edwards, *Gangraena* (2nd ed., London, 1646)

HMC   *Historical Manuscripts Commission, Reports*

LJ   *Journals of the House of Lords* 1578-1714, vols. 2-19 (London, 1767ff.)

Nickolls, OLPS   J. Nickolls, ed., *Original Letters and Papers of State Addressed to Oliver Cromwell* (London, 1743)

PRO   Public Record Office, London

RCC   *Records of the Churches of Christ, Gathered at Fenstanton, Warboys, and Hexham. 1644-1720*, ed. Edward Bean Underhill (Hanserd Knollys Society, London, 1854)

Rel. Bax.   Richard Baxter, *Reliquiae Baxterianae*, ed. Matthew Sylvester (London, 1696)

Seaver   Paul Seaver, *The Puritan Lectureships: The Politics of Religious Dissent* 1560-1662 (Stanford, 1970)

Shaw   William A. Shaw, *A History of the English Church During the Civil Wars and Under the Commonwealth*, 2 vols. (London, 1900)

TBHS   *Transactions of the Baptist Historical Society*

TCHS   *Transactions of the Congregational Historical Society*

Thurloe, *SP*   John Thurloe, *A Collection of State Papers of John Thurloe, Esq.*, ed. T. Birch, 7 vols. (London, 1742)

Tolmie   Murray Tolmie, *The Triumph of the Saints: The Separate Churches of London 1616-1649* (Cambridge, 1977)

Whitelocke   Bulstrode Whitelocke, *Memorials of the English Affairs*, 4 vols. (Oxford, 1853)

Wilson, *HADC*   Walter Wilson, *The History and Antiquities of Dissenting Churches and Meeting Houses, in London, Westminster, and Southwark*, 4 vols. (London, 1808-1814)

Preface
and Acknowledgments_____

   In the course of writing entries for the *Biographical Dictionary of British Radicals in the Seventeenth Century,* which I coedited with Robert Zaller, it became apparent that there was far more important material on the lives of some figures, hitherto largely unstudied, than could be included in their entries. These persons often played important roles in shaping the events and institutions of Stuart England, so that fuller accounts of their lives were obviously needed for a better understanding of the period. The seven men whose careers are explored in this study illustrate the diversity of the Nonconformist tradition in the seventeenth century and provide a salutary warning against the dangers of oversimplifying its characteristics. These seven lives alone display striking differences in political ideals, theological tenets, and ecclesiastical principles. This study is offered not only because these men are intrinsically important but also because their lives manifest the rich and varied tapestry of Stuart Nonconformity.
   It is a pleasure to record my gratitude to a number of fellow historians for their encouragement and assistance. The decision to pro-

ceed with this study was made after a stimulating discussion in Los Angeles with J. Sears McGee. Geoffrey Nuttall, who taught me so much about this period, drew on his unrivaled knowledge of Stuart Nonconformity to provide me with numerous leads and suggestions. Robert Zaller generously undertook a meticulous and invaluable critique of the entire manuscript. The two distinguished historians to whom this book is dedicated, Richard Schlatter and Leo Solt, have graciously provided inspiration and assistance for nearly two decades. It is also a pleasure to thank Leland Carlson, G. R. Elton, Christopher Hill, Martin Havran, Paul Seaver, Dewey Wallace, Ellen More, B. R. White, and T. L. Underwood. For their published work, I am especially indebted to B. S. Capp and Murray Tolmie.

The staffs of the following libraries were very helpful: the Public Record Office, Chancery Lane; the British Library; Dr. Williams's Library; the Henry E. Huntington Library; the William Andrews Clark Memorial Library; and the Strozier Library of Florida State University. I am also indebted to Mr. Frank D. Gatton of the North Carolina Division of Archives and History, and to the staff of the South Carolina Department of Archives and History.

The final stages of the research for this book were assisted by a fellowship from the American Council of Learned Societies under a program funded by the National Endowment for the Humanities.

To my wife, Judith, to my daughters, Sherry Elizabeth and Stephany Lynn, and to my parents I express my gratitude for their continuing support and unflagging enthusiasm.

Introduction _____

The world of Nonconformity in Stuart England is one of rich diversity and even conflicting ideology. Setting aside the more extreme sects, such as the Diggers, the Seekers, and the Ranters, there are still substantial and divisive differences among the more traditional Nonconformists, such as the Presbyterians, the Congregationalists, and the Baptists. Indeed, there is often more common ground between "Anglicans" (or Conformists) of the anti-Laudian variety and Presbyterians than there is between Presbyterians and General Baptists. [1]

---

[1]"Anglican" (or "Conformist") is an anachronistic term for the Elizabethan and early Stuart periods, but there is no substitute free of serious drawbacks. Even the British historian Patrick Collinson is forced to concede that "Puritanism often embraced a nonconformist resistance to some Anglican ceremonies, or even a more general rejection of Anglican worship and polity," and that "there would be little point in denying that it was as a protest against the policy of the Elizabethan Church that it acquired identity in the first place." Collinson, "Towards a Broader Understanding of the Early Dissenting Tradition," *The Dissenting Tradition*, ed. C. Robert Cole and Michael E. Moody (Athens OH, 1975) 10. The differences between "Anglican" and Puritan within the established church are best understood in

But apart from the decades of upheaval between 1640 and 1660, Nonconformists of nearly all stripes shared a common goal—the dream of a church conformable to the precepts of Scripture. In their own diverse ways, before the 1640s they envisioned substantive religious reforms that would radically alter the face of the church in England, while after 1662 they found themselves systematically excluded from the religious establishment. Indeed, it can be argued that the Restoration Church of England was more exclusive in many respects than its pre-Laudian counterpart. It was Laud's attempt to remake the established church in a medieval, sacerdotal, highly liturgical form that seriously frustrated the ongoing efforts of Calvinist reformers within the early Stuart Church of England and led to the religious upheavals that were so much a part of the tumultuous 1640s. Laudian reaction unwittingly fostered the explosion of religious radicalism.

In recent decades competent scholars have demonstrated intensive interest in the religious movements of this period. Although the phrase "Puritan Revolution" has been cast aside as a relic of Whiggery by those who find neither Puritan motivation nor a revolution in the events of the 1640s, no one has assayed to deny the importance of substantial religious change in the mid-century years. Among the best works of recent scholarship on Nonconformists are J. Sears McGee's provocative analysis of the differing emphases of Anglican and Puritan with respect to the two "tables" of the Ten Commandments, Christopher Hill's exciting exploration of the world of unconventional beliefs propagated especially in the 1640s and 1650s, and Murray Tolmie's corrective to Hill's studies, in which he argues for the fundamental continuity of English Nonconformity throughout the century.[2] Yet, as Tolmie recognized, there has been such a tendency for historians to concentrate on the religious history of the period 1640-1660 that its events acquire an undue and inappropriate uniqueness.

the context of a continuum, not absolutes or fixed parties. See Richard L. Greaves, *Society and Religion in Elizabethan England* (Minneapolis, 1981) 3-14. A healthy corrective to the more extreme revisionism is found in Dewey D. Wallace, Jr., *Puritans and Predestination: Grace in English Protestant Theology, 1525-1695* (Chapel Hill NC, 1982).

[2] J. Sears McGee, *The Godly Man in Stuart England: Anglicans, Puritans, and the Two Tables, 1620-1670* (New Haven, 1976); Christopher Hill, *The World Turned Upside Down: Radical Ideas During the English Revolution* (New York, 1973); Tolmie.

Perhaps with respect to the most extreme sects there may be some justification for this sense of uniqueness, but even here it is more likely that the expression of extremist views by such groups as the Ranters and Diggers was different in form but not substantially in content from what others had been espousing in earlier decades. The Family of Love, with its hodgepodge of radical ideas, was deeply rooted in Elizabethan England, and many of the revolutionary views of the mid-century sectaries were advanced much earlier by Elizabethan Separatists.[3] The sociopolitical atmosphere of the 1640s and 1650s made possible the more open and systematic expression of extreme notions as well as the more effective organization of their adherents into religious sects.

Christopher Hill has argued that later Nonconformity differs as much from Puritanism as vinegar does from wine.[4] If one means by later Nonconformity its Victorian manifestations, Hill is probably on the mark, but later Stuart dissent was at root much the same as that found in the early decades of the century. The ideas and experiences at the core of early Stuart Nonconformity continued to be its driving force and raison d'être in the post-1660 period. Tolmie's analysis of the Separatist movement from 1616 to 1649 has laid a partial foundation for this thesis. The present book intends to explore the validity of this thesis from another perspective, that of individual biographical studies. There is perhaps no better illustration of the continuity of dissent than the careful examination of the lives of individual Nonconformists.

What lives, however, should be selected for such a study? In the course of coediting a biographical dictionary of more than a thousand radicals in the Stuart era, many of whom were part of the Nonconformist tradition, it became obvious that the available options were legion.[5] Given the choice of seven names, no historian would likely

---

[3]Richard L. Greaves, "Radical Social Demands in Elizabethan England: The Case of the Separatists," *Red River Valley Historical Journal of World History* 4 (Winter 1979): 106-21; Greaves, *Society and Religion in Elizabethan England*, passim.

[4]Christopher Hill, *Puritanism and Revolution: Studies in Interpretation of the English Revolution of the 17th Century* (New York, 1964 edition; 1st pub., 1958) vii.

[5]*BDBR*.

compile a list identical to that of any other historian. My own selection was deliberately made so as to include persons who would represent the various major groups ranging from early Stuart Puritanism to the Presbyterians and Independents, and ultimately to the various types of Baptists (Particular, General, open-communion, and Seventh-Day). The group also includes two individuals who were Fifth Monarchists and two who were Antinomians.

Each of the seven Nonconformists was also selected because he illustrates some facet of the rich diversity of the dissenting tradition. Edmund Calamy represents the more moderate Nonconformists who were willing to explore the possibility of comprehension within a broad Church of England while working closely with Independent colleagues. Calamy is also typical of those Nonconformists who sought major reform in the church but still opposed the more radical programs of the sectaries, including the Baptists. In Richard Culmer one finds the manifestation of a fanatical religious zeal that was instrumental in fracturing the Nonconformist cause in Kent. George Griffith provides the fascinating study of an Independent whose leadership and longevity gave the Congregationalist movement a sense of continuity from the heady days of the 1650s to the period of settlement following the 1689 Act of Toleration. John Simpson and Henry Danvers were both fire-breathing Fifth Monarchists, but the former tempered his views after experiencing a healthy dose of Cromwellian incarceration. In contrast, Danvers went on to become one of the leaders of the radical underground throughout the period from the Restoration to the Glorious Revolution. Paul Hobson too was part of that underground, but unlike Danvers his social origins were humble and his fate in the 1660s much bleaker. Although he ranged over much of England from the southwest to the northeast, he was particularly active in Newcastle. In Francis Bampfield one discovers a combination of religious zeal, sectarian ideals, pronounced biblicism, and humanistic reform, as well as the story of a person whose pilgrimage took him from his early days as an Anglican and a Royalist to the culmination of his career as an imprisoned Seventh-Day Baptist.

The diversity of Nonconformity in these seven men is paralleled by their varied backgrounds and experiences. Danvers and Bampfield came from gentry families, but whereas the former inherited the ancestral estate in Leicestershire, Bampfield was the third son of a

Devon family and was therefore destined by his parents for the ministry. The families of Culmer from Kent and Griffith from Montgomeryshire may have been from the prosperous yeomanry. The Griffiths were friendly with Sir Robert Harley's family in Herefordshire, and a Richard Culmer, undoubtedly a relative of our Culmer, hoped to administer two manorial courts for Lord Cobham. In contrast, Calamy's father was an immigrant from Guernsey who became a London tradesman, whereas Hobson's father may have been a tailor in Buckinghamshire. Simpson was raised in London of unknown social origins. Three of the men—Danvers, Hobson, and Simpson—served in the parliamentary army, whereas Bampfield provided support to the Royalists in the Civil War.

Of these seven Nonconformists, only Hobson did not definitely attend a university. Danvers's situation is uncertain, but he may have spent some time at Trinity College, Oxford. The others were all university graduates. Two were Oxford men, graduating in the same year but from different colleges: Simpson was at Exeter (B.A. 1635, M.A. 1638), while Bampfield was from Wadham (B.A. 1635, M.A. 1638). Two others were Cambridge men and virtually contemporaries as students: Calamy studied at Pembroke Hall (B.A. 1620, M.A. 1623), and Culmer at Magdalene (B.A. 1618, M.A. 1621). Griffith was unique in taking degrees at both universities: B.A. (1642), Magdalen College, Oxford, and M.A. (1645), Emmanuel College, Cambridge. In age, the seven represent two generations, the oldest of which comprised Culmer (b.c. 1597) and Calamy (b. 1600), politically and ecclesiastically the more moderate men among the seven. Bampfield and Simpson were both born about 1615, Danvers and Griffith about 1619. Hobson was probably born in the late 1610s as well. Calamy, Culmer, Hobson, and Simpson all died in the mid-1660s, but Bampfield and Danvers lived to the mid-1680s, and Griffith until 1702.

At one time or another all seven found themselves in some difficulty with government authorities. Culmer and Calamy were victims of Laudian repression. Bampfield refused the Engagement, Hobson was harassed by Sir Samuel Luke and ultimately opposed the Protectorate, while Simpson was imprisoned by Cromwell for his radical beliefs. In contrast, Griffith and Danvers enjoyed some favor with the government in the 1650s. At the Restoration Bampfield, Calamy, Culmer, and Griffith were ejected from their livings, and had Simpson lived a bit longer, he would have been as well. Danvers and Hobson had no positions from which to be ejected. At one time or another all but Griffith were imprisoned after 1660, but even he was watched by government spies and fined for illegal preaching. Despite the similarities in the treatment they received, their attitudes toward the Restoration monarchy varied sharply. Calamy nearly accepted a bishopric, and Bampfield, Culmer, and Griffith, while repudiating the Church of England, offered no opposition to the secular authorities. Simpson's attitude is ambivalent, but Danvers and Hobson were active in the political underground.

In the course of their careers the paths of these men occasionally crossed. Calamy and Culmer enjoyed the patronage of the Earl of Warwick, and Culmer received the support of the Westminster Assembly—of which Calamy was a leading member—for his appointment to the living of Minster in Thanet, Kent. Culmer also had contact on at least one occasion with Sir Robert Harley, a family friend of the Griffiths. Calamy and Griffith must have known each other well. Both served on a committee in 1657 to resolve a dispute between the Scottish Resolutioners and Remonstrants; both were appointed in 1659 to a commission for the approval of ministers, and were members of an informal group established in the summer of 1659 to combat the spread of Quakerism. Both men preached to Parliament on 27 January 1658 and, with Hobson, were among those appointed to help establish a new university at Durham. They were also among those who recommended Henry Whitfield's 1652 book on missionary work among the Indians in New England.

Some of the contacts between these Nonconformists were less than pleasant. In 1644 Hobson was denounced for his views by Sion College, of which Calamy was a member, and the following year he actively supported a debate—ultimately cancelled by the Lord Mayor of London—between Calamy and several Baptists. Calamy openly objected to the Antinomian tenets of Simpson, and once actually lectured him on the errors of his ways. Simpson also had some difficulty with Danvers, who supported the militants in Simpson's congregation after Simpson retracted his Fifth Monarchist principles. Simpson, incidentally, may have met Hobson on a trip to the Newcastle area in 1653. Only Bampfield apparently had no contacts with any of the other six Nonconformists in this study, though his sabbatarian tenets were attacked by John Bunyan, a friend of Griffith and Simpson.

Each of these Nonconformists is significant enough in his own right to justify much fuller treatment than can be provided in biographical dictionaries. The most famous Nonconformists such as Richard Baxter, John Milton, John Bunyan, and John Owen are the subject of full biographies, and deservedly so. Although the seven men in this study were all authors—though only Bampfield wrote a spiritual autobiography—there is simply insufficient material to write a full biography on any of the seven. Yet the prominence given to persons such as Baxter, Bunyan, and Owen tends to be somewhat out of proportion to the roles they exercised in Nonconformist history. More biographical studies are essential and indeed are necessary complements to the more sweeping studies of Nonconformist history.[6] This volume is intended as a contribution toward that end; others are clearly needed.

---

[6]Of these the best is easily Michael R. Watts, *The Dissenters* (Oxford, 1978). Because of the scope of his survey (1532-1791), little more than passing mention could be given to most Nonconformists. Danvers is mentioned four times, Calamy and Hobson three, Bampfield and Simpson once, and Culmer and Griffith not at all. Geoffrey F. Nuttall's indispensable study of the Independents in the 1640s and 1650s, to cite but one other work, ignores Griffith but mentions Calamy once and Simpson on eight occasions. *Visible Saints: The Congregational Way 1640-1660* (Oxford, 1957).

chapter 1

"A Great Evangelist
of the New Way":
Edmund Calamy
and the Presbyterian Cause

The career of Edmund Calamy is representative of those adherents
of the Puritan tradition who strove to undertake major reforms in the
Church of England, but who simultaneously resisted the more radical
courses espoused by Independents and sectaries. With Stephen Marshall, Calamy became one of the foremost advocates of Puritan reform
during the tempestuous 1640s, but he was opposed to such radical acts
as Pride's Purge, the execution of Charles I, the forcible dissolution
of the Rump, the extension of de facto religious toleration in the
1650s, and the institution of the Protectorate. Throughout the 1640s
and 1650s Calamy worked tirelessly in the Presbyterian movement,
distinguishing himself as one of London's most prominent religious
leaders. A popular preacher who spoke before Parliament a number of
times, he published many of his sermons. When Richard Cromwell's
government collapsed, Calamy worked with General Monck to effect
a return to the monarchy, for which he was rewarded with a short-
lived royal chaplaincy. Like Richard Baxter, his goal was now to
achieve the reconciliation of Anglicans and Presbyterians in a comprehensive Church of England, but his efforts were nullified by the

recalcitrance of uncompromising Presbyterians and Anglicans alike. The "Reconcilers," as Baxter called them, failed. Unlike his colleague Edward Reynolds, Calamy refused the offer of a bishopric, preferring instead to devote his final years to strengthening the Nonconformist community in London.

The only son of tradesman and London citizen George Calamy, an immigrant from Guernsey who was possibly of Huguenot origin, Edmund Calamy was baptized on 24 February 1600 in the church of St. Thomas Apostle, London. He enrolled at the Merchant Taylors' School in London in 1613, and three years later, on 4 July 1616, was admitted as a scholar to Pembroke Hall, Cambridge. After graduating B.A. in 1620 and M.A. in 1623, he was appointed a fellow (*tanquam socius* was the official designation) of Pembroke in 1625. There he was known for his espousal of Calvinist tenets. Ordained to priestly orders at Ely on 5 March 1626, he became a chaplain to Nicholas Felton, Bishop of Ely, who made him Vicar of St. Mary, Swaffham Prior, Cambridgeshire, on 6 March 1626. During this period Calamy lived in Felton's house and "was ever after a thankful imitator of the piety, charity, and diligence of that good bishop, whom he used often to mention with honour." Felton, in fact, directed Calamy's early studies. Working sixteen hours a day, Calamy read all the controversies of Bellarmine as well as other Scholastics, particularly Thomas Aquinas, "in whom he was most exactly versed." He read the works of Augustine no less than five times, and studied the Bible and scriptural commentaries daily. Felton's household, where there were other Puritans besides Calamy, was in effect a seminary.[1]

After Felton died in October 1626, Calamy resigned the living at Swaffham in 1627 and took up duties as lecturer at Bury St. Edmunds, Suffolk, where he preached three times a week. At Bury he worked with Jeremiah Burroughs, later to become one of the leading Independents, until the latter's departure in 1631. On 18 June 1629 Calamy was licensed to preach in the diocese of Norwich, and in 1632 Cambridge University bestowed the B.D. degree on him. He apparently complied with the regulations of his bishop, Matthew Wren of Norwich, concerning clerical dress, but he preached against innovations

---

[1] Calamy, *Non. Mem.*, 1:76; *Calamy Revised*, s.v.; *Al. Cant.*, s.v. For Felton see *DNB*, s.v.

in religion, balked at having to read the required services in the Book of Common Prayer, and refused to bow to the altar. He was later accused by Laurence Womock, an Anglican apologist, of doing all these things and even of trying "to satisfie and to reduce such as sc[r]upled at these *Ceremonies* . . ." in order to procure their obedience.[2]

As Calamy's Puritan convictions intensified, he bridled at Bishop Wren's visitation articles (1636) and the imposition of the Book of Sports. In part the articles required raising the chancel, placing the communion table altarwise at the east end of the chancel and railing it, positioning the pews so worshipers could kneel facing the altar, kneeling at the communion rail to receive the sacrament of the Lord's supper, and curtailing prayer before sermons. Cited before Wren's commissioners with two other ministers, Mr. Jewel and Mr. White, in 1636, he was forced to "read Prayers *solemniter etc. ad altare* though with previouse reluctacion in private before us. The Chancells [in their churches] . . . are very long and the voyse very far distant which was their plea to us and will be after to your Lordship," that is, Bishop Wren. Although Calamy was offered £400 per annum to remain at Bury St. Edmunds, his disaffection with Wren was so strong that in November 1637, following the death of William Fenner, he accepted an offer of the rectory of Rochford, Kent, from one of the most prominent Puritan peers, Robert Rich, Earl of Warwick. This was done "in the hope, that under the wings of such a patron, and of a quiet bishop, he should have more repose. . . ." In Rochford, however, he contracted a quartan ague from which he suffered for years. The illness so affected his nervous system, particularly causing dizziness, that he was never again able to climb into a pulpit, but preached instead from a reading desk. Undoubtedly for reasons of health, he left Rochford to

---

[2]Calamy, *Non. Mem.*, 1:76; Edmund Calamy, *A Just and Necessary Apology Against an Unjust Invective* (London, 1646) 5; [Laurence Womock], *Sober Sadnes: Or Historicall Observations* ([Oxford], 1643) 32; *Fasti Oxon.*, 1:511-12. For Burroughs see *BDBR, s.v.* According to family tradition, Calamy's father was a Huguenot exile from the Normandy coast. Based on the claim that an old town and castle in Normandy bore the family name, the Heralds granted Calamy a coat of arms. Calamy, *Life*, 52-53. Referring to this tradition, E. C. Ratcliff has erroneously asserted that "Calamy, of Huguenot origin, was by mental inheritance perhaps too French willingly to accept compromise." "The Savoy Conference and the Revision of the Book of Common Prayer," in *From Uniformity to Unity 1662-1962* (London, 1962) 106.

succeed John Stoughton as minister and lecturer at St. Mary Aldermanbury, London, in 1639. Under the date of 27 May the vestry book
has this entry:

> The late election of our minister, Mr. Edward [sic] Calamy, was confirmed
> by a general consent, and ordered that he shall have for his maintenance
> £160 per ann. . . . And it was propounded whether every man would give
> the same rate which they formerly gave to Dr. Stoughton, and it was con-
> sented to without contradiction. And Mr. Calamy to come to us at Midsum-
> mer next, or presently after.

He was actually admitted to the living on 26 October. Three months
earlier he was incorporated B. D. at Oxford.[3]

Within a year of Calamy's arrival in London, Charles I summoned
the ill-fated Short Parliament to deal with the Scottish crisis. Under
Laudian direction the Convocation, which also met, approved seventeen bitterly controversial canons, including requirements that altars be at the east end of the church and railed off, and that worshipers
bow toward the altar upon entering and leaving the church. The Convocation also imposed the notorious "etcetera oath" on the clergy and
other professionals, insisting that they accept the polity of the church
as then established. Determined to resist, Calamy joined other Puritan leaders, including Cornelius Burgess and John Goodwin, at the
London home of John Downham on 6 August 1640 to formulate a petition against the canons and the "etcetera oath." The prominent role
that Calamy now assumed in the reforming movement was subsequently attested to by the conservative critic, Anthony Wood: "Upon
the approach of the troublesome times in 1640," Calamy, Burgess,

---

[3]Bodleian Library, Tanner MSS 68, fols. 29, 33-36, 45; John Browne, *History of
Congregationalism and Memorials of the Churches in Norfolk and Suffolk* (London, 1877) 85-
91, 157; Calamy, *A Just and Necessary Apology*, 5, 7; J. Granger, *A Biographical History
of England*, 6 vols. (5th ed., London, 1824) 2:364; Calamy, *Non. Mem.*, 1:76
(quoted); Seaver, 264; Vestry Minutes of St. Mary Aldermanbury, cited in T. W.
Davids, *Annals of Evangelical Nonconformity in the County of Essex, from the Time of Wycliffe
to the Restoration* (London, 1863) 534; *DNB, s.v.* Calamy subsequently served as a
trustee of the Earl of Warwick; among his co-trustees were the Presbyterian ministers Simeon Ashe and Anthony Tuckney. Acting in this capacity, they presented
the living of Moreton, Essex, to Calamy's son Edmund on 20 April 1659. *Calamy
Revised, s.v.* "Edmund Calamy [II]."

Stephen Marshall, Calybute Downing, and others "did first whisper in their conventicles, then openly preach that for the cause of religion it was lawful for the subjects to take up arms against their lawful sovereign." Wood, in fact, regarded the sermons of Calamy and his colleagues as a major factor in encouraging many Londoners to support the parliamentary cause at the outbreak of the Civil War.[4]

Although Wood has probably overstated the role of Calamy and his fellow Puritan clerics in contributing to the outbreak of hostilities in 1642, there can be no doubt about Calamy's central involvement in the movement for ecclesiastical reform. When, in December 1640 and January 1641, advocates of a root and branch reform of church government mustered forces to advance their cause, moderate Puritans countered by gathering petitions from around the country to urge a less severe course. When these petitions arrived in London in January, a meeting of over eighty reform-minded clergy, at which Calamy must have been present, formulated one general petition to which was appended a remonstrance detailing grievances. The resulting "Ministers' Petition and Remonstrance," with nearly a thousand signatures of the individual petitioners appended, was presented to the House of Commons on 23 January by Sir Robert Harley, who was accompanied by Calamy, Marshall, and several other clerics. On 1 February an attempt was made to discredit this effort by Lord George Digby on the grounds that some of the ministers whose signatures were affixed to the remonstrance now disavowed it. The following day seven ministers who supported the petition, including Calamy and Marshall, testified that the signatures had been affixed to the local petitions on which the remonstrance was based, and hence there was no impropriety. The fact that Calamy was one of the seven who testified in favor of the petition and remonstrance suggests that he was part of the group that initiated the moderate plan. The remonstrance indicated a willingness to accept a modified episcopacy, recognizing that bishops are not divinely instituted and that they must not ordain or discipline by themselves. There were also complaints that dioceses were too large and that bishops imposed unlawful oaths.[5]

---

[4]Seaver, 264; *Ath. Oxon.*, 3:682.

[5]Shaw, 1:23-25; William Haller, *Liberty and Reformation in the Puritan Revolution* (New York, 1955) 17; CJ, 2:72.

At Calamy's house, as he personally acknowledged, a group of Puritan ministers met early in 1641 to compose a reply to Bishop Joseph Hall's apology for *jure divino* episcopacy, *An Humble Remonstrance*. The Puritan response was published in March 1641 as *An Answer to a Booke Entituled, An Hvmble Remonstrance*, under the nom de plume Smectymnuus, a compilation of the authors' initials: Stephen Marshall, Edmund Calamy, Thomas Young, Matthew Newcomen, and William Spurstowe. Quoting extensively from scripture and the church fathers, the authors contended for clerical parity, insisting that in the early church presbyters and bishops were identical. Calling for the reform of episcopacy, they asserted that the bishops "have invaded this right and power of Presbyters and people in Church censures," and that they have no rightful place in secular affairs. The assertion "no bishop, no king," they argued, falsely implies that civil power depends on spiritual authority. In effect, episcopacy had "yoked Monarchy" in England. Not stopping with polity, Calamy and his colleagues also called for a reform of the liturgy, claiming that it retained too many vestiges of the popish mass, and they condemned the oath *ex officio mero* as contrary to civil law. In Calamy's personal judgment, this hard-hitting tract "was the first deadly blow to *Episcopacy* in *England* of late years." Moreover, it helped inspire John Milton to write no less than five spirited pamphlets against episcopacy, beginning in May 1641 with *Of Reformation*.[6]

Calamy still hoped for reform by peaceful means. In March he was summoned with other divines to meet with a subcommittee of the House of Lords, which was concerned with "the *Accomodating* [of] *Ecclesiastical Matters*. . . ." The House itself had appointed Archbishop James Ussher, John Prideaux, Seth Ward, William Twisse, and John Hacket. Empowered to call more learned divines, the committee added Calamy, Marshall, Cornelius Burgess, Daniel Featley, Richard Holdsworth, and others. A letter summoning the divines from Bishop Williams explained that "their Lordships do intend to examine all *Innovations* in Doctrine or Discipline, introduced into the Church with-

---

[6]"Smectymnuus," *An Answer to a Booke Entituled, An Hvmble Remonstrance* (London, 1641) 4 (quoted), 12, 21, 26-28, 32, 41 (quoted), 43-47, 85; Calamy, *A Just and Necessary Apology*, 9; Christopher Hill, *Milton and the English Revolution* (New York, 1978) ch. 7.

out Law since the *Reformation.* . . . " During the deliberations in the Jerusalem Chamber some progress was made towards an accord, and plans for a modified episcopacy were submitted by Archbishop Ussher and Bishop Williams. A paper was also prepared that suggested changes in the Book of Common Prayer and condemned doctrinal innovations. But as the younger Edmund Calamy noted, "the whole Design was spoil'd by the bringing in to the House [of Commons] the Bill against Bishops. . . ."[7] It is unclear whether Calamy's grandson was referring to the bill to deprive bishops and other clerics of secular offices and employments—which passed the House on 1 May but was rejected by the Lords on 8 June—or, more likely, the radical bill to abolish episcopacy, introduced in the Commons on 27 May by Oliver St. John. Debate on the latter bill continued sporadically until 3 August, when John Pym and his political associates quietly let it drop.

As the momentum for ecclesiastical reform temporarily slowed, a group of Presbyterian and Independent clergy met in November 1641 at Calamy's house. His residence by now had become the counterpart of Pym's home, where leading proponents of political reform met. Laurence Echard, in fact, aptly referred to Calamy's home as "the general Receptacle for all Presbyterian Ministers. . . ." The purpose of the November gathering was to forge a common unity that might provide a basis for further changes in the church. The resulting agreement, signed by Calamy (for the Presbyterians) and Nye (for the Independents), stipulated "that (for advancing of the publike *Cause* of a happy Reformation) neither side should Preach, Print, or dispute, or otherwise act against the other's way; And this to continue 'til both sides, in a full meeting, did declare the contrary. . . ." Dr. Lamont is probably correct in suspecting that Calamy, Marshall, and Herbert Palmer were in collusion with the Scottish Presbyterians during this period.[8]

---

[7]Calamy, *Non. Mem.*, 1:77; Shaw, 1:65-74; William Laud, *The History of the Troubles and Tryal of . . . William Laud, Lord Arch-Bishop of Canterbury* (London, 1695) 174-75 (quoted); Edmund Calamy, *An Abridgment of Mr. Baxter's History of His Life and Times* (London, 1702) 186.

[8]Laurence Echard, *The History of England* (3rd ed., London, 1720) 837; John Vicars, *The Schismatick Sifted* (London, 1646) 15-16; William M. Lamont, *Godly Rule: Politics and Religion, 1603-60* (London, 1969) 79-80. Cf. Tai Liu, *Discord in Zion: The Puritan Divines and the Puritan Revolution 1640-1660* (The Hague, 1973) 9.

As "a great evangelist of the new way," in Wood's words, Calamy was well known to reform leaders in Parliament. According to his grandson, he was the first person to testify before a parliamentary committee that bishops were not an order distinct from presbyters. The House of Commons first invited Calamy to preach before them on 8 August 1641, but due to more pressing business there was no time for the sermon. He and Marshall, however, were asked by the Commons to preach at fast services in connection with the Irish crisis on 22 December. In keeping with the occasion, Calamy declaimed: "Arise oh Lord and scatter the Irish rebels! Arise oh Lord and confound Antichrist." Troubled as much by the dissension within England as by the Irish rebellion, he exhorted the Commons "to the consummation of those blessed good things which you have begun to do for the Church of God in *England*." Warning specifically against further delays in reforming the church, he proclaimed that only "Nationall" repentance would avert judgment on the country and lead instead to blessings. Specifically he called for the convening of a national synod to discuss ecclesiastical reform, for the purging of all superstitious ceremonies, and for the establishment of a preaching ministry to take the gospel message to the dark corners of the land. Citing one of his favorite authors, John Bradford, he insisted that "we must first go to the Grammar-schoole of Repentance, before we can be admitted to the University of Praedestination." For their sermons, Calamy and Marshall were thanked for the House by Sir Arthur Ingram and Sir Thomas Barrington. Each received a plate worth £20. Calamy's was a large almsdish inscribed with his arms and the statement, "This is the Gift of the House of Commons to Edmund Calamy, B.D., 1641." In response Calamy and Marshall sent word to the House "that they give us hearty thanks and will daily pray to the Almighty for the good and prosperous success of this house." Printed under the title *Englands Looking-Glasse, Presented in a Sermon* (1642), Calamy's work was sufficiently popular to run through five editions.[9]

---

[9]*Fasti Oxon.*, 1:511-12; Calamy, *A Just and Necessary Apology*, 9; John F. Wilson, *Pulpit in Parliament* (Princeton, 1969) 14, 55-56; Calamy, *Englands Looking-Glasse, Presented in a Sermon* (London, 1642) sig. A4ʳ (quoted), 10 (quoted), 16-18, 22-23, 29, 39, 47, 61 (quoted); *The Journal of Sir Simonds D'Ewes*, ed. Willson Havelock Coates

SAINTS AND REBELS / 17

The same day that Calamy preached before the Commons, Charles I made a serious political blunder by placing Colonel Lunsford in charge of the Tower of London. The next day city activists petitioned the Commons, protesting Lunsford's appointment, and on the 24th the Commons resolved that Lunsford was unfit for the post. In the meantime, another petition bearing some 30,000 names had been received in protest against the presence of bishops and Catholic peers in the House of Lords. Although Lunsford was dismissed on the 26th, there were riots on the 27th, 28th, and 29th. Even Westminster Abbey was invaded by a mob intent upon destroying the altar and organ. Blame for the breakdown of order was subsequently cast by a conservative critic on Burgess—"the ring-leader of all sedition"—and his cohorts Calamy, Marshall, Downing, Harding, William Bridge, and Andrew Perne. They allegedly framed and submitted the petitions, replete with the names of people who had never seen them and who knew nothing of their contents.[10] While such charges are obviously exaggerations, they reflect the prominent role accorded Calamy in the critical winter of 1641-1642.

When the Long Parliament instituted its program of regular monthly sermons early in 1642, Calamy and Marshall were invited to give the inaugural sermons on 23 February at St. Margaret's, Westminster. The service lasted from shortly before 9:00 A.M. to 4:00 P.M., with Calamy preaching in the morning and Marshall in the afternoon after a short break and the singing of a psalm. In his sermon Calamy offered thanks for peaceful relations with Scotland, the hope of church reform, and the abolition of monopolies, the Laudian canons, Star Chamber, High Commission, the oath *ex officio mero*, and the "etcetera oath." Yet he pressed the Commons not to let their reforming ardor cool or be fainthearted in God's cause. Further reforms, including the establishment of a preaching ministry, were necessary in the church, and popery had to be rooted out of Ireland and Arminianism from England. He was particularly happy about the institution of the

---

(New Haven, 1942) 308, 334; *The Private Journals of the Long Parliament: 3 January to 5 March 1642*, ed. Willson Havelock Coates, Anne Steele Young, and Vernon F. Snow (New Haven, 1982) 329 (quoted); *DNB, s.v.* On the afternoon of the 22nd, Marshall too called for the convening of a national synod. *Reformation and Desolation* (London, 1642) 53.

[10]Griffith Williams, *The Discovery of Mysteries* (n.p., 1643) 21.

monthly sermons, which he likened to the twelve gates of the new Jerusalem (Rev. 21). The following day William Strode moved that Calamy and Marshall receive the thanks of the House, which were conveyed to them by Strode and William Wheeler. The House also gave both men sole authority to publish their sermons in the ensuing two months. Calamy's was published under the title, *Gods Free Mercy to England* (1642) and Marshall's as *Meroz Cursed* (1642).[11]

In the following months the conflict between the king and his critics in Parliament largely revolved around the explosive issue of control of the militia and the broader question of trust. Religious issues likewise remained unresolved. Ultimately, of course, the conflict led to the outbreak of war. For this the king cast a large share of the blame on Calamy and other prominent Puritan clergymen, including Marshall, Hugh Peter, Henry Burton, and Thomas Case. Accused of treasonous conduct for undermining the loyalty of subjects to the king, they replied collectively in *An Answer to the Articles*, placing responsibility for the debacle squarely on the shoulders of the prelates. Not only had the bishops replaced the gospel with popery, ceremonial superstition, and canonical innovations, but they had deluded the king himself. The abortive attempt to arrest Pym and his colleagues in January was blamed on the twelve prelates impeached for treason on 30 December 1641. They were also accused, in their "hell-nourished malice," of formulating the articles of treason against Calamy and his friends, and of withdrawing the people's obedience from their sovereign.[12] The charges and countercharges aptly reflect the heated atmosphere that contributed to the outbreak of war.

During the course of the war Calamy enjoyed considerable popularity in London. According to his grandson, "no Minister in the

[11]Calamy, *Gods Free Mercy to England* (London, 1642), epistle and 5-7, 20, 47-50; *Private Journals*, ed. Coates, Young, and Snow, 447, 458-59, 464, 469.

[12]*An Answer to the Articles* (London, 1642) 1-3. Echard subsequently charged Calamy with being "so much an Incendiary, and Promoter of the grand Rebellion, and Scotch Invasion, that his Actions cannot be vindicated. . . ." *History*, 837. As late as 1684, Thomas Long asserted that "by their *long Speeches* and *fair pretences*," Calamy, Stephen Marshall, and their colleagues "*deceived the hearts*, and *opened the purses* of the *deluded people.*" From this, Long argued, came the tumults that led to the attacks on the bishops and Catholic peers, and the trials of Strafford and Laud. *A Compendious History of All the Popish & Fanatical Plots and Conspiracies Against the Established Government in Church & State* (London, 1684) 59.

City was more follow'd; nor hath there ever bin a Week-day Lecture so frequented as his; which was attended not only by his own Parish, but by other Eminent Citizens, and many Persons of the Greatest Quality, and that constantly." His auditors heard him call not only for further reform in the church but for the zealous prosecution of the war, which he depicted as the Lord's battle in which those who died were martyrs. Further testimony to his zeal came early in 1643, following Hugh Peter's presentation of a *Humble Petition* to Parliament, calling for the collection of funds in the parishes of London, Westminster, and Southwark to transport urchins from Ireland and England to New England. Parliament responded by designating Calamy and Henry Walker as receivers of the donations. To assist him with his pastoral duties in these busy years, Calamy acquired a new assistant in 1643—his brother-in-law Matthew Newcomen—who also served as afternoon lecturer until 1648. [13]

On 15 June 1643, a day of thanksgiving following the discovery of Waller's Plot in which various peers were implicated in a royalist conspiracy, Calamy and Charles Herle preached before the House of Lords. Falling back on his Calvinist theology to explain what had transpired, Calamy informed the House that only a few of the nobles had been called by God, hence few remained loyal to the parliamentary cause. As in Christ's day, most of the elect were chosen from the humble and lowly. Calamy, however, stifled fears that the reformers ultimately strove to level society. There would be no attempt, he promised, to abolish the distinction between the nobility and commoners. The House of Lords could still prosper if, as in the days of Nehemiah, they dedicated themselves to reforming the church. Repeatedly he stressed the importance of faithfully serving God: "The excellency of a Christian is not so much in *taking a Covenant as in keeping of it when taken.*"[14]

---

[13]Calamy, *An Abridgment,* 186 (quoted); Roger L'Estrange, *The Dissenters Sayings: The Second Part* (London, 1681), cited in Capp, *FMM,* 39; Raymond Phineas Stearns, *The Strenuous Puritan: Hugh Peter, 1598-1660* (Urbana, 1954) 164; Seaver, 273. In 1640 Newcomen married Hannah, widow of Gilbert Rany and daughter of Robert Snelling of Ipswich, esq. Calamy's first wife was Hannah's sister, Mary.

[14]Calamy, *The Noble-Mans Patterne of True and Reall Thankfulnesse* (London, 1643), sig. A4ʳ; 1 passim, 45 (quoted), 46.

In the week preceding this sermon, the Parliament had given Calamy several additional responsibilities. On 12 June he was appointed one of the four London members of the Westminster Assembly of Divines. Later, in December 1643 and June 1644, the parliamentary Committee for the Advance of Money channeled funds for the Assembly through Calamy and Marshall. Two days after his appointment to the Assembly, Parliament also made Calamy one of twelve divines responsible for licensing books. His colleagues in this significant task included Joseph Caryl, Obadiah Sedgwick, and Thomas Gataker. In light of Parliament's concern with curtailing the publication of literature by religious extremists, Calamy's choice was fitting, for he was regarded as "a great Enemy to the Sectaries. . . ." When, in fact, the Assembly learned in June 1644 of the defeat of the parliamentary army of the Earl of Essex, Calamy rebutted the theory that this stunning blow was a warning to the divines not to suppress the sectaries.[15]

On 6 October 1643 Calamy spoke at the Guildhall in favor of raising a loan in the City to subsidize the Scottish army, a course he deemed essential to preserve the gospel.

> Let me tell ye, if ever . . . you might use this Speech, O *happy penny*, you may use it now, Happy money that will purchase my Gospel, happy money that will Purchase Religion, and Purchase a Reformation to my Posterity; O happy Money; and Blessed be God that I have it to Lend.

It was, however, a great shame to him that England had to rely on another country to help it safeguard its liberties and its Protestant faith. "To me it doth seem a very strange prodigy and a strange wonder . . . ," Calamy said, but he attributed it to divine punishment for the sins of England. It was God, he insisted, who blinded most Englishmen to the insidious plot to bring in popery and slavery. He lashed out against those who remained neutral in the misguided belief that all would be well whichever side won. It was because so many in England

---

[15]Firth & Rait, 1: 182, 186; David Masson, *The Life of John Milton*, 6 vols. (New York, 1946) 3: 270; *Calendar of the Proceedings of the Committee for Advance of Money, 1642-1656* (London, 1888) 1: 29; 3: 1494; Calamy, *An Abridgment*, 186 (quoted); George Gillespie, *Notes of Debates and Proceedings of the Assembly of Divines* (Edinburgh, 1846) 67.

were "malignant and disaffected to this great cause" that there was little hope of a parliamentary victory without Scottish assistance.[16]

Calamy preached before Parliament twice in 1644, the first time to the House of Commons on 22 October, two and a half weeks after he, Burgess, William Gouge, and others had been appointed presbyters to examine and ordain ministers. His fast sermon to the Commons, subsequently published as *Englands Antidote, Against the Plague of Civil Warre* (1645), stressed the theme of repentance, "the *onely way* to remove the man-devouring, and Land-devouring judgement that is now upon us. . . ." There must be, he insisted, repentance in Parliament, in the army, and among the people; and if this could be achieved, "what miracles might not they doe?" He also took this occasion to assert that Parliament must suppress Anabaptists and Antinomians or risk becoming such themselves.[17] The sermon had come at a crucial time, when animosities and recriminations threatened to rend asunder the anti-royalist forces, perhaps even the army of the Eastern Association itself. Calamy's words did not restore unity, but they may have helped to avert even more serious rifts.

In December the eyes of the political nation were on three crucial issues: negotiations with Charles I at Uxbridge, a New Model Army in conjunction with a self-denying ordinance, and the fate of William Laud. Two months earlier, Calamy's sermon to the Commons had been delivered in the context of the move to prosecute Laud by attainder, which was more politically expedient than impeachment, as the earlier condemnation of Strafford had graphically illustrated. Now, in late December, the Lords had not yet approved the bill. On Christmas day, Calamy addressed the Lords amid the Gothic arches of Westminster Abbey, entreating unity. "Divisions in a Kingdome, are like a *sweeping plague*, that devoures whole Kingdoms. . . ." Whether such divisions are political or religious, they are "infallible causes" of destruction. Peace, he argued, was the key to reunite war-torn England; to achieve this he was willing to negotiate with Charles

---

[16]*DNB, s.v.;* L'Estrange, *Dissenters Sayings,* 11; Davids, *Annals,* 535; *Evangelium Armatum* (1663) 3-12.

[17]Firth & Rait, 1:522; Calamy, *Englands Antidote Against the Plague of Civil Warre* (London, 1645) 11, 45.

1 as far as conscience allowed. Civil war, he lamented, was the worst form of war because it was unnatural, cruel, and treacherous. Only if the English remained loyal to the Solemn League and Covenant could ultimate destruction be averted.[18] Perhaps Calamy persuaded the Lords to join with the Commons to seal Laud's fate, for on 4 January the Lords approved the attainder, and six days later he was executed.

Calamy's concern for unity was a factor in his rejection of the sectaries, though his grandson later claimed—with some exaggeration—that he was "of known Moderation towards those of other Sentiments." For their part, at least some of the sectaries viewed Calamy hostilely. By 1646, for example, there were erroneous reports in sectarian circles about three of their critics: Calamy, they said, had broken his arm; William Twisse was dying; and Thomas Edwards was dead. Theologically, Calamy was at odds with the sectaries. On 3 December 1645 he was preparing to debate at Aldermanbury with three Baptists—Benjamin Cox, William Kiffin, and Hanserd Knollys—on the subject of paedobaptism, but the Lord Mayor, who had initially sanctioned the disputation, rescinded his permission on the evening of the 2nd in order to keep the peace. "And great Prudence it was in him to prevent it," insisted Edwards, "knowing what great preparations there was of most Sects, especially *Anabaptists, Kiffin* himself being left out from the Disputation, and put to do the drudgery, to fetch up members scattered too and fro in the Countreys neer the City, and others of them did the like good service (as *Hobson* the Taylor) in their places."[19]

---

[18]Calamy, *An Indictment Against England Becavse of Her Selfe-Murdering Divisions* (London, 1645) epistle and 3, 8-9, 21, 26. As late as 1682, Edward Pearse, arguing in defense of toleration for Nonconformists, cited Calamy's Christmas sermon. Calamy's argument that magistrates have the authority to regulate religion in order to prohibit matters that are blasphemous, heretical, and idolatrous was never meant by him, Pearse correctly argued, to deny the right to worship to "such as themselves, who were both sound and tolerable." *The Conformist's Second Plea for the Nonconformists* (London, 1682) 69. Calamy's sermon also expressed hostility to the way in which Christmas was typically celebrated, 41.

[19]Calamy, *An Abridgment*, 186; B. R. White, *Hanserd Knollys and Radical Dissent in the 17th Century* (London, 1977) 11; Benjamin Cox, William Kiffin, Hanserd Knollys, *A Declaration Concerning the Public Dispute* (London, 1645); *Gangraena*, 70, 87-88 (quoted).

Calamy was also in the forefront of the battle against the Antinomians in this period. When John Sedgwick wrote *Antinomianisme Anatomized, or, a Glasse for the Lawlesse* (1643), attacking John Eaton's Antinomian publications, *The Discovery of the Most Dangerous Dead Faith* (1641) and *The Honey-Combe of Free Justification* (1642), Calamy praised Sedgwick's refutation as "very necessary for these times." After Hanserd Knollys castigated all prescribed liturgies as idolatrous in a sermon at St. Christopher le Stocks, London, Calamy and a group of like-minded colleagues met at his house to deal with Knollys and John Simpson "in a Brotherly way. . . ." Although they persuaded Knollys and Simpson to sign a set of propositions dealing with the moral law and Ten Commandments, both men subsequently reneged on the agreement and returned to the advocacy of Antinomian tenets.[20]

Calamy also became embroiled in a rather acrimonious dispute with the Independent Henry Burton, who had been appointed to a lectureship at St. Mary Aldermanbury founded by voluntary contributions. On 23 September 1645 Burton expounded upon his Independent tenets in a sermon, during the course of which he urged his hearers to certify their faith through personal introspection rather than relying simply on the Westminster Assembly or Parliament to tell them what to believe. At Calamy's insistence, Burton was subsequently locked out of the church for fear that his separatist principles would quickly ignite "a City-devouring fire. . . ." Calamy was angry that Burton had lured one of his parishioners to Burton's gathered church. Burton defended himself and shifted the attack to Calamy in *Truth Still Truth, Though Shut out of Doors* (1645). In outrage, Calamy fought back in *A Just and Necessary Apology Against an Unjust Invective* (1646), defending himself against Burton's *ad hominem* charges that he had readily conformed to Laudianism in the 1630s. Calamy insisted that he had never bowed to the altar, read the Book of Sports, recited prayers at the high altar, justified the oath *ex officio mero*, or prosecuted anyone before the High Commission. Moreover he asserted that he

---

[20]R. T. Kendall, *Calvin and English Calvinism to 1649* (Oxford, 1979) 189; *Gangraena*, 129. The Presbyterian Zachary Crofton, Simpson's bitter enemy at St. Botolph's, Aldgate, in the 1650s, praised Calamy as "an eminent minister of this city." *The Morning Exercise Methodizd*, 6 vols. (London, 1669; reprint, Wheaton IL, 1981) 5: 414.

had often preached against innovations in religion. But because he had conformed to some degree "according to the light I then had," he "went to *Bury*, and there made in a Sermon, a *recantation and retraction* of what I had done, in the hearing of thousands. And this I did before the times turned against *Episcopacy*, not out of discontent, nor because I was disappointed of my expected preferment at Court." This recantation probably occurred in late 1639 or 1640.[21]

Calamy continued to occupy himself with a variety of activities in this period. In 1643 he wrote a commendatory epistle to William Fenner's posthumous book, *The Souls Looking-Glasse* (Cambridge, 1651). With Edward Reynolds, Anthony Burgess, Daniel Cawdrey, and Thomas Hill, he also composed a commendatory epistle to John Ball's posthumous *A Treatise of the Covenant of Grace* (London, 1645), a classic of covenant theology, which Simeon Ashe was responsible for publishing. In the epistle they praised Ball's previously published catechism and treatise on the life of faith, and they remarked that had he lived he might have been instrumental in reconciling the current disputes over ecclesiastical polity. With respect to this treatise Calamy and his colleagues urged readers to enhance their understanding of "the foederall transactions betwixt God and his people. . . ." When Matthew Hopkins undertook his crusade against witches, Calamy was appointed in 1645 to a Suffolk commission for their trial. On 20 October 1645 Calamy, Arthur Jackson, John Arrowsmith, and six laymen were appointed by Parliament as Triers in the sixth classis of the London Province. This appointment was renewed on 26 September 1646 and again on 29 August 1648. In this capacity Calamy was responsible for the approbation of elders. For his persistent hostility to the idea of toleration for the sectaries he was satirized by Richard Overton in 1645 as "a man but newly *Metamorphosed* by a figure which we Rhetoricians call METONOMIA BENEFICII from *Episcopallity* to *Presbytery*. . . ." Undaunted, Calamy returned to his campaign against the

---

[21]Samuel R. Gardiner, *History of the Great Civil War 1642-1649*, 4 vols. (London, 1894) 3:9; Calamy, *The Door of Truth Opened* (London, 1645) 4; Calamy, *A Just and Necessary Apology*, 8-9. Burton's charge that Calamy's earlier conformity indicates that he was a time-server was, according to Thomas Edwards, representative of accusations made against other Presbyterians. *Gangraena*, 75. Calamy may have preached to both Houses of Parliament on 5 November 1645. Wilson, *Pulpit in Parliament*, 246.

Independents in *The Great Danger of Covenant-Refusing*, a sermon on 2 Timothy 3:3 preached before the Lord Mayor on 14 January 1646. The Separatist notion of using a covenant to establish a gathered church, he contended, was nothing but human invention, devoid of scriptural sanction. He may have had a renewed attack of his ague that summer, for he declined invitations to preach to the Lords on 29 July and to the Commons on 26 August. He continued, however, to fulfill his duties as a censor, licensing in 1646 Robert Bolton's *The Last Visitation*. In the same year Baillie proposed that Calamy, Marshall, and Newcomen take on the additional responsibility of supervising the spiritual training of the king's children.[22]

Much of Calamy's attention was devoted to the deliberations of the Westminster Assembly, where he worked very closely with Marshall, Newcomen, Young, and the Scottish commissioners—especially Robert Baillie—on behalf of a presbyterian polity with a strong lay eldership. His contributions to the work of the Assembly were in three major areas: participation in the debates, service on numerous important committees, and service as an emissary to Parliament. In the latter capacity, for example, he was part of the committee that conveyed the Assembly's statement on ecclesiastical polity to the House of Commons in June 1645. With Caryl and Seaman, he was delegated by the Assembly to pray with the Lords, the Commons, and the Committee of Both Kingdoms in May 1646 as the first Civil War was drawing to a close. The same month the Assembly appointed him to a prestigious committee—whose members included Marshall, Seaman, Newcomen, Thomas Goodwin, Philip Nye, Obadiah Sedgwick, Simeon Ashe, and Richard Vines—which had to meet with the House of Commons to discuss the determination of scandalous sins. In June 1647, after the army seized the king, Calamy and George Gipps were sent by the Assembly to pray with the Lords and the Commons.[23]

---

[22]Calamy et al., epistle to John Ball, *A Treatise of the Covenant of Grace* (London, 1645), sig. A2ᵛ; *Calamy Revised, s.v.*; Firth & Rait, 1:794, 871, 1190; Shaw, 2:401; Richard Overton, *The Araignement of Mr. Persecvtion* (n. p., 1645) 16; Calamy, *The Great Danger of Covenant-Refusing* (London, 1646) epistle; Wilson, *Pulpit in Parliament*, 89; *Ath. Oxon.*, 2:516; Haller, *Liberty*, 35-36.

[23]Masson, *Milton*, 2:517; 3:20; 4:510; 5:98; *Minutes of the Sessions of the Westminster Assembly of Divines*, ed. Alexander F. Mitchell and John Struthers (Edinburgh, 1874) 104, 226, 233, 381.

Calamy participated in a number of significant debates in the Assembly in 1644 and 1645. During the discussion of marriage in November 1644 he categorized the rite as a civil ordinance, but agreed that the state had a right to declare it valid only if solemnized in public: "If we advise this, we shall do God a good service." In the debate on excommunication in December and January, he contended that persons excommunicated by the visible church were excluded only from participation in the sacraments, not the church invisible, hence they could still pray with the visible church. On the vexed question of which offenses merited excommunication, he affirmed simply that "whatsoever sin is admonishable, that sin is excommunicable." He spoke too in the disputations on appeals by excommunicated persons, on censure, predestination, and the fall of Adam.[24]

Calamy was especially caught up in the debate in October 1645 over the vexatious question of the extent of redemption, concerning which he espoused a moderate Calvinist position. While he carefully denied that he was an Arminian, he insisted that Christ had paid a redemptive price for all persons, absolutely for the elect and conditionally for the reprobate, in order that everyone "should be *salvabiles, non obstante lapsu Adami* . . . that Jesus Christ did not only die sufficiently for all, but God did intend, in giving of Christ, and Christ in giving Himself, did intend to put all men in a state of salvation in case they do believe." In arguing this position against those who were adamant that Christ died only for the elect, Calamy enjoyed some support in the Assembly from Marshall, Seaman, Vines, and Robert Harris. Referring to John 3:16, Calamy contended that Christ's love extended to the reprobate as well as to the elect. Because there was a biblical warrant to preach the covenant of grace to all, then Christ, in some sense, had to have redeemed all. The difference between the elect and the reprobate, according to Calamy, is that divine grace is made effectual only for the former, though tendered to both.

> The difference is not in the offer, but in the application. . . . There is a double love: general and special. A general love to the reprobate, and the fruit of this, a general offer, and general grace, and general reformation.

---

[24]*Minutes*, ed. Mitchell and Struthers, 5, 12, 26-27, 35, 42, 57-58, 151, 427.

For the chosen there was, averred Calamy, special election, whereas the reprobate, despite the general offer of redemptive grace, are condemned because they remain the *massa corrupta*. This, however, they deserve by virtue of their own choice: "By virtue of Christ's death, there is *ea administratio* of grace to the reprobate, that they do wilfully damn themselves." The thrust of Calamy's arguments to the Assembly thus focused on human responsibility and the universal extent of divine love.[25]

Calamy's committee work in the Assembly covered a wide spectrum of subjects, ranging from the printing of the Bible and the Confession of Faith to the problem of absenteeism and tardiness in the Assembly. He served on committees dealing with fasting and determining which children qualified for baptism. With Newcomen, Seaman, Sedgwick, John Dury, Thomas Temple and others, he was appointed to a committee in February 1646 that examined the subject of Christian liberty. The chapter on the Lord's supper in the Westminster Confession of Faith was the responsibility of Calamy, Cornelius Burgess, and Jeremiah Whitaker. With Burgess he was assigned the task of writing the commentary on the second commandment in the Larger Catechism, and he subsequently had to assist Edward Corbet (of Norfolk) and Samuel Gibson with the sixth commandment. Calamy was also a member of the committee that prepared the preface to the Shorter Catechism. On 14 September 1643 he was appointed to chair the committee concerned with Antinomianism and in May 1645 to the committee to deal with the preaching of Antinomians and other sectaries. In January 1646 he was appointed to the committee responsible for the examination of ministers, and in March 1647 to the committee delegated to handle clergy "sent for approbation of the Assembly, and come out of enemies' quarters." In the twilight of the Assembly he was delegated with Nye, Marshall, and others to thank the Church of Scotland in June 1648 for its "constancy and faithfulness in the cause of God wherein they and we have been engaged. . . ." As the Presbyterian cause waned that year, he offered to serve on a committee to muster evidence to substantiate that presbyterian pol-

[25]Ibid., lvi, 152-53 (quoted), 154, 156 (quoted).

ity was *jure divino* in nature. Clearly, Calamy was a major force in the deliberations and accomplishments of the Assembly.[26]

The shaky unity among the godly that Calamy had been striving to preserve was shattered in the summer of 1647. Although the king had surrendered to the Scots in May 1646 and Oxford had capitulated in June—ending the first Civil War—the quest for a settlement was unsuccessful. A rift between the New Model Army and Parliament widened, especially in May 1647, when the latter ordered mobilization. The king, who had been returned to the parliamentary leaders by the Scots, was seized by the army. The Grandees, fearing a social revolution, tried to negotiate with Charles on the basis of Henry Ireton's "Heads of Proposals." Although the Grandees were willing to accept monarchical government and an episcopal church (but with toleration for other Protestants), Charles rejected their terms in late July, emboldened by dramatic events in London. On the 21st a group of apprentices, watermen, and others signed an engagement to uphold the Covenant and restore the king to his throne. At the time some observers believed, probably erroneously, that Calamy and Joseph Caryl were among those who incited the apprentices to act. Two days later, a mob stormed the House of Commons and held the Speaker in his chair while a resolution recalling the king to London was passed. Fifty-seven members of the Commons and eight peers, including the Speakers of both Houses, thereupon took refuge with the army, which was advancing on the City. In the confusion Calamy, Simeon Ashe, and Anthony Burgess preached at the Guildhall on the 28th. Calamy had been supporting the efforts of the parliamentary peace party to achieve a negotiated settlement, but now he broke with them when they backed efforts in London to recruit troops to oppose the New Model Army. Further division was, for Calamy, intolerable. On 2 August, much to the discomfiture of his friend Robert Baillie, Calamy and some other members of the Westminster Assembly signed a petition urging the city leaders to negotiate with the New Model. Their efforts bore fruit, for when the army marched into London four days

---

[26]Ibid., 20, 72, 96, 110-11, 178, 187-88, 280, 295, 300, 334, 388, 394, 477, 490, 520, 525.

later, it was greeted by the Lord Mayor, the Aldermen, and the Common Council.[27]

Through the stormy years of the late 1640s, Calamy retained both his popularity and his outspokenness. When he gave his weekly lectures, sixty or more coaches could often be seen outside his church. Further testimony to his reputation is reflected in Lord Admiral Warwick's request that he and Samuel Bolton conduct sabbath services in July 1648 on the "Tilbury Hope." Yet Calamy remained embroiled in religious controversy. In December 1647 he was one of fifty-eight clergymen—including Ashe, Gataker, Case, and Christopher Love—who signed *A Testimony to the Truth of Jesus Christ* attacking Arminians, Antinomians, Anabaptists, Seekers, Unitarians, Mortalists, and proponents of toleration. Once again Calamy's salvos were primarily reserved for the radical Protestants, whom he deemed the greatest threat to a religious settlement. The following year, one of them, the General Baptist Edward Barber, interrupted Calamy while he was preaching at St. Benet Fink in the City. Barber had been invited by some members of the parish to hear Calamy preach and to add to or contradict what he said. Calamy, however, insisted that he be allowed to finish his sermon and accused Barber of "coming to make a disturbance in the Church of God." The congregation became tumultuous as some cried out to kill Barber by pulling him limb from limb. A constable rescued him, but not before a woman had scratched his face. Sympathetic members of the congregation urged Barber to visit Calamy at his house to resolve their disputes, but Barber was by then convinced that Calamy and his colleagues "were all anti-christian ministers."[28]

In 1648 the Independent John Price castigated Calamy, Case, and other Presbyterian leaders, especially those in the Westminster Assembly, for having disillusioned people in the 1640s. "Did not many godly, sober, wise and judicious Presbyterians, Parliament men and

[27]HMC 4, *Fifth Report*, 173; Valerie Pearl, "London's Counter-Revolution," in *The Interregnum: The Quest for Settlement 1646-1660*, ed. G. E. Aylmer (Hamden CT, 1972) 51-52.

[28]C. V. Wedgwood, *A Coffin for King Charles* (New York, 1964) 55-56; CSPD, 1648-49, 368; Edward Barber, *A Declaration and Vindication of the Carriage of Edward Barber* (London, 1648) passim.

others," Price asked, "joyne with you, stick unto you, engage for you, who now begin to decline[,] you being so greatly mistaken in you." Price's attack was part of a more general campaign by the Independents and sectaries against the Presbyterians in 1648 and early 1649, particularly as the time drew near to determine the fate of the king. The Presbyterian ministers were especially critical of the army leaders in the aftermath of Pride's Purge on 6 December, and Calamy himself was probably one of those who preached openly against the purge on 17 December. In the ensuing days, the Presbyterian clergy met frequently, resolving to continue in their opposition despite a warning from the Army Council. At least one of these meetings was held at Calamy's house, for Hugh Peter, who would shortly sign Charles's death warrant as a member of the regicide court, took a troop of soldiers and broke up the gathering. Irate, Calamy protested against this "knave" to General Fairfax. [29]

Against the background of the excitement sparked by Pride's Purge, the Army Council took up the second Agreement of the People. The crucial seventh article of the Agreement denied to the representatives of the people in the government the right to enact any legislation or impose any oaths or covenants that would compel individuals in matters of religion or restrain them from professing their faith, although "the instruction or directing of the nation in a publique way, for the matters of Faith, Worship, or Discipline (so it be not compulsive or expresse Popery) is referred to their discretion." On 14 December the Council took up the question of whether a magistrate should have compulsive or restrictive powers in religious matters. In addition to Council members, those present included a number of Presbyterian and Independent ministers as well as Levellers. The sectarian officers, the Levellers, and the more liberal Independents such as John Goodwin and William Packer opposed giving restrictive powers in religion to magistrates. In Goodwin's words, "God hath nott invested any power in a Civill Magistrate in matters of religion. . . ." Against this view, Commissary-General Henry Ireton and the Independent Philip Nye argued that magistrates must have some restrain-

---

[29]John Price, *The Pulpit Incendiary* (London, 1648) 52; David Underdown, *Pride's Purge: Politics in the Puritan Revolution* (Oxford, 1971) 163; Stearns, *Strenuous Puritan*, 332; Cromwell, *WS*, 1:732-33.

ing power in order to prevent persons from advocating unacceptable forms of behavior under the guise of religion and thus disrupting the peace of the state. After lengthy debate the Council adjourned without resolving the question.[30]

Because of the difficulty over this issue, the Council postponed further discussion of it until the 19th, but did arrange for a select group to examine the problem further on the afternoon of the 15th. This meeting was convened in the house of Colonel Robert Tichborne, who had taken little part in the debate on the 14th. In addition to Tichborne, eight others were delegated to attend, including the Leveller John Wildman, the sectarian officers Colonel Nathaniel Rich and Colonel Richard Deane, and the Independent John Goodwin. The Council directed that these men meet at Tichborne's with a contingent of ten men—mostly Presbyterians—who favored the recognition of some restrictive powers for magistrates in religious matters. Nye of course was there, as were Calamy, Ashe, Seaman, Burgess, and Marshall. When the meeting of this smaller group on the 15th failed to reach an accord, the Council directed that five more persons be added to the group to meet again on the 20th. Joining Calamy and the others were Dr. Paget, Dr. Cox, Dr. Jonathan Goddard, and two representatives of the army, Major John Carter and Captain Richard Hodden. This time the committee must have achieved a compromise, for on the 21st the Council agreed that the civil power would not have the right to interfere with Christians who did not disrupt the public peace, though it excepted those who advocated popery or prelacy. Calamy must have been reasonably satisfied with this decision. He and his Presbyterian colleagues had exerted sufficient pressure on the Army Council to prevent the adoption of the full-blown sectarian position on religious freedom.[31]

The Presbyterian ministers continued, however, to worry about the fate of the king. On 11 January 1649 they dispatched a delegation, which included Calamy and Marshall, to consult with Fairfax.

---

[30]*Clarke Papers*, 71-132 (73, 74 quoted). Cf. Tolmie, 179-80; H. N. Brailsford, *The Levellers and the English Revolution*, ed. Christopher Hill (Stanford, 1961) 384-87.

[31]*Clarke Papers*, 71-72, 134-35, 139-40; Gardiner, *History of the Great Civil War*, 4: 277.

After expressing their criticism of the army's actions, they agreed to additional meetings only insofar as they could be used to condemn the officers' "errors." A report on the 14th that Calamy, Cornelius Burgess, and others were ready to accept the king's conviction but not his execution was probably unfounded. Six days later fifty-eight ministers issued *A Vindication of the Ministers of the Gospel in, and about London*. Among the signatories were Calamy and his closest colleagues, including Burgess, Ashe, Case, Jackson, Love, and Watson. Regarding the trial as a violation of both Scripture and "the Fundamentall Constitution and Government of this Kingdome," they called for the people to be loyal to the Solemn League and Covenant. Their efforts were for nought, but Calamy was one of a group of ministers who went to St. James's on 30 January, the day of the king's execution, to offer him their services. The Independents Joseph Caryl and William Dell were also there, but the king politely refused their ministrations, preferring instead the company of Dr. Juxon, Bishop of London. To Calamy the act of regicide was abhorrent to "the principles of the Protestant religion, never yet stained with the least drop of the blood of a king."[32]

Although the triumph of the regicides troubled Calamy deeply, he remained committed to his ministerial responsibilities. During the early part of the year he served as the moderator of the fourth half-yearly provincial synod of London, a post to which his colleague Arthur Jackson succeeded at the commencement of the fifth synod in May. When the synod formulated its *Vindication of the Presbyteriall-Government* on 2 November 1649, it included Calamy's name at the end as an assessor. He also helped compose that body's *Jus Divinum Ministerii Evangelici, & Anglicani* in 1654. He continued to license books in this period, approving the publication of a Welsh translation (*Sail Crefydd Gristnogawl*) of William Perkins's *Foundation of the Christian Religion* in 1649 and Benjamin Woodbridge's *Justification by Faith* in May 1652.[33]

Calamy's service to the Presbyterians was further recognized in 1650 when he was named president of Sion College, London. This

---

[32]Underdown, *Pride's Purge*, 176-77; *A Vindication of the Ministers of the Gospel in, and About London* (London, 1648 o.s.) 5; *Ath. Oxon.*, 4:29; Calamy, cited in Burton, 2:320n.

[33]Masson, *Milton*, 4:60; *DNB*, s.v.; Calamy, *An Abridgment*, 187; Thomas Richards, *A History of the Puritan Movement in Wales* (London, 1920) 77; *Ath. Oxon.*, 4:159.

institution had three major goals: to bestow aid to the indigent, to provide books for students, and to serve as a center for the London clergy to assemble. Calamy had first been elected a member of the Court of Governors as far back as 1643, when Royalist members of the college fled London. At that time Calamy and Henry Roborough, Rector of St. Clement, Eastcheap, became assistants to the new president, Andrew Janaway. In the years that followed, the college was a center of Presbyterian activity and the usual meeting place of the Provincial Synod of London. Calamy served as junior dean of the college in 1644 and senior dean in 1649 before becoming president the following year. At the termination of his presidency in April 1651, he preached the customary Latin sermon, for which he received £1 0s. 3d. He installed Lazarus Seaman as his successor.[34]

In the spring of 1651 the City was rocked by the discovery of a broad royalist conspiracy involving prominent Presbyterian clergy. Love, Case, and William Jenkins (or Jenkyn), all of whom were co-signatories with Calamy of the 1649 *Vindication*, were arrested on 2 May, and it was widely expected that Calamy and Marshall would follow them to prison. A report that Calamy had been apprehended was apparently false, though one of the alleged conspirators, Thomas Coke, charged that Calamy and a small band of other Presbyterian clerics—including Love, Gouge, Case, and Jenkins—had been corresponding with other ministers throughout England. For his role, Love was condemned to death. In prison he was visited by two Independent ministers, John Owen and John Bond, who attempted to persuade him to take a conciliatory tone in his appeal for pardon. Worden is perhaps correct in suggesting that Calamy may have assisted them in this effort. Love was executed on 22 August after all attempts to save him failed. Calamy, Ashe, and Manton went with him to the scaffold, where he affirmed that though he had been "made a grief to the godly, a laughing-stock to the wicked, and a gazing-stock to all; yet, blessed be God, I am not a terror to myself. . . ." "Love's execution," as Worden observes, "broke the back of clerical opposition to the Rump." When the Rump was forcibly dissolved two

---

[34]Ernest Harold Pearce, *Sion College and Library* (Cambridge, 1913) 17, 92, 109-10, 112, 176-77, 344.

years later, Calamy condemned Cromwell's action as unlawful and impractical because " 'tis against the voice of the nation."[35]

In the following years Calamy openly demonstrated his respect for Love by seeing that his works were published posthumously. With Ashe, Allen Geree, William Taylor, and Jeremiah Whitaker, he prepared an introductory epistle to Love's sixteen sermons on 2 Peter 1:10, published in 1653 as a *Treatise of Effectual Calling and Election.* The next year Calamy, Ashe, and Whitaker wrote an epistle to Love's *Combate Between the Flesh and the Spirit,* a collection of twenty-seven sermons, and with Ashe, Taylor, and Geree he prepared an epistle to Love's *Christian's Directory,* another collection of sermons. Again in 1654 Calamy, Ashe, Whitaker, and Taylor composed an epistle for *Grace: The Truth, and Growth, and Different Degrees Thereof,* which contained more of Love's pulpit discourses. In 1657 the same group published Love's *The Penitent Pardon'd* and a *Discourse of Christ's Ascension into Heaven.* With Matthew Poole and Joseph Church, these four ministers also wrote epistles in 1657 for four more of Love's works: *The Dejected Soul's Cure; The Ministry of the Angels; Of the Omnipresence of God;* and *The Sinners Legacy to Their Posterity.* Calamy's work was obviously a clear sign that he and his colleagues held Love in high esteem and an indirect rebuke to the radicals responsible for his execution.

During these years Calamy continued apace with his own writings. Two sermons, *The Saint's Rest* and *A Sermon Preached . . . Aug. 24. 1651* appeared in 1651. On 19 October 1654 he preached a funeral sermon at St. Martin's, Ludgate, for Dr. Samuel Bolton, the late Master of Christ's College, Cambridge. Published in 1655 under the title *The Saints Transfiguration,* the sermon expounded upon the theme of the resurrection of the saints' bodies, using as the text Philippians 3:20-21. In the epistle to the sermon Calamy recorded his personal debt to both Bolton and the Earl of Warwick, to whom the sermon was dedicated. Perhaps depressed by Bolton's death, Calamy, preaching be-

---

[35]Cromwell, *WS,* 2:401, 414, 437, 626; HMC 29; *Portland Manuscripts,* 1:584-85; Benjamin Brook, *The Lives of the Puritans,* 3 vols. (London, 1813) 3:132; Blair Worden, *The Rump Parliament 1648-1653* (Cambridge, 1974) 243-48. Cf. Leland H. Carlson, "A History of the Presbyterian Party from Pride's Purge to the Dissolution of the Long Parliament," *Church History* 11 (June 1942): 118-22. For the case against Love see John Hall, *A Gag to Love's Advocate* (London, 1651).

fore the Lord Mayor and Aldermen on 10 December 1654, lamented that self-seeking had obstructed the reformation and destroyed the Parliament, the ministry, and the gentry. The sermon was published as *The Monster of Sinful Self-Seeking, Anatomized* in 1655.[36]

Among Calamy's special interests was the conversion of the Indians in America. *The Sun-shine of the Gospel Breaking Forth upon the Indians in New England* (London, 1648), written by Thomas Shepard, a minister at Cambridge, Massachusetts, carried an epistle dedicatory to Parliament in which the Indians are described as "the *saddest* spectacles of *degeneracy* upon earth. . . ." Signed by Calamy, Marshall, Ashe, Whitaker, Thomas Goodwin, Philip Nye, Sidrach Simpson, William Greenhill, John Downham, William Carter, Thomas Case, and Samuel Bolton—an impressive group of Presbyterians and Independents— the epistle remarked on the progress that had been attained in converting the Indians. For this Parliament deserved some credit, they thought, but they also hoped that further assistance would be forthcoming to "*help the day of small things among them.* . . ." The same group of Presbyterian and Independent ministers also wrote an epistle to the reader for Shepard's book, noting that his text would encourage pastors dismayed by a seeming lack of success. Merchants who read the book would, they thought, be more willing to provide financial support to carry the gospel message to the dark corners: "Whither you *traffick* you *take much* from them, [but] if you can *carry* this to them, you wil make them an *abundant* recompense."[37]

A similar opportunity to further missionary endeavors to the Indians was presented to Calamy with the publication in 1652 of Henry Whitfield's book, *Strengthe out of Weaknesse: Or a Glorious Manifestation of the Further Progresse of the Gospel Among the Indians in New-England.* The epistle dedicatory to the Rump Parliament was the work of a dozen Independent ministers, including Griffith, Owen, Caryl, and Thomas Goodwin. Calamy and five other Presbyterians—Seaman, Whitaker, Spurstowe, Ashe, and William Gouge—joined them in signing the epistle to the reader. Three years later Calamy supported the publication of John Eliot's *A Late and Further Manifestation of the Progress of the*

---

[36]Calamy, *The Monster of Sinful Self-Seeking, Anatomized* (London, 1655) 31.

[37]*CMHS*, 3rd ser., 4: 27-35.

Gospel Amongst the Indians in New-England (London, 1655). Caryl wrote the epistle to the reader, but Calamy, Ashe, Whitfield, and John Arthur observed that the book was worthy of publication in order to encourage the godly in England to give thanks for missionary activity among the Indians and to support such work financially. Taking the gospel to the Indians, they wrote, is "so much conducing to the Glory of God, the Salvation of soules, and the Inlargement of the Kingdome of Christ upon Earth." The last point, in particular, fit in well with the millenarian expectations of the age.[38]

Although Calamy's grandson asserted that "in *Oliver's* time [Calamy] . . . kept himself as private as he could," in reality he remained active in a variety of religious activities. Just before John Dury, the tireless advocate of Protestant ecumenicity, left for the continent on 5 April 1654 to work for an Evangelical Protestant Alliance, Calamy was a signatory to a letter from English Protestants to their European counterparts urging the formation of a league against the Antichrist. Among the forty-one other signatories were not only such longtime Calamy allies as Marshall, Seaman, and Ashe, but prominent Independents such as John Owen, Thomas Goodwin, Philip Nye, Joseph Caryl, Thankful Owen, and Sidrach Simpson. Calamy's interest in continental Protestants was manifest again the following year when the Council of State appointed him in May as a treasurer to receive funds to assist persecuted Protestants in the Piedmont. Among his fellow commissioners were the Independents Caryl and Nye, the Baptists Edward Cresset and William Kiffin, and the Fifth Monarchist Thomas Harrison. Although Calamy willingly cooperated with religious radicals in these ventures, it is still something of a surprise to find him intervening with the government in this period on behalf of the Socinian John Biddle, who had been exiled to St. Mary's Castle on the Isle of Scilly. Calamy had developed a more tolerant attitude toward those on the religious left by this time, and his intercession for Biddle stemmed primarily from such humanitarian motives. Like the Baptist Jeremiah Ives and others who urged Biddle's release, Calamy was probably also motivated by respect for Biddle as a scholar.[39]

---

[38]Ibid., 4: 155-59, 263. For a fuller discussion of Whitfield's work see below, ch. 3.

[39]Calamy, *An Abridgment*, 186; *Corr. of Owen*, 68-70; *CSPD, 1655*, 182, 197, 369; H. J. McLachlan, *Socinianism in Seventeenth Century England* (Oxford, 1951) 212; *BDBR*, *s.v.* Jeremiah Ives.

Because of Calamy's earlier work in Sussex verifying cases of witchcraft, Thomas White suggested to Richard Baxter in 1655 that he call on such ministers as Calamy and Richard Vines to help him determine the authenticity of reports from other clergymen regarding "Providences" and "Spiritual Experiences." The interest in this subject was directly associated with the millennial fervor of the 1650s. When Baxter himself was contacted in 1657 by Matthew Poole about a co-operative endeavor to register "Illustrious Providences," Baxter suggested that Poole solicit the assistance of Calamy and two or three other clergymen. [40]

More routinely, Calamy's time was taken up with normal religious and educational concerns. "He commonly had the chair among the city ministers at their meetings, and was much esteemed for his prudence and propriety of conduct." He continued to be involved in the business of the London Province. When ministers in Hereford inquired about establishing means for ordaining clergy in their area, Calamy was delegated to write the response in February 1656. The previous month he joined with other London clergy to ask the Council of State to inquire into the qualifications of a schoolmaster about whom they apparently had doubts. Because of his interest in education, Calamy was named in March 1656 to the committee charged with preparing the statutes for the new college at Durham. Among the others appointed to this committee were John Lambert and the Independents Thomas Goodwin, Joseph Caryl, and George Griffith. In May 1658 Calamy joined with Ashe, Jenkins, and Bartholomew Beale to provide a certificate of recommendation to the Commissioners for Ejecting Scandalous Ministers regarding the fitness of John Jackson, the minister of St. Benet, Paul's Wharf, London. With the master and ten other fellows of Pembroke Hall, Calamy testified concerning the godliness and learning of one of its students in July 1659. Such activities, extending from London and Cambridge to the Council of State, reflect the primary areas of Calamy's influence. [41]

Calamy took time out from his ministerial activities in the spring of 1657 to consult with Cromwell concerning the latter's considera-

[40]William M. Lamont, *Richard Baxter and the Millennium: Protestant Imperialism and the English Revolution* (London, 1979) 30-31, 325.

[41]Calamy, *Non. Mem.*, 1:77 (quoted), Shaw, 2:158; *CSPD*, 1655-56, 136, 218; *CSPD*, 1658-59, 14; *CSPD*, 1659-60, 10.

tion of an assumption of the crown under the terms of the Humble Petition and Advice. According to the account of the meeting by Henry Neville, a member of the Council of State, Cromwell had invited Calamy and other leading clergymen in the City to discuss the Humble Petition with him "as if he made it a Matter of Conscience to be determin'd by their Advice." To Cromwell's face Calamy insisted that the proposal was both illegal and impractical. Cromwell, after retorting that the safety of the nation made such a recourse legal, asked Calamy why assuming the crown was impractical. He replied:

> Oh it is against the Voice of the Nation; there will be Nine in Ten against you. Very well says *Cromwel*; but what if I should disarm the Nine, and put the Sword in the tenth Man's Hand, would not that do the Business?

Even allowing for some exaggeration in the story stemming from Neville's hostility to the Humble Petition, the basic notion of Calamy's opposition to the scheme is compatible with his general principles. [42]

And still he wrote. The first edition of Calamy's very popular collection of five sermons, *The Godly Mans Ark*, appeared in 1657; by 1683 it had gone through eight editions. The first sermon, explaining why Christians suffered afflictions, was preached at the funeral of Elizabeth Moore, whose brother, John Hancock, was one of Calamy's printers. The remaining sermons reflect typical Puritan piety, concentrating on the Word of God and its usefulness to the saints, as well as the proper way to meditate on and apply the promises of God. Calamy wrote a prefatory epistle to *Evidence for Heaven*, a book of more than two hundred pages whose author, a "Gentlewoman" in his congregation, insisted that her name remain anonymous. The treatise itself explains how a person can gain assurance of salvation—a question of great import for many Calvinists. Calamy's funeral sermon for his longtime friend, the Earl of Warwick, was published in 1658 as *A Patterne for All*. In it he aptly pointed to the significance of a godly life for those of eminence: "Great men are like looking glasses according to which all the country dresse themselves, and if they be good they do

---

[42]Calamy, *Cont.*, 8.

a world of good."[43] The same year Calamy joined with three other Presbyterian ministers—Ashe, Humphrey Chambers, and Richard Byfield—to publish Obadiah Sedgwick's book, *The Shepherd of Israel.* Calamy used his epistle to Samuel Hudson's *A Vindication of the Essence and Unity of the Church Catholick Visible* (London, 1658) to warn Independents of the dangers of separation.

In this period Calamy continued to follow events in Scotland, where an acrimonious struggle was occurring between the Resolutioners and the Protesters (Remonstrants). The Church of Scotland was rent by a schism early in the decade when the Remonstrants, led by Patrick Gillespie, criticized the government for making an alliance with Charles II too hastily and for working with "Malignants" who had not taken the Covenant. As the struggle for control of the church dragged on, theologian Samuel Rutherford complained in January 1657 to Calamy's colleague Simeon Ashe that the churches were filled with "Malignants" and that godly persons were not accepted as ministers. Presbyterian leaders in London were consequently angry with the Resolutioners, who dominated kirk government. Robert Baillie, Calamy's friend and the leader of the Resolutioners, countered with letters of explanation to Ashe and Francis Rouse, a member of the Council of State, swinging Presbyterian opinion back in the Resolutioners' favor. Cromwell tried various expedients to mediate the dispute, including the appointment of a committee of fifteen, seven of whom were clergymen. Of the latter, three—Manton, William Cooper, and a Mr. Bramford—were Presbyterians and four—George Griffith, John Owen, Joseph Caryl, and William Carter—were Independents. The committee produced a report favorable to the Protesters, but before this could be sent to Scotland, complaints from London Presbyterians—probably including Calamy—led to its withdrawal. Even a more moderate letter failed to meet with the Council of State's sanction. Cromwell finally decided to refer the dispute to the Scottish Council of State and so informed Archibald Johnston of Wariston, a representative of the Protesters, on 25 September 1657. Cromwell, Johnston recorded in his diary, "thought the Remonstrators ever contending for the power of godlynesse and uthers [Resolu-

---

[43]Calamy, *A Patterne for All* (London, 1658) 34.

tioners] for the forme, yet he thought the course taken not indifferent nor healing but wydening differences." Cromwell, moreover, let Johnston know that "moderat men" such as Calamy and Ashe preferred the Resolutioners, "tho they differd from them." Thus Calamy and Ashe were instrumental in persuading the Cromwellian government not to endorse the Protesters' cause.[44]

In January 1658 Calamy was once again invited to preach before the House of Commons. The occasion was a day of humiliation on the 27th for which the House desired two sermons, one from Calamy and the other from George Griffith. The invitation was extended to Calamy on the 20th by Major Richard Beke, Colonel Richard Lilburne's brother-in-law. Calamy's sermon on Isaiah 9:12 was, according to Thomas Burton, "very good," though it "smelled Presbyterian." While Griffith's sermon was favorable to the Cromwellian regime, Calamy "professed himself never to have been a Court flatterer." For his efforts Calamy received a resolution of thanks and a request to publish his sermon, which he seems not to have done.[45]

Calamy was optimistic at the outset of Richard Cromwell's Protectorate. With Presbyterian leaders such as Manton, Jenkins, Ashe, and Seaman, he sent Edward Reynolds to express support to the new Protector on 11 October 1658. From Scotland, General George Monck conveyed advice to the new ruler that included a recommendation to favor such moderate Presbyterian ministers as Calamy, Reynolds, and Manton. Richard ignored both this suggestion and Monck's proposal to summon a new assembly of divines to work out a plan of religious accommodation.[46]

Early in Richard's Parliament, Calamy became indirectly embroiled in the mounting political struggles. On 28 January a controversy developed in the Commons regarding the selection of four

[44]CSPD, 1657-58, 28; F. N. McCoy, Robert Baillie and the Second Scots Reformation (Berkeley, 1974) 134-38, 189-95; Sir Archibald Johnston of Wariston, The Diary of Sir Archibald Johnston of Wariston, ed. George M. Paul, David H. Fleming, and James D. Ogilvie, 3 vols. (Edinburgh, 1911-1940) 3:98 (quoted). See ch. 3 for the dispute between the Resolutioners and the Remonstrants.

[45]CJ, 7:579, 588; Burton, 2:320, 372-73 (quoted).

[46]The Publick Intelligencer, no. 147, p. 912; Thurloe, SP, 7:388.

ministers to preach to the House on 4 February, a day of humiliation. After Edward Reynolds and Thomas Manton were chosen unanimously, Calamy was nominated by the Commonwealthsmen Arthur Haselrig and John Weaver, with the support of General Monck's brother-in-law, Thomas Clarges, a Presbyterian member. The Independent John Owen was the choice of John Lambert and Thomas Kelsey, whose support for a military protectorate ran counter to the Commonwealthsmen's plans for a civilian republic. After a "great debate," the Commons agreed to invite all four. Three of those chosen were Presbyterians—Reynolds, Manton, and Calamy—a victory for the moderates. Reynolds used his sermon to encourage the House to order a crackdown on religious radicals by the magistrates. The House thanked all four and asked them to publish their sermons, though again Calamy seems not to have done so.[47]

Although Calamy's actions in the ensuing months are largely unknown, it is clear that he became increasingly convinced of the need for the restoration of monarchical government. By August 1659 the Royalists too had come to the conclusion that their goal could best be attained with the assistance of Presbyterian leaders such as Calamy and Reynolds. When the more militant Presbyterians and Royalists rebelled against the government in the summer of 1659, particularly under the leadership of Sir George Booth in Lancashire and Cheshire, there were hopes that the Presbyterians in London would support the rising. On 26 August Alderman James Bunce wrote to Calamy, Ashe, Newcomen, Jenkins, and other Presbyterian ministers to solicit their aid, but by the time the letter arrived the insurrection had been quashed. The defeat of the militants did not dampen the willingness of Royalists to seek an accommodation with Presbyterians aimed at restoring the monarchy. At this time Calamy himself was involved in ecumenical discussions with Independent and Baptist leaders as well as other Presbyterians in order to attain some degree of unity and oppose the Quakers. The others involved in these summer meetings were the Independents Owen, Caryl, and Griffith, the Baptists

---

[47]*DNB, s.v.; CJ,* 7: 594, 599; Ivan Roots, "The Tactics of the Commonwealthsmen in Richard Cromwell's Parliament," in *Puritans and Revolutionaries,* ed. Donald Pennington and Keith Thomas (Oxford, 1978) 287-88; Burton, 3: 11-12; E[dward] R[eynolds], *The Substance of Two Sermons* (London, 1659) 14.

Henry Jessey, William Allen, Richard Deane, and John Griffith, and the Presbyterians Reynolds, Seaman, Jenkins, and Thomas Jacomb. The negotiations were, however, unsuccessful.[48]

In January 1660 Sir Edward Hyde, Charles II's key advisor and future Lord Chancellor, dispatched George Morley to England to consult with the Presbyterians, even offering preferment where appropriate. Calamy and Reynolds were the first men he consulted. Calamy responded to Hyde that they would endorse a modified episcopalian polity. Calamy must have been further encouraged by the promise of another royal emissary, Lord Mordaunt, that Charles would accept an ecclesiastical settlement akin to that of Scotland. About the same time the Earl of Lauderdale was able to persuade Calamy, Ashe, and William Taylor to help prepare the way for the arrival of General Monck in London on the grounds that he favored "a good parliament." After his arrival in the City on 3 February, Monck even announced his support for a presbyterian polity. His subsequent appointment of Calamy as one of his chaplains further confirmed his intention, as did his receipt of the Lord's supper at Calamy's hands and his consultations with Calamy concerning ministerial appointments. When Edmund Ludlow visited Monck at his London house on 13 February, Monck "was at the time of my coming in a private gallery, conferring with Mr. Edmund Calamy and others of the clergy." According to Baxter, both Calamy and Ashe with the concurrence of Bates, Manton, and other City ministers pressured Monck to restore the monarchy.[49]

[48]*Calendar of the Clarendon State Papers,* ed. O. Ogle, W. H. Bliss, W. D. Macray, F. J. Routledge, 4 vols. (Oxford, 1869-1932) 4: 340; George R. Abernathy, Jr., "The English Presbyterians and the Stuart Restoration, 1648-1663," *Transactions of the American Philosophical Society,* n.s. 55, pt. 2 (1965): 32-33.

[49]*State Papers Collected by Edward, Earl of Clarendon,* ed. R. Scrope and T. Monkhouse, 3 vols. (Oxford, 1767-1786) 3: 546, 722; Ethyn Williams Kirby, "The Reconcilers and the Restoration (1660-1662)" in *Essays in Modern English History* (Cambridge MA, 1941) 51-54; Robert Wodrow, *The History of the Sufferings of the Church of Scotland from the Restoration to the Revolution,* 4 vols. (Glasgow, 1828) 1: 8; Stearns, *Strenuous Puritan,* 411; Robert Halley, *Lancashire: Its Puritanism and Nonconformity,* 2 vols. (Manchester, 1869) 2: 104; *The Memoirs of Edmund Ludlow,* ed. C. H. Firth,

Monck, probably apprising Calamy of his intentions, quickly made it known that he favored the readmission to Parliament of the members formerly secluded by Colonel Pride as well as early elections for a free Parliament. Following the return of the secluded members on 21 February, Calamy and Manton were selected to preach on the day of thanksgiving celebrating the return. The new Presbyterian majority prepared for a Presbyterian settlement in the church by adopting the Westminster Confession, ordering the annual reading in the churches of the Solemn League and Covenant, and replacing the Cromwellian Triers with a Commission for the Approbation and Admission of Ministers of the Gospel. Most of the leading Independent clergy, such as John Owen, Thomas Goodwin, and Philip Nye, were not included, though George Griffith and Joseph Caryl were. The new commission was dominated by Presbyterians, including Calamy, Reynolds, Ashe, Manton, and Case. Under the provisions of the act, which established the commission, all future appointments to benefices and lectureships required the commission's approval. Although a quorum of the thirty-one members was fixed at only five, as few as nine negative votes could block an appointment. The Independents thus had a voice on the commission but no control. Not until most of the major religious legislation had been enacted by Parliament did the Committee on Religion appoint clergymen to advise it. On 5 March Calamy, Reynolds, Manton, Ashe, and two others were asked to assist the committee, just in time to influence the selection of the commissioners. [50]

Calamy and his colleagues were sufficiently satisfied with the religious program of the restored Long Parliament to be chary about its

---

2 vols. (Oxford, 1894) 2: 225; *Rel. Bax.*, pt. 2: 214. According to Calamy's grandson, during the course of a sermon before Monck after the Restoration he preached on the topic of filthy lucre. Money is so-called, he averred, because it tempts people to do base and filthy things. Then, waving his handkerchief towards Monck's pew, he asserted that some men were willing to betray three kingdoms for the sake of such gain. There is no other evidence to substantiate this story, which is probably apocryphal. Calamy, *Non. Mem.*, 1: 77.

[50]*CJ*, 7: 850; Firth & Rait, 2: 1459; *CSPD, 1659-60*, 392; HMC 29, *Portland Manuscripts*, 3: 219.

dissolution and the idea of free elections, which they feared might lead to the restoration of episcopal polity. Nevertheless their principal liaison with members of Parliament was James Sharp, who was in England specifically at Monck's behest to serve as a link between the general and the Presbyterians. Sharp also had been commissioned on 6 February by Scottish ministers meeting in Edinburgh to represent their interests to Calamy, Ashe, Manton, and William Cooper. Sharp subsequently reported back to Robert Douglas that Calamy, Ashe, and Taylor were "honest, and after his own heart." They in turn thought Sharp could be useful to them and asked him to speak with members of Parliament as well as with Monck and his officers on matters that concerned them. The following week Monck sent his coach for Calamy, Ashe, and Sharp, and engaged in a lengthy, private discussion with them. They agreed that a commonwealth was impractical and were persuaded that the Long Parliament had to be dissolved and new elections held. According to Sharp, in a letter of 13 March to Douglas, "we urged much upon him [Monck], that the presbyterian interest he had espoused, was much concerned in keeping up this house, and settling the government on terms; but in regard he had so lately declared against the house of lords, and continuing of this house, he could not do it so reputably." But, according to Baxter, if Monck was persuasive here, Calamy and Ashe were among those most responsible for urging Londoners to support a restored monarchy.[51]

Monck and Sharp continued to work closely with Calamy and his Presbyterian allies. "With our noble prisoners" Sharp was at St. Mary Aldermanbury in early March to hear Calamy and Taylor offer public thanks for the prison release of those who had refused the Engagement. Monck's desire for the continued support of Calamy was sufficiently strong for him to let Calamy and Sharp determine who would preach before him. Commencing about 18 April, Monck began urging Sharp to visit Charles in exile and to persuade him to write a letter to Calamy intended for dissemination to the Presbyterian clergy, to the effect that the king would endorse "the godly sober party" and uphold the Protestant faith.[52]

---

[51]Abernathy, "The English Presbyterians," 43-45; Wodrow, *History*, 1:5, 9 (quoted), 11 (quoted); *Rel. Bax.*, pt. 2:214.

[52]Wodrow, *History*, 1:11, 19, 21.

When the newly elected Convention Parliament met on 25 April 1660, Calamy, John Gauden, and Richard Baxter were selected to preach to the Commons on the next fast day, 30 April. To moderates such as Ralph Josselin, this was an encouraging sign: "If wee judge of the temper of the houses (the Lords satt) by the ministers they choose to preach unto them, it presents hopes, being Calamy, Gaudon, Baxter." Reynolds preached to the Lords. The Presbyterians, however, were already experiencing internal divisions that seriously undermined their chance to achieve a Presbyterian settlement. Politically they split over whether to require Charles to accept acts specifically restricting royal power. In the meantime, to pave the way for a possible agreement on the religious issues, Gauden organized a meeting in the lodgings of John Barnard at Gray's Inn. Calamy was not present, but Baxter and Manton explained the Presbyterian cause to Gauden, a moderate Episcopalian. Although Baxter quarreled with Gauden and subsequently with Morley, communications between the two sides remained open. Lord Mordaunt was able to inform Hyde on 9 May that Morley had convinced Calamy and Reynolds to accept an episcopal polity and a slightly modified liturgy, "but as yet they cannot undertake for their brethren." This willingness to compromise clearly worried the Scots, for on 12 May David Dickson, Robert Douglas, James Hamilton, John Smith, and George Hutchison wrote from Edinburgh to Calamy, Ashe, and Manton pressing them to oppose the restoration of episcopacy and the Book of Common Prayer.[53]

In the meantime, on the 7th a meeting of the "Generall Assembly" at Sion College, having read and approved the Declaration of Breda, "ordered That an humble Addresse to the King's most Excellent Ma[jest]y (now in Holland) be presented by the Ministers in & about the Citty of London." On 11 May Calamy, Reynolds, Manton, Case, and others left for the Netherlands to consult with Charles, who, said

---

[53]White Kennet, *An Historical Register and Chronicle of English Affairs* (London, 1744) 126; Masson, *Milton*, 6:425; Ralph Josselin, *The Diary of the Rev. Ralph Josselin 1616-1683*, ed. E. Hockliffe (Camden Society, 3rd ser., 15; London, 1908) 134; Halley, *Lancashire*, 2:107; *State Papers Collected by Clarendon*, 3:744; Wodrow, *History*, 1:26-27. According to Sir Thomas Wharton, the king's divines liked what they heard in Calamy's sermon on 30 April, "as to the point of moderation." *A Collection of Original Letters and Papers*, ed. Thomas Carte, 2 vols. (London, 1739) 2:338.

the radical Edmund Ludlow, "must yet carry it faire with the presbyterians . . . [who have] gone to meete him, . . . promising themselves
a great share in his favour." Calamy, according to his grandson with
undoubted exaggeration, "was reckon'd to have the greatest Interest in
Court, City and Country of any of the Ministers, and therefore [was]
extreamly caress'd at first. . . ." Meeting with Charles in his bed-
chamber, Calamy and his companions gave the king a letter signed by
more than eighty ministers at Sion College. When the delegation assured Charles of its loyalty and expressed a willingness to accept a
moderate episcopacy, he responded by promising that Parliament
would settle the ecclesiastical question. "They expressed much satisfaction with his majesty's carriage towards them, speaking him to be
a prince of a deep knowledge of his own affairs, of singular sweetness
and moderation, and great respectiveness [sic] towards them. . . ." To
the delegates' request in subsequent informal sessions that the king
cease using the Book of Common Prayer and requiring his chaplain to
wear the surplice, he retorted that he wished to enjoy the same liberty
that he was prepared to grant others. Calamy and his colleagues returned to England confident of Presbyterian comprehension in a national church.[54]

Calamy's prominence in the Restoration was reflected in his appointment, along with Reynolds and Gauden, to preach the fast sermons to Parliament at St. Margaret's, Westminster, the same month.
On the 26th, the day after the king landed at Dover, he met with
Hyde and Gilbert Sheldon, the future Bishop of London and Archbishop of Canterbury. It was probably in that meeting that Charles
reached his decision to name ten Presbyterians, including Calamy,
Reynolds, Ashe, Baxter, Manton, and Case, as his chaplains-in-or-
dinary. Calamy only accepted his appointment after some soul-

---

[54]Pearce, Sion College, 118 (quoted); Edmund Ludlow, A Voyce from the Watch Tower,
Part Five: 1660-1662, ed. A. B. Worden (Camden Society, 4th ser., 21; London,
1978) 157-58; Calamy, An Abridgment, 187; Kirby, "The Reconcilers," 58-59; Edward
Hyde, The History of the Rebellion and Civil Wars in England, ed. W. Dunn Macray, 6
vols. (Oxford, 1888) 6:231-32; Kennet, Register, 139, 152. Several of the sermons to
the Convention were published: Reynolds, The Avthor and Svbject of Healing in the
Church (London, 1660), preached on 25 April; Reynolds, The Meanes and Method of
Healing in the Church (London, 1660), preached on 1 May; Baxter, A Sermon of Repentance
(London, 1660), preached on 30 April.

searching. According to the Scottish observer James Sharp, "Mr. Cal-amy . . . [was] at a stand whether to accept of being king's chaplain, and I think it will not be much pressed upon him." Ludlow's view of these appointments was understandably jaundiced: "For the presby-terian party were not yet altogether out of hopes of doing something on the behalfe of their interest, Charles Steward thinking it adviseable to give them faire words, and some casts of his favour, the army being not yet disbanded." When the king entered London on 29 May, he was greeted by a delegation of ministers in St. Paul's churchyard and pre-sented with a Bible by the Presbyterian minister Arthur Jackson. Cal-amy was probably there, for the decision to conduct such a ceremony had been approved in Sion College.[55]

Much of June was occupied with negotiations between Anglican and moderate Presbyterian leaders. Some Presbyterians, led by Jen-kins and Lazarus Seaman, opposed any settlement short of one mod-eled on Scottish Presbyterianism, but this was not Calamy's position. Like Baxter, he favored negotiations with Anglican leaders designed to achieve accommodation. In mid-June Charles himself passed on a suggestion from Baxter that Calamy and Reynolds select ten of their colleagues to meet with Gauden and eleven other proponents of epis-copal polity to "decide the business of Church Government." The king promised to serve as moderator. Several meetings—with Charles present—took place, usually at the Earl of Manchester's house. Hyde and the Earl of St. Albans also attended. With Baxter, Reynolds, Ashe, and Manton, Calamy argued that nonessentials must not be re-quired in the church, that biblical discipline must be imposed, and that only godly clergy must have benefices. If these conditions were met, episcopal polity was acceptable. In turn the king promised to work for comprehension and asked both sides to prepare their pro-posals for the polity of the church.[56]

In the honeymoon period following Charles's return, the Presby-terians had cause to hope. On 1 June, the king acceded to a request

---

[55]HMC 4, *Fifth Report*, 181, 204; Masson, *Milton*, 6:62; Wodrow, *History*, 1:37, 40 (quoted); Ludlow, *A Voyce*, 167 (cf. *Memoirs*, 2:283); Kirby, "The Reconcilers," 59-60; Pearce, *Sion College*, 118-19; Kennet, *Register*, 162, 178, 180.

[56]*Rel. Bax.*, pt. 2:230-32; HMC 4, *Fifth Report*, 168; Kirby, "The Reconcilers," 61; Masson, *Milton*, 6:62; Wodrow, *History*, 1:42.

from the Convention Parliament that incumbents in both clerical and lay posts could not be deprived without either legal eviction or a parliamentary order. In the third week of June Calamy, Ashe, Baxter, and Reynolds had a conference with Charles in which they were satisfied with his politeness and moderation. The king impressed upon them the necessity of compromising with the Anglicans and requested a written statement indicating the concessions they felt they could make. Because the Presbyterians were concerned that the Anglicans might not compromise in turn, Calamy turned to Sharp for assistance, but the latter declined on the grounds that any compromise undermined the religious "settlement" between the English and Scottish Presbyterians. Calamy and his Presbyterian colleagues in the City subsequently met with Presbyterian delegates from the country at Sion College to assess the situation.[57]

At Sion College the Presbyterians finally agreed to ask Calamy, Reynolds, and Dr. Worth to draft a proposal to present to the king. In essence it embraced "the true antient primitive episcopacy or presidency as it was ballanced with a due commixtion of Presbyters." In particular they were willing to accept a modified episcopacy as Archbishop Ussher had earlier proposed, with a major role accorded to suffragans chosen by the respective synods. They also insisted that there must be no oaths or promises of obedience to bishops as prerequisites for ordination or ministerial appointment. With respect to the liturgy, Calamy, Reynolds, and Worth called for a revision of the Book of Common Prayer, and for the abolition of the surplice, the sign of the cross in baptism, and bowing toward altars and at the name of Jesus. They also called for kneeling at the Lord's supper and the observance of humanly instituted holy days to be made voluntary. On 10 July these proposals were politely received by Charles, who promised to bring the two sides together for negotiation.[58]

---

[57]*LJ*, 11:46; *Cobbett's Complete Collection of State Trials*, ed. T. B. Howell, vol. 6 (London, 1810): 2-3; Wodrow, *History*, 1:46. Calamy was troubled with the gout in late June. Wodrow, *History*, 1:45.

[58]*State Trials*, 6:2-7; Abernathy, "The English Presbyterians," 68-69. Calamy kept Sharp apprised of the discussions. Wodrow, *History*, 1:49.

The king's interest in achieving an accommodation stemmed wholly from political considerations and not from religious convictions. Of his ten Puritan chaplains, only five—Calamy, Baxter, Reynolds, Spurstowe, and Benjamin Woodbridge—actually preached before him, and then only once apiece. They were not required to use the Book of Common Prayer, but only to give the sermon. Samuel Pepys heard a rumor in the spring that Calamy had preached before the king at Whitehall wearing a surplice, but the rumor proved to be false. Although the king was accommodating in not insisting upon the more formal clerical garb, he had no personal sympathy for the views of his Puritan chaplains. From his informants Ludlow learned that while these men were preaching, Charles and his brother, the Duke of York, spent most of the time looking at pictures in their Bibles. In part, such a response must have been occasioned by Calamy's determination to use the pulpit to lecture the king. When he preached at Whitehall on 12 August on the text, "To whom much is given, of him much is required," Calamy, according to Pepys, "was very officious with his three reverences [sic] to the King, as others do." Nevertheless, according to Calamy's grandson, "about this Time, he was often with his Majesty at the Lord Chamberlain's Lodgings, or elsewhere; and was always smil'd on, and graciously receiv'd."[59]

By the late summer Calamy was increasingly troubled, having seen "whither things were tending," but continued to work for Presbyterian interests. When Thomas King, Rector of Sudborne-cum-Orford, Suffolk, was threatened with the loss of his living, Calamy came to his defense. Faced with a choice between working for accommodation with the Anglicans in a state church or accepting a policy of toleration, Calamy opted for the former, fearing that toleration would benefit Catholics and sectaries. With Manton and Ashe, he expressed this decision to the Scottish divines David Dickson, Robert Douglas, James Hamilton, John Smith, and George Hutchison in a letter dated 10 August. The key to accommodation, they argued, was to alter episcopacy into a form of synodical government, with both sides compromising on lesser issues.

---

[59]Calamy, *Non. Mem.*, 1:20; Kirby, "The Reconcilers," 60; Wodrow, *History*, 1:42; *The Diary of Samuel Pepys*, ed. Henry B. Wheatley, 9 vols. (London, 1910-1918) 1:160, 204; Ludlow, *A Voyce*, 167; Calamy, *Cont.*, 89.

The general stream and current is for the old prelacy in all its pomp and height, and therefore it cannot be hoped for, that the presbyterial government should be owned as the public establishment of this nation, while the tide runneth so strongly that way; and the bare toleration of it will certainly produce a mischief, whilst papists, and sectaries of all sorts, will wind in themselves under the covert of such a favour: therefore no course seemeth likely to us to secure religion and the interests of Christ . . . but by making presbytery a part of the public establishment; which will not be effected but by moderating and reducing episcopacy to the form of synodical government. . . . This is all we can for the present hope for. . . .

Most Anglican leaders, however, were unwilling to compromise.[60] Faced with an apparent impasse, Charles offered the outlines of a solution in a preliminary draft dated 4 September. Despite some concessions, the moderate Presbyterians found the compromise inadequate and commissioned Baxter to compose a reply. His response, however, was so intemperate that Calamy and Reynolds, supported by the leading political Presbyterians—the Earl of Manchester, Denzil Holles, and Arthur Annesley—insisted upon revision. The version submitted to the king asked for five major concessions: the appointment of suffragan bishops in large dioceses; ordination and the imposition of discipline by bishops and presbyters together; confirmation only with the local minister's approval; revision of the Book of Common Prayer and provision for alternate forms of worship; and making ceremonies such as kneeling at communion optional. To reconcile the differences, the Presbyterians asked for a conference, at which they were represented by Calamy, Baxter, and Reynolds. Neither side yielded.[61]

Charles and Hyde, unwilling to abandon their hope of accommodation, requested that the moderate Presbyterians give them their proposed alterations to the king's preliminary draft. On 22 October a special conference was convened at Hyde's home, with the king himself present. Seven Presbyterians were invited: Calamy, Baxter, Ashe,

[60]Calamy, An Abridgment, 187; CSPD, 1660-61, 233; Wodrow, History, 1:54.

[61]Rel. Bax., pt. 2:259-64 (the draft), 256-76 (the response); Abernathy, "The English Presbyterians," 74-75. Annesley was raised to the peerage as Lord Anglesey in 1661.

Reynolds, Manton, Spurstowe, and John Wallis. The eight-member Anglican delegation included Sheldon, Morley, and Gauden. In the heated exchanges, both sides stood firm, with Calamy and Baxter arguing vociferously against the Anglican view of episcopacy and Anglican demands for the reordination of ministers not in episcopal orders. Calamy, testified Baxter, "answered Dr. [Peter] *Gunning* from Scripture very well against the Divine Right of Prelacy as a distinct Order." After the meeting, Manchester, Holles, and Annesley urged the Presbyterian ministers to offer more compromises, to which Baxter wanted typically to respond by publishing a paper setting forth the differences within the Presbyterian camp. Calamy wisely objected. Baxter nevertheless did correctly insist in his history of these negotiations that there was a difference in the positions taken by those Presbyterians unwilling to compromise on the one hand and the "Reconcilers" who would accept a modified episcopacy on the other. Looking in retrospect upon Calamy's role, Baxter observed that "he pleaded for no more than I did, whatever his Judgment was; only at the Meeting before the King, he pleaded well that the words *Bishops* and *Presbyters* are in Scripture of the same signification. . . ."[62]

Resolved to publish a final version of his declaration, the king appointed a select committee to make the last revisions. To it he named the Reconcilers Calamy and Reynolds, the Anglicans Morley and Humphrey Henchman, and two moderators, Holles and Annesley. When the declaration was published on 25 October, it contained major concessions to the Presbyterians on nearly every matter of substance, including a provision to revise the Book of Common Prayer. Calamy was undoubtedly one of those Presbyterian leaders who urged the London ministers to accept the declaration, as most in fact did. He and Baxter, however, then channeled their efforts toward procuring parliamentary legislation to give the king's solution more perma-

---

[62]Huntington Library, Hastings MSS, HA 5586; *Rel. Bax.*, pt. 2:276-78; Abernathy, "The English Presbyterians," 75. According to Anne Whiteman, the Presbyterian William Bates also attended the conference at Worcester House. "The Restoration of the Church of England," in *From Uniformity to Unity*, ed. Nuttall and Chadwick, 70, n. 2. The principal Reconcilers were Calamy, Baxter, Reynolds, Newcomen, Spurstowe, Ashe, Manton, Bates, Thomas Jacomb, and Anthony Tuckney.

nence. In their efforts they received some encouragement from Hyde.[63]

The seriousness with which Charles viewed the accommodation was further manifest when he offered bishoprics to the three leading Reconcilers: Lichfield to Calamy, Hereford to Baxter, and Norwich to Reynolds. The three men met several times to discuss the offer, agreeing that a bishopric could be accepted under the terms of the royal declaration without violating their earlier oaths to the Solemn League and Covenant or recognizing *jure divino* prelacy. They had doubts, however, whether the declaration would become law or whether it was simply a ploy to lure them irretrievably into the episcopal camp. For his part Calamy "desired that we might all go together, and all refuse, or all accept it."[64]

Having previously advocated moderate episcopacy, Reynolds and Baxter thought they could accept the sees with only minimal negative repercussions, but Calamy, having publicly opposed episcopacy, and having "done so much against it[,] . . . . never Presbyterian would be trusted for his sake" if he accepted. Following Baxter's advice, Reynolds accepted in September, but Baxter himself preferred to remain at Kidderminster. Baxter declined to advise Calamy, who, pressed by his wife and Matthew Newcomen, eventually declined. According to Baxter, "the true Reason of Mr. *Calamies* delay (which few men knew better than my self), was because perhaps he would have accepted a Bishoprick as altered by the Kings Declaration about Ecclesiastical affairs, and to be used according to that Declaration, but not according to the ancient Laws and Customs of the Land and Church, though of this much he was unresolved." A somewhat different perspective was provided to Thomas Birch by John Tillotson, who recounted "that the good old man deliberated about it some considerable time, professing to see the great inconvenience of the Presbyterian parity of ministers." According to Tillotson, if Calamy had accepted the see of Lichfield, William Bates would have been appointed his dean and John Miles and Tillotson himself would have been made canons. Although Cal-

---

[63]*Rel. Bax.*, pt. 2:277-78, 284-85, 287; *LJ*, 11: 179-82; Abernathy, "The English Presbyterians," 75-77. For the text of the declaration see *State Trials*, 6: 11-21.

[64]*Rel. Bax.*, pt. 2:281-83.

amy was ready to agree, Tillotson said, his wife "over-ruled her husband, and so the matter went off." Their refusals seem to have surprised the Anglicans. Dr. Thomas Smith rather caustically observed that Calamy and Baxter "make a little nice of accepting" the sees. Professor Abernathy is undoubtedly correct in concluding that the refusals of Calamy and Baxter were a major reason for the failure of the proposed accommodation. A bill to confirm the royal declaration by statute was defeated in the Convention's House of Commons.[65]

Despite the setbacks, Charles was not ready to abandon his efforts. The conference proposed in the declaration to revise the liturgy was convened at the bishop of London's lodgings in the Savoy in April 1661. To Calamy and Reynolds fell the task of selecting the twelve Presbyterian representatives and their alternates. At the outset Bishop Sheldon informed the Presbyterian delegation that the conference had been convened at their request and they must therefore prepare their "Exceptions" to the liturgy in writing. This was done primarily by Calamy, Reynolds, Bates, Newcomen, Jacomb, John Wallis, and Samuel Clarke. The final document listed eighteen "Exceptions" based on the principle that "the prayers and other materials of the liturgy, might not be clogged with any thing that was doubtful or questioned among pious, learned and orthodox persons." To these "Exceptions" the Anglicans responded with a lengthy "Answer" that was uncompromising in tone. The scruples that troubled the godly, averred the Anglicans, had no validity unless proven unlawful: "For otherwise, if the bare pretence of scruples is a sufficient plea to discharge us from obedience, all law and order can signify nothing." Calamy drafted a substantive "Reply" to the Anglican "Answer" and Baxter prepared a "Reformed Liturgy," which the Presbyterians generally sanctioned. Calamy also helped draft a "Petition for Peace," which the conference

---

[65]Ibid.; Baxter, *An Apology for the Nonconformists Ministry* (London, 1681) 106-107; Thomas Birch, *The Life of the Most Reverend Dr. John Tillotson, Lord Archbishop of Canterbury* (London, 1752) 404; Abernathy, "The English Presbyterians," 77; *CSPD, 1660-61*, 308; Calamy, *An Abridgment*, 187. Reynolds accepted on 9 September; Calamy was still considering the offer on 17 November, but had declined by 6 December. *CSPD, 1660*, 262; *CSPD, Addenda, 1660-85*, 13; HMC 4, *Fifth Report*, 145, 158. His grandson estimates that if Calamy had accepted the see, he might have had £20,000 to bequeath to his family or "expend for pious uses. . . ." Calamy, *Life*, 55.

did not consider. In the debates it is interesting to note that Calamy accused the bishops of espousing Anabaptist tenets because they insisted on godfathers or sureties to answer for infants at their baptism. Increasingly dispirited and divided among themselves, the delegation of Reconcilers at the conference, dominated by Baxter, was ineffective. In July the conference broke up without having achieved its goals. Once again, the hopes of both the king and Calamy for comprehension were dealt a serious blow. Although there was a rumor to the effect that Calamy had told the king and some of his councillors "that there was nothing in the church to which he could not conform, were it not for scandalizing others," Baxter insisted that those who were with him throughout this period heard him repeatedly protest that "several things in conformity . . . [were] intolerable sins."[66]

While the Savoy Conference carried out its ill-fated discussions, Anglican leaders pressured Charles to summon Convocation. After the writs were issued on 10 April, the ensuing elections returned few Presbyterians or Reconcilers. Baxter and Calamy, who "was much esteem'd for his Prudence and Conduct" in the City, were nominated by the London ministers, but Bishop Sheldon "excused" them from attending, exercising his right to select the delegates from those nominated in the diocese. Both in Convocation and in the recently elected Cavalier Parliament the prevailing mood was hostile to an accommodation with the Presbyterians. Moderates were disappointed. John Wilkins, who was rewarded with the bishopric of Chester for conforming (despite being Cromwell's brother-in-law), was disappointed by Calamy's exclusion. Wilkins "had such an opinion of his judgment about church-government, as to wish he could have conformed, that he might have confronted the bold assertors of the *Jus Divinum* of episcopacy in the convocation. . . ."[67]

---

[66]*Rel. Bax.*, pt. 2:303, 307, 355; *State Trials*, 6:28-31 ("Exceptions"), 31-41 ("Answer"), 41-42 (28, 32 quoted); Calamy, *Cont.*, 89; Calamy, *Non. Mem.*, 1:78 (quoted). The commission for the conference is printed in *State Trials*, 6:25-27. The conference documents are also printed in *The History of Non-Conformity, As It Was Argued and Stated* (London, 1704). See also HMC 63, *Egmont*, 2:2-3. Calamy was scheduled to preach before the king during Lent, 1661. *The Lauderdale Papers*. ed. Osmund Airy, 2 vols., Camden Society, n.s. (1884-1885) 1:74-75.

[67]*Rel. Bax.*, pt. 2:333; Abernathy, "The English Presbyterians," 80-81; Calamy, *An Abridgment*, 187; Calamy, *Non. Mem.*, 1:78.

The unfriendly temper of Parliament and Convocation was reflected among the populace as well. In the theater crowds flocked to see a revised version of Ben Jonson's *Bartholomew Fair,* which satirized Calamy and Baxter. As William Hooke described it to John Davenport in New England, "prayers were made in imitation of the Puritan, with such scripture expressions as I am loath to mention. . . ." In October 1661 the king himself enjoyed the play, along with the Earl of Manchester, the Bishop of London, and two other prelates. "And in a play made of the late warr," Ludlow reported, "the English and Scots presbyters are brought in, giving thancks for the severall victoryes, as Mr. Marshall, Calamy, Baxter etc., with which representation the King expressed himselfe *highly* pleased." Ludlow and Pepys were convinced that Charles personally countenanced such satire. Yet since he still hoped for some plan of reconciliation, he must have approved the satire as good humor and not in a malicious spirit. [68]

For Calamy the times were all the more difficult because of several personal matters. Early in the year he had fallen, "and at first it was feared his leg was out of joint." In October Lady Anne, wife of his friend Sir William Waller, the former parliamentary general, died. On the 31st Calamy preached her funeral sermon at New Church, Westminster, trying to strike a theme of consolation and hope. The death of a saint, he averred, is only a blessed, comfortable sleep. Although the bodies of the godly, while in the grave, are asleep in Jesus, they will eventually be resurrected and taken to heaven. The living must therefore neither fear death nor mourn immoderately for the dead. The sermon was published the following year under the title, *The Happinesse of Those Who Sleep in Jesus.* [69]

The struggle for a comprehensive religious settlement entered its final stage in the fall of 1661. The Savoy Conference had now collapsed and the Presbyterians were in serious disarray. Early in January the House of Commons passed a bill that would require the ouster from their livings of all ministers not in episcopal orders. In the Lords

---

[68]Robert S. Bosher, *The Making of the Restoration Settlement: The Influence of the Laudians* (New York, 1951) 238-39; Mather Papers, *CMHS,* 4th ser., 8: 177 (quoted); Ludlow, *A Voyce,* 290-91.

[69]*CSPD, 1660-61,* 537; Calamy, *The Happinesse of Those Who Sleep in Jesus* (London, 1662) 3, 7, 13, 16-17.

Hyde, the Lord Chancellor, successfully lobbied to amend the bill so that Presbyterian clergy could retain their livings. Among those who followed the Chancellor's lead was Calamy's longtime colleague, Bishop Reynolds. Calamy, Baxter, and William Bates were delegated by the Presbyterians to express their gratitude to Clarendon on 3 February. But the Commons refused to approve the bill in its revised form, and subsequent efforts of the Lord Chancellor and the king to save the policy of comprehension failed. The Presbyterians were of little help, for they were, according to William Hooke, "in extreme contempt, &c[.], there former forwardnes to bring in the K: not at all regarded. . . ." Calamy himself, now "a Lame man with one fall after another," kept urging moderation on the Presbyterians "lest the Gospell [be] quite lost. . . ."[70]

Finally, on 19 May 1662 Charles agreed to accept the Act of Uniformity, though various schemes to mitigate its effects on the Presbyterians followed. One of these, advanced by Clarendon at the king's request, called for selected ministers—including Calamy, Manton, and Bates—to petition the crown for dispensations from the act. The London Reconcilers were convinced that Charles would approve a plan for toleration, and so informed their colleagues in the country: "His Majesty will write to all the bishops that it is his pleasure that those ministers that cannot subscribe shall notwithstanding be allowed to preach, if the Common Prayer be read in their churches. This favour was obtained by non-subscribers, particularly by Dr. Jacomb, Dr. Bates, Mr. Calamy, Dr. Manton."[71]

Calamy's farewell sermon on 2 Samuel 24: 14 to his congregation was preached on 17 August. God, he told his parishioners, was taking away the gospel ministry because his people had lost their first love. "Are there not some of you [who] have itching ears, and would fain have Preachers that would feed you with dainty phrases, and begin not to care for a Minister that unrips your Consciences, speaks to your hearts and souls, and would force you into heaven by frighting you out of your sins?" Ten days later Calamy, Manton, Bates, and several oth-

---

[70]Abernathy, "The English Presbyterians," 81-84; Bosher, *The Making*, 242; Mather Papers, *CMHS*, 4th ser., 8: 195 (quoted), 197 (quoted).

[71]Abernathy, "The English Presbyterians," 84-85; *Mercurius Publicus* (1662) no. 35, p. 579, cited in Bosher, *The Making*, 260.

ers petitioned the king for dispensations as Clarendon had recommended.

> *May it please Your most Excellent Majesty,*
>
> Upon former Experience of Your Majesty's Tenderness and Indulgence to Your Obedient and Loyal Subjects, (in which Number we can with all Clearness reckon ourselves) we some of the Ministers within Your City of *London,* who are likely by the late Act of Uniformity to be cast out of all publick Service in the Ministry, because we cannot in Conscience conform to all Things requir'd in the said Act, have taken the Boldness humbly to cast ourselves and Concernments at Your Majesty's Feet, desiring that of Your Princely Wisdom and Compassion, you would take some effectual Course whereby we may be continu'd in the Exercise of our Ministry, to teach Your People Obedience to GOD and Your Majesty. And we doubt not but by our Dutiful and Peaceable Carriage therein, we shall render ourselves not altogether unworthy of so great a Favour.

When he delivered this petition Calamy informed Charles that he and his cohorts were as loyal as any to the king, but that they did not expect to be treated as they had been, nor would they make any petitions apart from this one. The king promised to consider the petition and in fact brought it to the Privy Council the following day. Although Charles looked upon the petition favorably, he declined to act without finding a way around the provision in the Act of Uniformity that allowed bishops and patrons to present persons in episcopal orders to benefices held by Nonconformists. On this issue Sheldon, who had already ejected clergy, refused to budge, prompting the king to back off from the idea of issuing dispensations.[72]

Although ejected, Calamy attended services at St. Mary Aldermanbury. When its minister failed to appear on 28 December,[73] Cal-

[72]Calamy, *The Fixed Saint Held Forth in a Farewell Sermon* (London, 1662) 17-18; Calamy, *Cont.*, 10-11 (quoted); Kennet, *Register*, 753; Abernathy, "The English Presbyterians," 85-86. *The Fixed Saint* is reprinted in *Farewel Sermons Preached by Mr. Calamy* (London, 1663). The same collection includes his funeral sermon for Simeon Ashe (d. 1662), dealing with the meaning of death for saints, 222-40. Originally published under the title, *The Righteous Mans Death Lamented*, the sermon was preached at St. Augustine's, London, on Isaiah 57:1. Kennet, *Register*, 746-47.

[73]After Calamy's ejection, the people of St. Mary Aldermanbury elected Tillotson as his successor, perhaps at Calamy's recommendation. Tillotson, however, declined to serve, whereupon the congregation chose Richard Martin on 28 January 1663. Birch, *Tillotson*, 24.

amy agreed to preach rather than have the parishioners return home without a sermon. Conversations with lawyers had led him to understand that an occasional sermon did not violate the Act of Uniformity. As the theme of his sermon on 1 Samuel 3: 13, he warned that England was in danger of losing the ark. "There is not one sin for which God hath taken away the ark from any people, but that sin may be found among us." He urged his hearers to recognize "that the Gospel is not entailed upon *England; England* hath no Letters Patents for the gospel. . . ." In particular he cautioned of the peril resulting from the presence of Jesuits and priests in England. For this sermon Calamy was arrested and imprisoned in Newgate on 6 January on a warrant from the Lord Mayor. According to the mittimus he had also preached illegally at St. Mary's on 26 August, which is possible since the king had encouraged Calamy and his friends to stay in their pulpits as long as possible. The mittimus specifies that Calamy was to remain in Newgate without bail for three months. "And O what insulting there was by that Party, in the Newsbook, and in their Discourses, *That* Calamy *that would not be a Bishop was in Jail!*"[74]

Two days prior to Calamy's sermon, the king had issued a Declaration of Indulgence. Calamy himself had helped urge Charles to take this course: "Upon Mr. *Calamy's* advising with his friends at court, a petition for indulgence was drawn up, and presented to his majesty." However, the royal declaration was essentially a statement of opposition to religious persecution rather than an offer of indulgence. In it the king expressed his hope that Parliament would pass legislation recognizing his authority to dispense with the provisions of the Act of Uniformity. Because Charles expressly intended to aid the Catholics, the Presbyterians were hostile to the declaration, though it received support from the Congregationalists. It was probably as part of his efforts to secure Presbyterian support that Charles ap-

---

[74]*CSP Venetian, 1661-64,* 229; Pepys, *Diary,* 3:5; Calamy, *Eli Trembling for Fear of the Ark* (Oxford, 1663) 11-12, 15; Abernathy, "The English Presbyterians," 85; *CSPD, 1663-64,* 8; *Rel. Bax.,* pt. 2:386 (quoted). The mittimus is printed with *Eli Trembling,* and in *Mercurius Publicus,* 1 (1-8 January 1663) 14-16; and *Kingdomes Intelligencer,* 2 (5-12 January 1663) 17-20. Laurence Womock responded to Calamy's sermon in *Aron-bimnucha* (1663). In the same year, Calamy was satirized, along with other Nonconformist leaders (including George Griffith), in *Cabala, or an Impartial Account of the Non-conformists' Private Designs,* reprinted in *Somers Tracts,* 7:567-86.

proved a warrant for Calamy's release on 13 January 1663. Baxter had interceded for him. In prison Calamy had become something of a martyr and the government was embarrassed "when it was seen what a Resort of Persons of all Qualities there was to him in Newgate; and how generally the Severity was resented." His incarceration even sparked two poets—Samuel Butler and Robert Wild—to refer to the event in their verse. Wild wrote:

> Shame and disgrace
> Rise only from the crime, not from the place,
> Who thinks reproach or injury is done
> By an eclipse to the unspotted sun?
> He only, by that black upon his brow,
> Allures spectators, and so do you.
> Let me find honey, tho' upon a rod,
> And prize the prison when the keeper's God.
> Newgate or Hell were Heaven if Christ were there,
> He made the stable so, and sepulchre.

Wild himself had been ejected from the rectory of Tatenhill, Staffordshire.[75]

Sometime after Calamy's release and before 2 March, the king summoned him along with Manton, Bates, and possibly Baxter. In return for supporting his policy of indulgence, the king offered to return them to their livings, bringing momentary respect at court. "Before they went in to the King, people said, 'What do these Presbyterians here?' but when they came out, they said, 'Your servant, Dr. Calamy, &c.'" There was, however, no agreement. When the House of Commons debated the indulgence issue in February, there was some discussion of Calamy's imprisonment, for at his release the king had claimed that the Act of Uniformity did not permit longer incarceration. It was probably in the context of this indulgence that an An-

[75]Calamy, Non. Mem., 1:79 (quoted); Abernathy, "The English Presbyterians," 87-88; CSPD, 1663-64, 10; Michael R. Watts, The Dissenters (Oxford, 1978), 1:247; Calamy, An Abridgment, 187 (quoted); Calamy, Life, 56-57; Ath. Oxon., 1:899; Wild, quoted in Davids, Annals, 537. For Wild see DNB, s.v.; Calamy Revised, s.v. While Charles was drafting an earlier version of his declaration in October 1660, Calamy and Baxter expressed to him their support for the public maintenance of ministers. Thomas Richards, Religious Developments in Wales (1654-1662) (London, 1923) 181.

glican critic compiled a collection of the earlier reformist views of Calamy, Marshall, Caryl, Case, and others, publishing them—with an intent to discredit—under the title, *Evangelium Armatum. A Specimen, or Short Collection* (London, 1663).[76]

Little is known of Calamy's last years. With his longtime associate Jenkins, he was a funnel for channeling money to support needy Nonconformist ministers. About 1664 he had £500 for this purpose. On 24 May of that year, a general day of humiliation "kept by all sects" in London, Calamy was one of the preachers, along with Arthur Jackson, Nathaniel Strange, John Vernon, John Skinner, John Rowe, Ralph Venning, and others. Calamy also participated in conventicles, which met at the house of his son-in-law Mr. Bayly, with whom Watson was also associated. Until he was taken ill, Calamy reputedly preached every Sunday after evening service in his home. Frequent fasts were also held at his house, and in May 1665, a government informant reported that he had returned from a trip and planned to resume holding conventicles there. One in fact was held as early as the 14th of that month. Calamy apparently maintained contact with exiles in the Netherlands, for in September 1666 Colonel Bampfield dispatched Joseph Hill, a minister at Leyden, to meet with Calamy, Jenkins, and others.[77]

After the Great Fire devastated much of London on 3 September 1666, Calamy was driven through the City in a coach, "and seeing the desolate Condition of so flourishing a City, for which he had so great an Affection, his tender Spirit receiv'd such Impressions as he could never wear off. He went home, and never came out of his Chamber more; but dy'd within a Month." Following his death at Enfield on 29 October, Calamy was buried in the ruins of his old church, St. Mary Aldermanbury, on 6 November.[78]

---

[76]*Mather Papers*, CMHS, 4th ser., 8:208; *CSPD, 1663-64*, 53, 64; *Rel. Bax.*, pt. 2:429. Hooke wrote to John Davenport on 5 March that Charles gave Calamy, Bates, and Manton "ful assurance that a Bill should be brought into the House which would introduce most of them into there places againe." *Mather Papers*, loc. cit.

[77]PRO SP 29/67/54; 29/99/7; 29/100/7; 29/109/56; 29/121/38; *CSPD, 1663-64*, 12; *CSPD, 1664-65*, 144, 363; *CSPD, 1666-67*, 146.

[78]Calamy, *An Abridgment*, 187. The date of the funeral is given as 7 November in Francis Peck, *Desiderata Curiosa: Or, a Collection of Divers Scarce and Curious Pieces*, 2 vols. (London, 1779) 2:545.

A few of Calamy's writings were published posthumously. *The Art of Divine Meditation* is a collection of sermons printed from the notes of a listener concerning divine meditation as a means of begetting and increasing grace and trust in Christ. The sermons explain where and when to meditate, what meditation entails, and the proper objects of meditation, such as God's commandments, threats, promises, and ordinances. "You would be tall Christians in grace if you did accustom your selves to this duty; the reason why you are such Dwarfs in Christianity . . . is for the want of the practice of this duty. . . ." His sermon on Acts 26: 8 dealing with the resurrection of the dead was published in the *Morning-Exercise at St. Giles's Cripplegate*. Calamy's ability to turn a phrase led to the inclusion of some of his aphorisms in a compilation entitled *Saints Memorials: or, Words Fitly Spoken, Like Apples of Gold in Pictures of Silver* (1674). One example of his pithiness must suffice: "Ingratitude is the Epitomy of Impiety." This compilation also included Calamy's "Exhortations to the Service of the Lord," much of which consists of biblical quotations.[79]

Calamy was married twice. By his first wife, Mary, daughter of Robert Snelling of Ipswich, esq., a member of Parliament in the latter part of James I's reign, he had two sons—Edmund (c. 1635-1685), like his father an ejected minister, and Jeremy (born in November 1638)—and a daughter (Mrs. Bayly). By his second wife, Anne Leaver, a committed Presbyterian of Lancashire, he had three more sons—Benjamin (1642-1686), James, and John (born 2 August 1658)—and four daughters—Susan, Elizabeth, Rebecca, and Anne. Calamy's will, dated 4 October 1666, was proved on 14 November of the same year. He owned property in Kent and Suffolk as well as his house in St. Nicholas Lane, London. His grandson, Edmund, was the historian of the Nonconformists and a primary source of information for his grandfather's life.[80]

From the early 1640s to his death in 1666, Calamy was remarkably consistent in the principles to which he adhered. The Presbyterianism

---

[79]Ibid.; Calamy, *The Art of Divine Meditation* (London, 1680) 48-56, 105, 139-40, 206 (quoted); anon., *Saints Memorials* (London, 1674) 39.

[80]*DNB*, s.v.; *Calamy Revised*, s.v.; Birch, *Tillotson*, 388; Will, Prerogative Court of Canterbury, 14 November 1666.

he espoused for two and a half decades was neither narrow nor rigidly intolerant. To be sure, he repudiated both *jure divino* episcopalians on the right and sectaries on the left, but he also sought a working unity with Independents, primarily in the 1650s, and with Anglicans at the Restoration. Theologically he worked in the Westminster Assembly to modify the tenets of the strict Calvinists, yet he repudiated both Arminianism and Antinomianism. His path in both theology and polity was essentially one of moderation and comprehension, not exclusiveness. His inclination to unify was also readily apparent in the mid and later 1640s as he became dismayed by the ever more radical course of events. Nevertheless his own crucial support among the Puritan clergy for major reforms in the church and ultimately for the defense of religious and parliamentary principles in the first Civil War was itself radical in its implications. Calamy did not act out of self interest or economic motivation, but in devotion to the cause of a church that he believed must be brought more closely into agreement with the precepts of Scripture. His firm hand helped prevent Presbyterian disintegration in the 1650s just as it helped preserve Presbyterian independence and identity in the 1660s. Moved by conscience, his commitment to the Presbyterian cause remained unshaken from the days of near triumph in the mid-1640s to the resumption of persecution two decades later.

"One of the Most Daring Schismaticks in all that Country": Richard Culmer, Divisive Zealot*

The unity that Edmund Calamy sought was threatened by a host of factors ranging from conflicting perspectives on how to prosecute the Civil War and deal with the king to divergent religious aims. There was another cause of divisiveness within the reform movement, which is too easily overlooked, namely, the fanatical zeal of those who challenged not only the more overt problems in the church but the traditional mores of the people. There is perhaps no better illustration of the depth of conflicting religious ideology and the bitter divisiveness within local communities during the Civil War than the career of Richard Culmer. Puritan, iconoclast, controversialist, pamphleteer, and outspoken proponent of the parliamentary cause, Culmer, like Calamy, was supported by the influential Earl of Warwick as well as the Westminster Assembly of Divines, yet his enemies assaulted and slandered him, refused to pay him tithes, and even attempted to assassinate him. Rather than being a balm to heal the wounds of a di-

---

*This chapter is a revised version of an article published in the *Historical Magazine of the Protestant Episcopal Church* 50 (December 1981): 359-68.

vided community, his ministry exacerbated tensions and inflamed feelings. In this respect his career was strikingly different from that of Calamy.

Born about 1597 in the Isle of Thanet, perhaps at Broadstairs, Kent, Culmer was a student at King's School, Canterbury, where he studied under Roger Raven. On 8 July 1613 Culmer was admitted to Magdalene College, Cambridge, where he graduated B.A. in 1618 and received the M.A. degree three years later. He was ordained a deacon in the Diocese of Peterborough on 23 September 1621 and a priest the following day. On 20 July 1624 he married Katharine Johnson at Harbledown, Kent, and by her had seven children, five of whom were still living in 1662. Culmer was incorporated at Oxford University in July 1628.[1]

In 1630 Culmer was appointed Vicar of Goodnestone, Kent, but he was suspended early in 1635 by Sir Nathaniel Brent—acting for Archbishop Laud—because he refused to read the Book of Sports. Two other ministers—John Player of Kennington and Thomas Heiron of Hernhill—were suspended at the same time for this offense and had their annual incomes reduced £20. In contrast, Culmer, who was already acquiring a reputation as an outspoken critic of the Laudian church, was required to forfeit his entire income, notwithstanding the fact that he had a wife and seven children to support. His difficulties were compounded when his successor attacked him in print. When Culmer became suspicious that his troubles were due to Edward Boys of Bonnington in Goodnestone, he accused Boys in July 1635 of plotting a rising to protest Ship Money. Because the charge could not be substantiated, Culmer was imprisoned in the Fleet.[2]

---

[1]*Al. Cant., s.v.; Al. Oxon., s.v.;* Richard Culmer, Jr., *A Parish Looking-Glasse for Persecutors of Ministers* (London, 1657) 3, 39. On 18 December 1601 a Richard Culmer, almost certainly one of Culmer's relatives and possibly his father, wrote from Canterbury to Sir Henry Brook, Lord Cobham, Lord Warden of the Cinque Ports, informing him of the location of the records of the manorial courts of St. Austin's and of Minster in Thanet. Because he knew the customs, he offered to hold the courts for Lord Cobham. HMC 4, *Fifth Report,* 139.

[2]*CSPD, 1635,* 301, 368; *1641-43,* 545; William Laud, *The History of the Troubles and Tryal of . . . William Laud, Lord Arch-Bishop of Canterbury* (London, 1695) 344; Peter Clark, *English Provincial Society from the Reformation to the Revolution: Religion, Politics and Society in Kent 1500-1640* (Hassocks, Sussex, 1977) 369-70; Culmer, Jr., *A Parish Looking-Glasse,* 3-4. *Calamy Revised, s.v.,* makes Culmer Curate of Goodnestone.

Repeatedly Culmer petitioned Laud to lift his suspension, but the archbishop's passion for order and obedience made him unsympathetic to Culmer's pleas. To Culmer, Player, and Heiron, Laud retorted: "If you know not how to Obey, I know not how to Grant your Petition." Culmer's persistence clearly irritated Laud, who on a subsequent occasion fumed: "Consideration! I will take nothing into consideration, and if you conform not all the sooner I'll take a more radical course with you." It was not until after the Scots invaded England that Culmer was again permitted to preach. By now, however, his enmity for Laud ran deep and in the elections for the Short Parliament Culmer vigorously opposed the return of the archbishop's secretary. In the violence-marred election, Sir Edward Master and his son-in-law, John Nutt, were returned.[3]

Culmer was now serving as the assistant to Robert Austin at Harbledown, near Canterbury. In his Puritan zeal, Culmer declaimed against inebriety and sabbath violations, prompting irate parishioners to protest by playing cricket before his door on the sabbath. Although he successfully forced them away, they subsequently played in a nearby field and stoned Culmer's son when he was ordered to spy on them. When Culmer denied the sacrament of the Lord's supper to the churchwarden's wife, her husband petulantly boarded up the pews. As Culmer extended the Puritan practice of denying communion to unworthy persons, hostility to him intensified. The parishioners voiced objections to Austin that Culmer did not administer the sacrament according to Church of England rites, "that he raised scandals of the Parish in the Pulpit: That he made differences between Neighbors," and that some people refused to listen to his sermons because he was not edifying. It is particularly significant that some of the hostility toward Culmer already stemmed from the divisive effect of his ministry on the community. Austin, however, refused to remove Culmer, but the latter was forced out of Harbledown when Austin accepted another benefice. During his period in Harbledown, Culmer,

---

[3]Laud, *History*, 344 (quoted); *CSPD*, 1644, 15; Culmer, Jr., *A Parish Looking-Glasse*, 4; Alan Everitt, *The Community of Kent and the Great Rebellion 1640-60* (Leicester, 1966) 74.

unwilling to forget his persecution at Laud's hands, petitioned the Long Parliament for redress on 3 February 1641.[4]

From Harbledown Culmer went to Canterbury where he continued to preach. Still very much the center of controversy, he was defended in an August 1642 declaration from the mayor, aldermen, and leading citizens of the town, who praised him as "a man of exemplary Life and Conversation."[5] The following year he became embroiled in a dispute over the vacant living of Chartham, near Canterbury.

The rectory of Chartham was in the gift of Laud, who was instructed by the king to bestow it on Mr. Reading, "a Man of good Note in the Church. . . ." Culmer, who wanted the living for himself, appealed for assistance to the Earl of Warwick on 31 January 1643, warning that Laud intended to give it to "one of the tribe of Lambeth." Because "malignants" must not have the power to advance their cause, he wanted Warwick to halt Laud's "tyrannous patronage." Warwick thereupon made a special trip to visit Laud in the Tower in the hope of obtaining the benefice for Culmer, who in Laud's eyes was "ignorant, and with his Ignorance, one of the most daring Schismaticks in all that Country" of Kent. Although Warwick produced a statement showing that the House of Lords had already recommended on 4 February that Culmer receive the benefice, Laud asserted that he was merely adhering to a royal directive. Culmer himself then went to Laud protesting that he was in conformity with the Church of England. "I think," Laud later wrote, "the Man forgot that I knew both him and his ways." Unwilling to quit, Culmer then allegedly offered one of Laud's servants a bribe of £150 to assist him in acquiring the living. For his part, Warwick reported Laud's intransigence to the Lords, but another peer pointed out that the benefice was now in the keeping of the Earl of Essex. Faced with objections that the Lords had acted in Culmer's behalf with only a minority present, Warwick dropped the matter, "and so," said Laud, "the Business slept. . . ." At Essex's request, the rectory of Chartham was awarded to Edward Corbet. The episode is instructive for the light it throws on Culmer's

---

[4]Culmer, Jr., A Parish Looking-Glasse, 4-5 (quoted); CSPD, 1640-41, 453-54.

[5]Culmer, Jr., A Parish Looking-Glasse, 9.

relationship to Warwick, perhaps the greatest of all the Puritan patrons.[6]

The vehemence of Culmer's Puritanism was amply revealed after Parliament appointed him in 1643 to be a commissioner for "the utter demolishing . . . of all monuments of superstition" in Canterbury Cathedral. For three days Culmer and his fellow iconoclasts wreaked havoc, demolishing thirteen statues of Christ and his disciples as well as beautiful stained-glass windows. At one point he was personally "on top of the city ladder, near sixty steps high, with a whole pike in his hand rattling down proud Becket's glassy bones." As a guide in his destructive efforts, Culmer used a work prepared by the Canterbury antiquary, William Somner, which enabled him "to sail by in that cathedral ocean of images." Culmer later remarked that he ruined the figure of Jesus in stained glass in Becket's chapel but left the devil because "he had an order to take down Christ, but had no order to take down the Devil." While the iconoclasts smashed the images, hostile crowds gathered outside the cathedral, forcing the authorities to lock the doors in order to protect Culmer and his cohorts. At one point the beleaguered Puritan, unable to leave the church because of the angry demonstrators, yielded to the call of nature and urinated in the cathedral—an act his enemies never let him forget. Eventually the mayor had to dispatch a file of musketeers to escort Culmer home. Even as late as June 1645, Culmer received a receipt for £8 11s. 2d. from Sir Robert Harley as the proceeds from burning embroidery called "The Glory" from the cathedral's high altar.[7]

The controversy that surrounded Culmer did not deter his supporters. On 9 October 1643 the Mayor of Canterbury, Edward and John Boys of Betteshanger, Sir James Oxinden, and others petitioned the Committee for Plundered Ministers to provide a benefice for Culmer, and on 2 February 1644 the Earl of Warwick asked that Culmer receive the cure of Ickham, near Sandwich, Kent. The committee,

---

[6]HMC 4, *Fifth Report*, 70; Laud, *History*, 200-201, 207; *LJ*, 5:588. Calamy correctly questioned the factual basis for Laud's charge that Culmer offered his servant a bribe. *Non. Mem.*, 2:346. The date of the Lords' bestowal of Chartham on Culmer is erroneously given as 4 January by Shaw, 2:307, and in *Calamy Revised*, s.v.

[7]Everitt, *The Community of Kent*, 200-203; Culmer, Jr., *A Parish Looking-Glasse*, 5-6; *Fasti Oxon.*, 1:447-48; HMC 29, *Portland*, 3:133.

however, also received a report dutifully forwarded by the mayor accusing Culmer of breaking the pipes conveying water to Canterbury
and advocating the execution of those who refused to contribute to
the parliamentary cause. Notwithstanding these charges, Culmer received the vicarage of St. Stephen's, Hackington, near Canterbury,
following the imprisonment of John Gouge for delinquency in 1644.
Culmer assumed his duties at the direction of the deputy-lieutenants,
but was removed by 17 April 1645. In the same year Culmer provided
evidence in Laud's trial with respect to the charge that the archbishop
had punished clergymen for refusing to read the Book of Sports. In
June Culmer passed on material against the archbishop from Player,
who was too ill to testify in person. Laud in turn criticized Culmer for
bribing one of his servants to acquire the rectory of Chartham, castigated him for urinating in Canterbury Cathedral, and damned him
as "both Wilful and Ignorant. . . ."[8]

At his own request Culmer was appointed one of six preachers as
well as a prebend at Canterbury Cathedral on 4 October 1644, the
same year he published a diatribe entitled *Cathedrall Newes from Canterbury*. Referring to the cathedral and its chapter as "that Augean stable,"
he condemned the paucity of sermons, the "Tyrannous" patronage of
livings, the manifestations of prelacy and popery, the icons that had
decorated the cathedral, the "profane" Book of Sports, the cathedral
clergy's support for the Bishops' Wars, and the use of organ music in
church worship. Laud, the dean, the canons, and other ecclesiastical
officials were scathingly castigated.[9] The reaction was predictable:
"Immediately upon the first publishing of it, the nest of Cathedral
Hornets at *Canterbury*, and their waspish Malignant Adherents, flew
about M. Culmers ears. . . ."[10] The counterattack came in *The Razing
of the Record* (1644) and *Antidotum Culmerianum* (1644), which included
charges that Culmer had been infamous at Cambridge as a football

[8]Culmer, Jr., *A Parish Looking-Glasse*, 8-10; *Fasti Oxon.*, 1:447; *Calamy Revised, s.v.*;
CSPD, 1644, 15, 217; Laud, *History*, 344.

[9]*LJ*, 7:10; Richard Culmer, Sr., *Cathedrall Newes from Canterbury* (1644), sig. A2ʳ,
5-7, 11. The book was approved by Joseph Caryl; a second edition was published in
1649. As a Six Preacher, Culmer received augmentations for his stipend from the
sale of dean and chapter lands. Shaw, 2:534, 568.

[10]Culmer, Jr., *A Parish Looking-Glasse*, 6.

player and a swimmer, which is plausible, and had been expelled from
the university, which was untrue.

Following the ejection in 1645 of Meric Casaubon from the living
of Minster in Thanet, Kent, the Committee for Plundered Ministers
gave the position to Culmer. There was trouble from the outset. His
curate was a common tippler and sabbath-breaker, and people from
Harbledown and Canterbury traveled to Minster to voice their hostility to Culmer. Even before he formally received the living, local folk
protested to the Westminster Assembly of Divines. In the Assembly,
however, Herbert Palmer, William Gouge, and others came to his defense, and the Assembly recommended that the committee bestow
the living on him. His opponents even petitioned a group of peers,
including Warwick, to assist them in keeping Culmer out of Minster,
but Warwick supported him as an honest man and made it clear that
if Culmer did not receive this living, Warwick would give him another. The enmity toward Culmer in Minster was so intense that some
villagers contemplated sending a band of women to waylay him at
Sarre Wall on his return and throw him in a ditch. Subsequently they
plotted to embarrass him by assigning him an illegitimate maiden as
a servant.[11]

Repeatedly a faction at Minster endeavored to have Culmer deprived of his living. One angry parishioner even pledged £500 to
drive him away. Complaints against him were made to the County
Committee at Canterbury, but Sir James Oxinden and Edward Boys
of Betteshanger defended him. On 12 June 1645 the committee ordered that Culmer take a turn speaking in the weekly lecture at St.
John's in the Isle of Thanet, but after he preached, hostility from "the
Cavalier party" was so intense that the lectures had to be terminated.[12]
At Sandwich, Culmer's critics demanded that the County Committee
remove him, but this time he was supported by Sir Edward Boys, constable of Dover Castle.

Boys also came to his defense, commending his sizable loans to
the state, when accusations were made before the County Committee

---

[11]Ibid., 10-12.

[12]Calamy, *Non. Mem.*, 2:346; Culmer, Jr., *A Parish Looking-Glasse*, 13. Those who
signed the order were Sir Anthony Weldon, Sir Richard Hardres, John Boys, William Kenwricke, Robert Scott, and William Miller.

at Eastry. Boys, in fact, had even written to the Committee for Plundered Ministers on Culmer's behalf as early as 27 January 1645. Culmer's enemies so hated him that they raised over £300 to instigate proceedings against him in the committee, where they accused him of being a "narrow brain'd man," of having refused to pay parliamentary taxes, and of having urinated in Canterbury Cathedral. When these charges were judged insufficient for his ejection, the determined critics offered him all the revenues due him from the living (£200 p. a.) for life if he would leave and allow them to support a minister of their liking. To their chagrin, he refused. [13]

An examination of the factors responsible for this persistent, intense hostility to Culmer suggests one fundamental reason why the quest of the godly to rule England ultimately failed. Culmer deeply divided the communities in eastern Kent in large measure because of his Puritan assault on traditional sociocultural practices and symbols. He spoke out, for example, against the erection of a maypole in Minster, and his antagonism to traditional holy days was manifested in his refusal to preach on Christmas day (for which he was assaulted in the churchyard). Moreover, he not only declined to use the Book of Common Prayer at Harbledown and Minster, but he would not perform graveside services at funerals. Insisting that "he would not be Chaplain to the wormes, to say grace to them before they go to dinner and feed on the dead corps," he offered only to preach in the church after interment. On top of this he continued his iconoclastic work at Minster, destroying the crosses on the steeple and breaking stained-glass windows; he even spent £5 of his own money on this activity. [14]

There was also resentment to Culmer over tithes, an issue that frequently led to outbursts of anticlericalism in this period. Some of Culmer's foes were irate because of his refusal to compound for tithes, whereas others, including sectaries and at least one Leveller, opposed tithes in principle as props of an ungodly church. The dispute over tithes became increasingly ugly. Whereas some parishioners organized a campaign to withhold all tithes from Culmer, others blatantly stole his tithe corn in 1646 and 1647. When his servant tried to collect

---

[13] Culmer, Jr., A Parish Looking-Glasse, 14, 18-20.

[14] Ibid., 12, 17, 18, 24. Because of his antipathy to wearing black, Culmer was known as "Blue Dick of Thanet." Fasti Oxon., 1: 447-48.

tithes, he was physically beaten. The campaign to withhold tithes was effective enough to prevent Culmer from paying his taxes and force him to borrow. His plight was exacerbated when ten soldiers were stationed in his home. On several occasions Culmer went to London to instigate legal action against those who refused to pay tithes, ultimately enjoying some success in 1648.[15] The tithing problem bothered him so much that he finally wrote two tracts justifying tithes: *The Ministers Hue and Cry* (1651) and *Lawles Tythe-Robbers Discovered* (1655). If better laws were not passed to ensure the payment of tithes, Culmer was willing to consider the radical notion of voluntary maintenance to support ministers.[16]

The enmity to Culmer, which was sparked by the tithes controversy and his attack on traditional symbols and practices, periodically led to violence. On one occasion Culmer's antagonists locked him and his congregation out of the church, but on the second Sunday he gained access through a broken window. As he conducted services he was physically assaulted until he vomited blood. When he persisted in trying to preach, a riot ensued between his supporters and detractors. The following week the clappers were removed from the church bells to prevent him from summoning people to services, but he substituted his wife's iron pestle, rang the bells, and held the services anyway. When Culmer's supporters finally appealed to the Earl of Warwick at Walmer Castle, a warrant was issued to keep the peace. Subsequently, however, a hostile parishioner relieved himself in a pew, whereupon an unsuspecting London gentlewoman, having knelt in the excrement, stripped off her white petticoat in the midst of the service. It may have been in reference to these problems that the "principal" parishioners of Minster complained in 1647 to Casaubon that "for the last three Sabbaths they had tumults in their church between the poor people and Mr. *Culmer.*"[17]

---

[15]Culmer, Jr., *A Parish Looking-Glasse*, 10-11, 20-23. While he insisted on receiving tithes, Culmer did try to maintain the medieval ideal of using a portion of them to assist the destitute. Ibid., 18.

[16]In *The Ministers Hue and Cry* (1651) Culmer also expressed concern that the growth of religious toleration enabled some people to absent themselves from all religious services, to the detriment of themselves and their families.

[17]Culmer, Jr., *A Parish Looking-Glasse*, 25-27, 29; Calamy, *Non. Mem.*, 2:346 (quoted).

Far more serious were the overt dangers of 1647-1648. In Canterbury on Christmas day, 1647, an unruly mob pelted Culmer with mud and then tried to hang him. Shortly thereafter he appealed for help to Oxinden, and the trained bands quelled the rioters. As Alan Everitt has demonstrated, the Christmas riot was in fact the commencement of a chain of events that led to the Kentish rebellion in 1648. The riot itself was sparked by an attempt to enforce the parliamentary ordinance proscribing religious festivals. Considering Culmer's support from various county leaders, it is likely that his influence was a factor in the County Committee's decision to implement this ordinance. As conditions worsened in 1648, Culmer publicly defended parliamentary taxes, which he contrasted with the "illegally" imposed Ship Money of Charles I, and spoke against disbanding the army. During the uprising he was forced to flee Minster and was nearly captured in Deal before finding refuge in Deal Castle with Colonel Thomas Rainsborough. Taken to London, Culmer preached at St. Mary, Bermondsey, but was also assaulted at Billingsgate. Returning to Kent with Sir Thomas Fairfax's forces, he discovered that his house had been plundered. The collapse of the Kentish rising enabled Culmer to spend another decade promulgating his divisive Puritan message. [18]

For Culmer the 1650s were less turbulent than the previous decade, but hardly free of either dispute or danger. According to his son, about 1650 Culmer was visiting London when he was assaulted at the Minories without Aldgate. In Minster, dissension continued over his strict view of the sabbath and his declamations against inebriety. More furor was raised by his attempt to exclude unworthy communicants from the Lord's supper, so that "the Communion-Table Carpet was cut into Breeches, slanders raised, [and] Tythes detained." He even became embroiled in a controversy with a man who barred a common sheep-track. About 1657, a libelous piece of doggerel circulated in Canterbury, insisting that

Blew Dick must out of Mynster,
His wife must now turn Spinster:
He lov'd the Parliament;

---

[18]Culmer, Jr., *A Parish Looking-Glasse*, 29-32; Everitt, *The Community of Kent*, 231-59.

But now he doth lament:
The Bishops he did hate;
But now Dick's out of Date.

There were further attempts to extrude Culmer from Minster in 1657, prompting his son Richard to come to his defense in *A Parish Looking-Glasse for Persecutors of Ministers* (London, 1657). His father's tormentors, he argued in a half truth, were "those of the Popish, Prelatical and Cavalier Party that never saw him, because of his activenesse against their Cause." Culmer had indeed achieved considerable notoriety by his enthusiastic espousal of the Puritan and parliamentary causes, but a goodly number of his critics through the years not only knew something of him from direct experience, but also included a broader range of Kentish folk than those of the Cavalier cause.[19]

At the Restoration Culmer was ejected from Minster, enabling Casaubon to return to his former vicarage. Culmer moved to nearby Monkton, where even his last years were not free of controversy. He was suspected of complicity in Thomas Venner's rising and was briefly imprisoned in London, though the charges were unfounded.[20]

After a long illness Culmer died at the Monkton vicarage on 20 March 1662, leaving behind two sons (Richard and James) and three daughters (Anne, Katharine, and Elizabeth); his other two children predeceased him. His funeral sermon on Revelation 14:13 was preached on the 22nd by his good friend, Nicholas Thoroughgood, shortly to be ejected as Vicar of Monkton. Culmer's will, dated at Monkton on 18 March 1662, was proved on 13 May. In it he claimed that "many sums of mony are due unto me from occupiers of Lands in the said parish of Mynster and otherwise dureing the time of my being possessed of the sequestration of the said Vicarage there." The

---

. [19]Culmer, Jr., *A Parish Looking-Glasse*, 3, 33, 35, 37.

[20]Edward Hasted, *The History and Topographical Survey of the County of Kent*, 10 (Canterbury, 1800) 293; *Fasti Oxon.*, 1:447. According to Mr. Lewis, a correspondent of the historian Edmund Calamy, Culmer went to St. Peter's, Broadstairs, Kent, after his ejection from Minster, and there "he led a useless vicious life, giving himself in a manner up to drinking." According to a note on the manuscript, however, this behavior was subsequently attributed to Culmer, Jr. Calamy, *Non. Mem.*, 2:346-47.

younger Richard Culmer, biographer of his father, had been admitted a pensioner at Queens' College, Cambridge, on 18 May 1646, and graduated B.A. in 1650. He was licensed as the master of the school at Sandwich on 6 August 1673. Culmer's other son, James, had moved to Ireland where his father owned 400 acres.[21]

To the Enlightenment historian Edward Hasted, Culmer was a "noted fanatic," while the modern Kentish specialist Alan Everitt plausibly refers to Culmer's "pathological spleen." A frustrated Laud, of course, had depicted Culmer as one of the most daring sectaries in Kent. Mr. Lewis, a correspondent of Calamy the historian, asserted that Culmer was "of a very warm and violent temper, and had a zeal which was not according to knowledge. . . ." Culmer, moreover, "acted more the part of a bully, than of a christian minister. He was often engaged in broils, and being a very strong man, cared not whom he fought with."[22] Yet it must be recognized that among Culmer's prominent supporters were some of the leading Kentish moderates, such as Sir James Oxinden and Sir Richard Hardres, as well as political radicals such as the Earl of Warwick, Sir Anthony Weldon, Sir Edward Boys, and William Kenwricke. This breadth of support continued into the mid-1640s, but by the time of the Kentish rising in 1648 some of Culmer's former supporters were among the petitioners whose actions triggered the rising. For his part, Culmer was firmly in the parliamentary camp, undoubtedly because there he found support for his iconoclastic activities and sabbatarian ideals. While the intensity of his Puritan views is often striking, it must be remembered that the Isle of Thanet was so lawless that the County Committee in Kent even considered making it a separate shire with its own legal officers.[23] The endemic lawlessness of this region could only have enforced Culmer's convictions to campaign against sabbath violators, drunkards, and holy day celebrations.

---

[21]Calamy, Non. Mem., 2:347; Al. Oxon., s.v.; Al. Cant. s.v.; Calamy Revised, s.v.; White Kennet, An Historical Register and Chronicle of English Affairs (London, 1744) 645.

[22]Hasted, History of Kent, 10:288; Everitt, The Community of Kent, 60; Lewis, in Calamy, Non. Mem., 2:346.

[23]Everitt, The Community of Kent, 127-28.

To many of the people in Culmer's parishes, his violent declamations threatened not only traditional religion with the aesthetic
beauty of its icons but traditional customs, ranging from maypoles to
burial services. Perhaps then, in the zeal of Richard Culmer—iconoclast, nemesis of Laud, Puritan firebrand—we can see the seeds of
the eventual failure of the Puritans to achieve their reforming goals.
As the moderates began to part forces with Puritan zealots in the late
1640s, they doomed the latter's dream of creating in England a New
Jerusalem.

chapter 3

"A Notorious Independent": George Griffith and the Survival of the Congregational Tradition

The history of English Nonconformity from the heady days of the 1650s, through the decades of persecution under Charles II, to the age of toleration after the Glorious Revolution is poignantly reflected in the career of the Congregational minister George Griffith. In the Cromwellian era he moved in the circle of the leading Independent divines, imbibing Congregational principles from some of the greatest figures in the history of the movement. His own fame spread quickly; he preached before both Oliver Cromwell and Parliament. At the Restoration, however, he was forced from his lectureship and into ties with the radical Protestant underground in London, for which he was in serious trouble with the state in the early 1680s. He was not, however, a political revolutionary and his links to the underground were more in the nature of a spiritual brotherhood. Faced with an impending revolution, James II looked to Griffith for support in 1688 but came away empty-handed. In his last years Griffith devoted himself to his preaching ministry, to achieving unity with the Presbyterians, and to strengthening the Nonconformist cause. His lengthy career, which had begun on the eve of Charles I's execution, concluded like that of his last sovereign, William III, early in 1702. Congregation-alism owes its survival as a major religious force in England to the per-sistent efforts of Griffith and his colleagues through the trying period from 1660 to 1689, yet his work has seldom been recognized by mod-ern scholars.[1] More than any other individual, Griffith provides the personal link between the era of the Independents in the 1650s and the age of toleration and consolidation commencing in 1689.

Griffith (or Griffiths), a younger son, was from Montgomery-shire. His father was still living in March 1640 and his mother, a brother, and a sister, in 1658. The family was on friendly terms with Sir Robert and Lady Brilliana Harley of Brampton Bryan, Hereford-shire, and George was known to Stanley Gower, rector of that village and a former chaplain to Archbishop James Ussher. Griffith matricu-lated at Magdalen College, Oxford, on 2 November 1638 at the age of nineteen. There he was a servitor to Sir Robert's son Edward, a fu-ture captain in the parliamentary army and governor of Dunkirk. When Griffith grew "weary of saruis" he obtained Sir Robert's ap-proval to commence the study of theology, though he retained his contacts with the Harleys for years to come. A number of letters from Lady Brilliana to her son Edward in the period December 1638 to Feb-ruary 1643 mentioned Griffith or his family, though often only in connection with such routine matters as the delivery of goods or let-ters. The correspondence indicates that Lady Brilliana sometimes wrote to Griffith, though these letters apparently have not survived. Early in 1641 Griffith sent his brother to Sir Robert Harley either to provide assistance or for employment. Later that year, when Edward contemplated leaving Oxford to attend Lincoln's Inn in London, Lady Brilliana became quite upset with Griffith: "I much wonder at Gorge Griffits, whoo has had so many tyes to you, that he so neglects what

---

[1]There is, e.g., no mention of Griffith in the following accounts: Michael R. Watts, *The Dissenters* (Oxford, 1978); Gerald R. Cragg, *Puritanism in the Period of the Great Persecution 1660-1688* (Cambridge, 1957); R. W. Dale, *History of English Congre-gationalism* (London, 1907). Neither is he included in the *Dictionary of Welsh Biography* or in Richard Williams, *Montgomeryshire Worthies* (2nd. ed., Newtown, [1894]). George Griffith(s) is sometimes confused with the General Baptist minister John Griffith. Nor must he be confused with the George Griffith who was sequestered from the rectory of Woolsthorpe, Lincolnshire, before 28 January 1647 for delin-quency. A. G. Matthews, *Walker Revised* (Oxford, 1948) 251.

you would haue done. I hope your father will not let you goo to Lin-consine as longe as he is in Loundoun." A few days later, after a visit from Griffith's father in June, Lady Brilliana learned that he was going to provide George with £20 for the coming academic year. The pur-pose of the visit had been to inform the Harleys that Mr. Griffith's eldest son was going to marry the daughter of a Mr. Knight. The mar-riage had occurred by 23 July 1641. (This brother of George's may have been Edward, who was still living in Montgomeryshire in 1702.) When the Civil War broke out, at least one member of the Griffith family suffered, for on 28 January 1643 Lady Brilliana informed Ed-ward that one of the Griffiths had been "cruelly used, but he is now seet at liberty. But the poore drumer is still in the dungon, and Griffits says he fears he will dye." A final reference to George Griffith appears in a letter of 25 February 1643 from Lady Brilliana to her son in which she mundanely notes that William Griffith (a brother of George?) has taken linens from her that will be delivered to Edward by George Griffith.[2]

On the eve of the Civil War Griffith graduated B. A. (14 June 1642), and three years later he received an M. A. degree from that vir-tual seminary of Puritanism, Emmanuel College, Cambridge. By a parliamentary order of 13 February 1646, he was appointed a Fellow of Trinity College, Cambridge.[3]

Griffith's long association with London began on 6 June 1648 when he was named to the post of preacher at the Charterhouse in London. By a special indulgence in 1651, his wife Elizabeth was per-mitted to live there with him, the first time a woman had ever lived in the Charterhouse. Further testimony to his ability came in 1650, when the Haberdashers' Company selected him to succeed John Downham as the William Jones Lecturer at St. Bartholomew Ex-

---

[2]Al. Oxon., s.v.; Geoffrey F. Nuttall, The Welsh Saints 1640-1660 (Cardiff, 1957) 9; Letters of the Lady Brilliana Harley, ed. Thomas Taylor Lewis (Camden Society; Lon-don, 1854) 15, 21, 35, 86, 88, 105, 114, 134, 135 (quoted), 137, 142, 187 (quoted), 190; Francis Peck, Desiderata Curiosa: Or, a Collection of Divers Scarce and Curious Pieces, 2 vols. (London, 1779) 2:507; Calamy Revised, 237; HMC 29, Fourteenth Report, Ap-pendix, pt. 2:54. A letter of Griffith's dated 3 September 1653, probably to Colonel Edward Harley, is extant; see HMC 29, Fourteenth Report, Appendix, pt. 2:204.

[3]Al. Cant., s.v.; Al. Oxon., s.v.; Firth & Rait, 1:831.

change. Because the Haberdashers had a number of ecclesiastical preferments in their control, Griffith was assigned the responsibility of
examining candidates for the positions. Perhaps because of this experience as well as his growing prominence in London religious circles, he was appointed an assistant to the Commission for Ejecting
Scandalous Ministers in London on 28 August 1654, two days after
Cromwell's empowering ordinance for the commission had been issued. The commission had the responsibility to examine and eject
ministers and schoolmasters who were scandalous, ignorant, or irre-
sponsible. Among the other ministers assigned to assist the London
commissioners were the Independent Philip Nye and the Presbyterians Lazarus Seaman, Thomas Gouge, and Arthur Jackson. Five days
later, on 2 September, Griffith was appointed a commissioner for the
Approbation of Public Preachers—a Trier—in which capacity he was
charged with determining the suitability of potential incumbents for
positions in the state church. In this connection he was, according to
Thomas Richards, an unofficial representative of Wales, and as such
saw to it that Puritan ministers were sent to his native Montgomeryshire. Yet he was surely selected for these responsibilities because of
his stature in London rather than his family background. In any case,
at this stage in his career Griffith must have worked very closely with
Sidrach Simpson, a Trier and the Rector of St. Bartholomew Exchange
until his death in 1655.[4]

During the 1650s Griffith revealed a marked interest in theological issues. Because of his theological expertise, he was one of ten ministers chosen to meet with a committee of the House of Commons in
February 1652 to prepare a formal condemnation of the Racovian Catechism (*Catechesis Ecclesiarum Poloniae*, 1605), a Socinian confession of
faith, which denied the divinity of Christ and insisted that the truths
of revelation could never contradict reason. In addition to Sidrach
Simpson, his colleague at St. Bartholomew's, the committee also included such eminent Independent divines as John Owen, Philip Nye,
William Bridge, and William Strong. It may have been on this committee that Griffith first met John Dury, the tireless advocate of Prot-

[4]Seaver, 286; Wilson, *HADC*, 2:516; Firth & Rait, 2:981, 1026; Thomas Richards, *Religious Developments in Wales (1654-1662)* (London, 1923) 8; Richards, *Wales Under the Indulgence (1672-1675)* (London, 1928) 179.

estant union and educational reform. The next year (1653) Griffith wrote to Dury indicating a willingness to correspond with Baxter. Griffith and Baxter were certainly on good terms no later than the 1660s.[5]

Griffith was concerned with the spread of Protestant principles in foreign lands. With eleven other prominent Independent ministers—John Owen, Thomas Goodwin, Joseph Caryl, Sidrach Simpson, Philip Nye, William Greenhill, William Bridge, William Carter, William Strong, Henry Whitfield, and Ralph Venning—he was a signatory of a 1652 letter to the Rump Parliament endorsing Whitfield's book, *Strengthe out of Weaknesse: Or a Glorious Manifestation of the Further Progresse of the Gospel Among the Indians in New-England* (1652), which printed letters from New England describing the conversion of Indians to Christianity. It was the hope of Griffith and his colleagues that Parliament would give "encouragement unto this Worke, and . . . open a Doore for the reliefe of those Eminent Instruments in the hand of the Lord who carry it on," particularly since they provided the Indians with physical as well as spiritual food. This letter of the Independents was reprinted in 1657 when the book was published under the title, *Banners of Grace and Love.*[6]

In addition to the epistle dedicatory to Parliament, a separate preface to the reader was prepared by a group of eighteen ministers—including the twelve who wrote the epistle—and Calamy, Lazarus Seaman, William Gouge, Simeon Ashe, William Spurstowe, and Jeremiah Whitaker. The mission to the Indians, they argued, enlarges the kingdom of Christ (fulfilling the promise in Revelation 11: 15), rescues souls from the snares of the Devil, and propagates the gospel abroad at a time when many at home reject it. Griffith and his colleagues saw eschatological significance in missionary activity to the Indians: "*Hereby the fullnes of the Gentils draws neere to be accomplished,* that the calling of the *Jewes* may be hastned. . . ." This may be, they hoped, the "*first fruits of those great Nations*" that would embrace the gospel.

---

[5]Nuttall, *Welsh Saints,* 43, 80; Peter Toon, *God's Statesman: The Life and Work of John Owen* (Exeter, 1971) 83-84. Some of Griffith's notes on biblical passages have survived; British Library, Birch MS 4275, fol. 254.

[6]*Corr. of Owen,* 56-58. The letter is also reprinted in *CMHS,* 3rd ser., 4 (1834): 151-54.

There was also a sense of satisfaction in knowing that those who actively worked with the Indians and were being divinely blessed had been forced out of England because of their religious beliefs. Justice, they believed, had triumphed.[7]

The breadth of Griffith's concerns was manifested again in 1656, this time regarding the persecution of Protestants in the Vaudois valleys of the Piedmont by the Duke of Savoy. The Cromwellian government reacted with alarm to the news that the Duke had plundered their estates, burned their homes, and imprisoned or slaughtered the people. In addition to promoting a national fast and exerting diplomatic pressure on Savoy, Cromwell's Council of State appointed a committee to aid the Piedmont Protestants. Along with Griffith and the Independent minister Peter Sterry, the committee included such prominent political leaders as the Protector's brother Richard, Oliver St. John, William Packer, and William Purefoy. The committee was especially concerned with raising funds to assist victims of the persecution.[8]

The Council of State turned to Griffith once more the following year for assistance in resolving a dispute between the Scottish Resolutioners and Protesters (Remonstrants). The two groups had originally differed in large part over the latter's insistence that only those loyal to the Covenant could participate in the military campaign against England. By 1657 the Protesters were demanding an equal share with the Resolutioners in the government of the church and the power to purge the church of malignants. Throughout the first half of 1657 both sides presented their case at Westminster, but when the dispute remained unresolved, Cromwell and the Council of State appointed a committee of referees to hear the arguments in July. Seven of the referees were ministers—three Presbyterians and four Independents, including Griffith, Owen, and Caryl. The representative of the Resolutioners, James Sharp, was convinced that Griffith, Owen, and Caryl were prejudiced against his group. In fact the committee report, presented on 4 August, endorsed the demands of the Protest-

[7]*CMHS*, 3rd ser., 4: 155-59.

[8]Bulstrode Whitelocke, *Memorials of the English Affairs* (London, 1732) 626; *CSPD, 1655-56*, 100.

ers. When, however, the Presbyterian clergy in London objected to the report, the Council of State returned it to the committee, which withdrew the report in favor of a letter to the Scottish ministers asking them to resolve the dispute themselves. The Council, however, decided against sending even this letter to the factious Scots. Although the efforts of Griffith, Owen, and Caryl were largely in vain, they underscore the extent to which these men were committed to the strict standards of spiritual discipline espoused by the Protesters.[9]

Even before his service to the Council of State in the Scottish dispute, Griffith had been asked to assist in a domestic matter of import. On 10 March 1656 the Council appointed a blue-ribbon committee to draft statutes for a new college at Durham, which had been petitioning for a school since the dissolution of the cathedral and collegiate chapters in April 1649. Cromwell himself approved the project as "a matter of great concernment and importance, as that which, by the blessing of God, may much conduce to the promoting of learning and piety in those poor rude and ignorant parts. . . ."[10] In addition to Griffith, the committee included his Independent colleagues Goodwin and Caryl as well as such prominent Cromwellians as John Lambert, Charles Fleetwood, Colonel Robert Lilburne, and Viscount Lisle. The committee deliberated until at least 5 September 1656, and on the following 15 May Cromwell's writ of Privy Seal officially established the college as a place for "the promoting of the Gospel" and the "prudent education of young men. . . ."[11] With a faculty that included the political theorist William Sprigge and Samuel Hartlib's friend Ezerell Tonge, the new college offered instruction in subjects ranging from religion to mathematics and geography.[12] Following Cromwell's death the grant of university authority was suspended due to oppo-

[9]F. N. McCoy, *Robert Baillie and the Second Scots Reformation* (Berkeley, 1974) 137-38, 189-95; *CSPD, 1657-58,* 28.

[10]Richard L. Greaves, *The Puritan Revolution and Educational Thought: Background for Reform* (New Brunswick NJ, 1969) 56-57; *The Letters and Speeches of Oliver Cromwell,* ed. Thomas Carlyle and S. C. Lomas, 3 vols. (London, 1904) 2: 186-87.

[11]*CSPD, 1655-56,* 218; Cromwell, *WS,* 4: 522-23.

[12]G. H. Turnbull, "Oliver Cromwell's College at Durham," *Research Review,* no. 3 (September 1952): 1-7.

sition from Oxford and Cambridge, and the college was officially disbanded in 1660. Nevertheless, Griffith's appointment to the eminent
committee that drafted the statutes is testimony to the high regard in
which he was held by the Cromwellian authorities.

Further testimony to Griffith's stature came in the fall of 1656
when he preached to the House of Commons at St. Margaret's, Westminster, on 30 October, a fast day, in company with John Owen and
Thomas Goodwin. The following day the Commons voted a resolution of gratitude to the three ministers and asked that their sermons
be printed. The House's thanks were extended to the preachers by
three prominent political radicals: to Griffith and Owen by the
Cromwellian officers Edward Whalley and Thomas Kelsey respec-
tively, and to Goodwin by Sir William Strickland. There is no indication that Griffith published his sermon. [13]

Parliament turned to Griffith again that December when it had to
consider the enigmatic case of the Quaker James Nayler. In October
Nayler, inclined like other Quakers to use vivid symbolism in trans-
mitting the gospel, reenacted Christ's entry into Jerusalem at Bristol,
aided by a small group of followers, including devoted female disciples. In the House of Commons, where Nayler was accused of blasphemy, tempers flared as some members demanded harsh punishment.
More temperate minds were reluctant to go to such extremes, partly
because they feared the negative effects of such action on the Cromwellian policy of toleration. On 20 December the House appointed a
committee of ministers to confer with Nayler in the hope of procuring
a retraction from him. The committee included such influential clergymen as the Independents Griffith, Nye, and Joseph Caryl and the
Presbyterians Thomas Manton and Edward Reynolds. Whether the
committee actually consulted with Nayler is unclear, for John Lambert, a leader of the moderates on this issue, reminded the House
shortly after the committee was appointed that "nobody is suffered to
come at him." In any event, Nayler insisted he had nothing of which
to repent, for the Bristol event had only been intended as an allegorical
act and not a claim of his messiahship. The House nevertheless found
him guilty of blasphemy and sentenced him to be pilloried, whipped,

---

[13]CJ, 7:447.

branded, and imprisoned. What Griffith thought of such savagery is unknown.[14]

Griffith remained active in the 1650s with a variety of religious responsibilities. The hostile critic Anthony Wood referred to him as "a notorious Independent, a frequent preacher before Oliver and the parliaments in his time. . . ."[15] To those in the Puritan tradition he was "very conversible, and much the gentleman. He was reckoned a man of great invention and devotion in prayer."[16] Because of Griffith's skill in examining candidates for ministerial positions, he served as an assistant not only to the London Commission in 1654, but also to the Middlesex Commission in 1657. In August of the latter year the Council of State asked him to join with Nye and others to determine the fitness of Christopher Newstead, the minister of Maidenhead, Berkshire, and a year later the Council asked him to work with Nye and Caryl to judge the qualifications of a prospective cleric.[17]

Griffith was invited to preach to the House of Commons again on 27 January 1658, a day of humiliation. The proposal for him to give the sermon had been made a week earlier by Major-General Kelsey and John Trenchard. Calamy too was invited to preach, and the lengthy service extended from 10:00 A.M. to 5:30 P.M. According to Thomas Burton, who kept a diary of this Parliament, the two gave "very good sermons." Griffith, who preached on 2 Chronicles 20, defended the Cromwellian policy of toleration, speaking "for church government, but against imposing spirits. . . ." The sermon, noted Burton dryly, "tasted a little of Court holy water." In his sermon Griffith also urged that more money be provided for the maintenance of godly ministers, especially in Wales and the North. Following his sermon there was support for this idea, particularly from Major Lewis Audley and Alderman William Gibbs, and a collection was taken. The House passed a resolution of thanks to Griffith and asked him to

[14]Burton, 1:183-84.

[15]*Fasti Oxon.*, 2:8.

[16]Calamy, *Non. Mem.*, 1:207.

[17]*Calamy Revised*, 237; *CSPD*, 1657-58, 69; *CSPD*, 1658-59, 109.

print his sermon. Once again, however, he apparently declined to publish it.[18]

On 3 March 1658 Griffith was appointed lecturer to the Independent congregation, which met in Westminster Abbey. He had been close to that congregation's first Independent rector, William Strong (d. 1654), and had written (with the Independent John Rowe and the Presbyterians Thomas Manton and Richard Vines) a preface to Strong's sermons, *The Heavenly Treasure* (1656). The following year he joined with Rowe and Manton to compose a preface to Strong's *A Treatise Shewing the Subordination of the Will of Man unto the Will of God.* As lecturer, Griffith probably worked closely with Strong's successor, John Rowe, and his assistant, Seth Ward. The respect accorded to Griffith in the City is underscored by his inclusion with other leading Independents—Caryl, Venning, Matthew Barker, Thomas Brooks, and William Tuttle—in the will of Sheriff Stephen Estwick, a prominent politician and a member of Barker's congregation.[19]

Griffith played a key role in the summoning of the Savoy Conference, which produced one of the classic documents of Congregationalism, "A Declaration of the Faith and Order Owned and Practised in the Congregational Churches in England." This was preceded by a meeting of elders from Independent churches in the London area called by Henry Scobell, clerk of the Council of State, in June 1658. The meeting took place in Griffith's house. At Oxford the next month, leading Independent ministers were determined to hold a general meeting at the Savoy Palace in London in late September, especially, as Goodwin said, "to clear ourselves of that scandal . . . viz. That Independentism . . . is the sink of all Heresies and Schisms." To Griffith, one of the "elders" of the Congregational movement, fell the task of writing to prominent Independent clergy in England and Wales to get their support in arranging for delegates from churches in their areas. His letters are not extant, but some of the responses addressed at Griffith's request to Henry Scobell have been preserved.

---

[18]Burton, 2: 321, 372-73; CJ, 7: 579, 588.

[19]Ira Boseley, *The Independent Church of Westminster Abbey* (1650-1826) (London, 1907) 99; James E. Farnell, "The Usurpation of Honest London Householders: Barebones's Parliament," *EHR* 82 (January 1967): 27-28.

One of the letters went to the influential Welsh radical, Vavasor Powell, a "kinsman" of Griffith, who responded directly to the latter expressing his fear of writing to anyone as closely associated with the government as Scobell. As a Fifth Monarchist, Powell had aroused Cromwell's ire for opposing the Protectorate. "I hope," Powell wrote, "your ends are good, & your actions lawful; if soe, you may not doubt of the concurrence of the poor Welsh churches. . . . But if you go upon political & worldly accounts, or by a humane spirit, to work, you may expect God to blast the work." When the conference met, the articles of the proposed confession were drafted by a select committee—Owen, Goodwin, Nye, Caryl, Greenhill, and Bridge—and then read to the full synod each morning by Griffith. The resulting "Declaration" was officially approved on 12 October, due in no small part to the labors of Griffith.[20]

Following Cromwell's death on 3 September, the Protectorate rapidly disintegrated under the ineffectual leadership of his son and successor, Richard, who was little more than a cipher of the army leaders Charles Fleetwood and John Desborough. The more junior officers' hostility to Richard's Parliament, elected on the traditional franchise, led to its dismissal. In late April and early May of 1659, critical discussions were held relative to the recall of the Rump Parliament, in which John Owen was an intermediary between the senior officers

---

[20]Peck, *Desiderata Curiosa*, 2: 501; *The Savoy Declaration of Faith and Order 1658*, ed. A. G. Matthews (London, 1959) 12 (quoted), 13-14, 16-18, 34. Peck prints responses to Griffith's letter from the following: William Sheldrake of Wisbech, Cambridgeshire; William Hughes of Marlborough, Wiltshire; Bankes Anderson of Boston, Lincolnshire; Vavasor Powell; Edward Reyner of Lincoln; Isaac Loeffs of Shenley, Hertfordshire; Samuel Basnet of Coventry; William Bridge of Yarmouth; Thomas Gilbert of Edgmond, Shropshire; Samuel Crossman of Sudbury, Suffolk; Comfort Starr of Carlisle; Anthony Palmer of Bourton on the Water, Gloucestershire, and Carnsew Helme of Winchcomb, Gloucestershire; Thomas Palmer of Aston on Trent, Derbyshire; John Wright of Woodborough; and John Player of Canterbury, a colleague of Richard Culmer. For all these men except Wright see *Calamy Revised, s.vv. Desiderata Curiosa*, 2: 505-12. Several of these men made personal references to Griffith in their letters. Powell described him as "his endearedly honoured friend," 508, and Gilbert referred to him as "my worthy friend," 509. To Bankes Anderson, Griffith was "a person of that worth and value, that I durst not question any thing about the truth, much less disobey the reasonable commands of that letter," 506.

and the Protector. Griffith too was involved, for Sir Archibald Johnston of Wariston reports that on 30 April he met with Griffith, Owen,
William Sydenham, and finally Fleetwood himself. From this he
learned that "they had agreed to [a]byde be another and manteane
civil and spiritual libertyes already obteaned, and submitt to what
government God shal inclyne them to."[21] The decision to recall the
Rump was made on 6 May, apparently with the support of Griffith
and certainly of Owen. When Baxter subsequently accused Owen
"and his assistants" of being the prime movers in the Protector's fall,
he was surely thinking of Griffith in that number, though the accusation itself is an overstatement.[22]

The situation facing the godly was sufficiently alarming to prompt
various leaders to meet that summer in the hope of establishing some
degree of cooperation as well as denouncing the Quaker challenge. In
addition to Griffith, the participants included the Independents
Owen and Caryl, the Presbyterians Calamy, Reynolds, Seaman, William Jenkins, and Thomas Jacomb, and the Baptists Henry Jessey,
William Allen, John Griffith, and Richard Deane. Discussions proceeded at an agonizing pace, prompting Allen to appeal in September
to Baxter to come to London and assist with the negotiations. Two
military officers prominent in the Good Old Cause, Colonel William
Goffe and Major-General Edward Whalley, were present at some of
the meetings, underscoring the goal of staving off a restoration of
monarchy and episcopacy. The discussions, however, failed to produce an accommodation between the respective groups, partly because they were not supported by more conservative Presbyterians.
Seaman also believed that the deliberations required the backing of
members of the Rump and officers more influential at this stage than
Goffe and Whalley, whose influence was waning.[23]

---

[21]*The Diary of Sir Archibald Johnston of Wariston*, ed. George M. Paul, David H.
Fleming, and James D. Ogilvie, 3 vols. (Scottish History Society; Edinburgh, 1911-
1940) 3: 106.

[22]*Rel. Bax.*, pt. 1: 101.

[23]Johnston, *Diary*, 3: 134-35; George R. Abernathy, Jr., "The English Presbyterians and the Stuart Restoration, 1648-1663," *Transactions of the American Philosophical Society*, n.s. 55, pt. 2 (1965): 32-33. Allen's letter of 7 September to Baxter is
in the Dr. Williams's Library, Baxter MSS, Letters III, no. 47/24.

Although the Rump's hostility to the military brought its dissolution in October, it was recalled in December in the face of General
Monck's mobilization of the army in Scotland. As the newly created
commander-in-chief, Monck, who occupied London on 3 February
1660, restored the excluded members of the Long Parliament on the
27th. Within three weeks, on 17 March, Parliament voted its dissolution and issued writs for the election of a Convention Parliament.
Three days earlier Griffith and Caryl had been appointed commissioners for the Approbation and Admission of Ministers to Benefices
and Public Lectures, renewing their old responsibilities as Triers.
Faced with the virtual certainty of a restored monarchy, the Independent leaders split. Nye and Brooks expressed a willingness to support
Desborough's plan to preserve the republic by the use of force, but in
April Griffith and Caryl opted instead to accept the determinations of
the Convention, which assembled on the 25th. When it had accepted
the concessions made by Charles II in the Declaration of Breda, he
was proclaimed king, and by the end of May was securely on his
throne. The same month Griffith joined with nineteen other Independents in signing an address of loyalty to Charles in which they hoped,
with reference to the Declaration of Breda, for religious toleration. [24]

Die-hard radicals, unwilling to submit to the restored monarchy,
mounted a desperate insurrection in January 1661. Led by Thomas
Venner and using as its slogan, "King Jesus, and their heads upon the
gates," the rising failed miserably. Congregationalist ministers rushed
to dissociate themselves from the revolt. With twenty-four others—
including Caryl, Nye, Thomas Goodwin, Brooks, Barker, and
George Cokayne—Griffith signed *A Renuntiation and Declaration of the
Ministers* (1661), repudiating Venner.

Ejected from his position at the Charterhouse, where he was succeeded by Dr. Timothy Shircross on 2 November 1661, Griffith, who
was apparently unwilling to take the oath prescribed by the 1662 Act
of Uniformity, resigned the Jones lectureship at St. Bartholomew Exchange on 27 September 1662. He was, however, able to recommend
his replacement, Francis Raworth, the ejected lecturer at St. Anthol-

---

[24]Firth & Rait, 2:1459; *CSPD, 1659-60*, 409; Richards, *Religious Developments*,
406.

in's, who later conformed and also was appointed Vicar of St. Leonard, Shoreditch.[25]

The loss of preferments did not silence Griffith, who continued to preach to Nonconformist groups in London. Sir Henry Bennet, a secretary of state, received a report in January 1663 identifying Griffith as a suspicious person. One of Sir Joseph Williamson's spies reported the same year that Griffith, who was then living in Broad Street, was conducting religious services in St. Laurence Lane near the Guildhall in conjunction with Owen, Thomas Goodwin, Barker, and Cokayne. Because of Griffith's long-standing interest in foreign Protestants, there was hope in April 1664 of getting him—along with Baxter, Owen, and Goodwin—to help raise funds to relieve Polish Protestants. Whether he did or not is unknown. Apparently the government took no further notice of Griffith in the 1660s. With other Congregationalists, including Owen, Goodwin, Caryl, Barker, Nye, and Thomas Brooks, Griffith was especially active after the fire of London. He even preached in the City's streets, undoubtedly taking advantage of the burned-out ruins to warn of divine judgment and the promise of mercy to those who would repent. According to Baxter, "the *Nonconformists* were now more resolved than ever, to preach till they were imprisoned. . . ." More people, he claimed, now attended their services than those of the parish churches.[26]

Throughout this period Griffith maintained a cooperative attitude toward other Nonconformists. It was because of this outlook that Baxter had approached him, probably early in the 1660s, with some proposals designed to work out the differences between Independents and Presbyterians. These propositions by Baxter were originally intended to serve as the basis for a discussion by the respective parties in an open forum, but the Restoration had made this impossible; hence he gave them to Griffith as the person most likely to instigate some move toward union. Baxter, however, became disillusioned when Griffith did nothing with the proposals over the space of a year,

---

[25]Wilson, *HADC*, 2: 516; Seaver, 286-87. Griffith is mentioned only once (1660) in the St. Bartholomew Vestry Minutes (Seaver, 372).

[26]*CSPD, 1663-64,* 27, 555-56; G. L. Turner, "Williamson's Spy-Book," *TCHS* 5 (1912): 247, 258; Richards, *Wales Under the Indulgence,* 168; *Rel. Bax.,* pt. 3: 19.

and finally retrieved his manuscript. Another manifestation of Griffith's cooperative spirit was his participation by 1669 in a "combination" lectureship at Hackney with the Presbyterians William Bates and Thomas Watson as well as the Congregationalists Owen, Nye, Brooks, and Peter Sterry. During the difficult 1660s Griffith even sent money to Wales to assist Baptist as well as Independent ministers.[27]

Griffith's status in Nonconformist circles remained high. Even the conservative cleric George Vernon, Rector of Bourton-on-the-Water, Gloucestershire, testified to Griffith's stature when he accused him of being an officer in a Congregational spy ring masterminded by Owen. The Independent church at Hitchin, Hertfordshire, sought the advice of Griffith and Owen in 1669 respecting the excommunication of two members of Francis Holcroft's Congregational church at Cambridge, an excommunication Griffith and Owen thought was undeserved. Their intent in writing both to the church at Hitchin and especially to Holcroft's congregation at Cambridge was to heal "that scandal, that hath come upon the way of the gospel, by the precipitant and undue casting out of persons out of the visible kingdom of our Lord Jesus Christ. . . ." The Hitchin church was also in need of counsel concerning five of its members who had separated themselves from the congregation, apparently over a matter of doctrine or discipline. On this matter Griffith and Owen advised patience. "We account," they admitted, "that they are overtaken in a fault, in this present continued separation of theirs, but we also desire you would . . . shew yourselves so spiritual, as to seek the restoring of them in no other way than the spirit of meekness. . . ." Such advice provides insight into the way Griffith presumably handled his own congregation—patiently and with an eye to the maintenance of peace within the congregation and between churches. By temperament and conviction Griffith was a reconciler.[28]

Griffith's recognition extended to the American colonies. On 21 August 1671 the magistrates and ministers of Massachusetts wrote to Griffith, Owen, Thomas Goodwin, Nye, Caryl, and fifteen other

---

[27]Rel. Bax., pt. 2: 193; C. E. Whiting, *Studies in English Puritanism from the Restoration to the Revolution, 1660-1688* (London, 1931) 75; Richards, *Religious Developments*, 9.

[28]DNB, s.v. John Owen; *Corr. of Owen*, 146-48.

Nonconformist ministers regarding the physical infirmity of Harvard President Charles Chauncy, the poor state of the Harvard buildings, and the small number of students. Specifically, they hoped for a donation of £1000, recommendations for a successor to Chauncy, and student recruits from England. With his colleagues, Griffith responded on 5 February 1672, noting that they had discussed the Massachusetts situation "as the providence of God hath permitted to us opportunities of meeting together." They observed that Nonconformists could contribute little money in their present straits, recommended Leonard Hoare as Chauncy's successor, and promised to encourage young people to consider studying at Harvard. "You cannot expect (as things stand with us) to receive that fruit that either your need calls for or our love would produce, were we not ourselves, together with the churches of Christ in these nations, intangled in many straits. . . ." In particular Griffith and his colleagues explained that Nonconformist churches and their ministers throughout England looked for essential financial support to the congregations in London. "The exhausted purses" of the Nonconformist financial backers simply could not make a substantial contribution to Harvard.[29]

The state renewed its interest in Griffith's activities in 1671, suspicious that he might be hiding Richard Cromwell. On 22 June a warrant was issued to search his house for arms, suspicious papers, and Cromwell. Although the results of the search are unknown, Griffith could not have been incriminated in anything serious since he, Owen, Caryl, and John Collings were involved in the ordination of the Congregationalist Matthew Mead at Stepney in December. For a time conditions improved for the Nonconformists as the result of Charles II's 1672 Declaration of Indulgence, for which Griffith, Owen, and Anthony Palmer personally thanked the king on the morning of 28 March. They were followed later that day by a Presbyterian delegation comprised of Manton, Bates, Lazarus Seaman, and Thomas Jacomb. Under the provisions of the Declaration, on 22 April Griffith received a license to preach at his home in Addle Street, London. Little is known of his activities in the ensuing decade, though he surely continued as a leader of the Congregational movement. In December

---

[29]*Corr. of Owen,* 149-53.

1677 his congregation learned of the difficulties of Nonconformists in the West Country. Griffith's church was one of those visited by John Bunyan on his trips to the City, and the Bedford congregation regarded it as an acceptable place for its members to transfer if they moved to London.[30]

In the aftermath of the Exclusion Controversy, conditions for Nonconformists worsened. In July 1682 the government was informed that Griffith, Mead, and Samuel Annesley were zealously warning people of the dangers of popery and arbitrary government. Griffith was now preaching at Plasterers' Hall, but he was also traveling to Tunbridge Wells, Kent, to meet with other Nonconformists. This fact, coupled with the earlier discovery of his contacts with Nonconformists in the West Country, indicated that Griffith was still one of an inner circle of Congregational ministers who formed the hub of a network extending from the capital throughout the kingdom. That network was strengthened late in 1681 when a member of Griffith's church, Timothy Jollie, son of the Congregational minister Thomas Jollie, left with Griffith's blessing to assume the pastorship of the Congregational church at Sheffield. Griffith similarly assisted the younger Matthew Clarke, son of the Congregational minister Matthew Clarke. For two years (1682-1684), Clarke stayed in London with Griffith as he prepared himself for the ministry. When he was ready, Clarke left to work with his father in Leicester.[31]

Griffith's activities were of sufficient interest to prompt the state to issue a summons to him, along with Owen, Baxter, and others in July 1682. Griffith may have been under suspicion for complicity in the Rye House Plot. In April 1683 Mr. Manning, a member of his congregation, confessed that Griffith knew Richard Goodenough, a member of the radical underground and a prime suspect in the plot. There is, however, no evidence to link either Manning or Griffith to

---

[30]*CSPD*, 1671, 335; A. T. Jones, *Notes on the Early Days of Stepney Meeting, 1644 to 1689* (London, 1887) 50; *CSPD*, 1671-72, 28-29, 332, 366-67, 609; *CSPD*, 1677-78, 529; *The Church Book of Bunyan Meeting, 1650-1821*, facsimile edition with intro. by G. B. Harrison (London, 1928) 45-46, 48-49.

[31]*CSPD*, 1682, 303, 610; The Mather Papers, *CMHS*, 4th ser., 8 (1868): 326; *DNB*, s.v. Matthew Clarke.

the plotting. Surveillance continued, and on 22 March 1684 Griffith was fined £20 at the Guildhall Sessions for illegal preaching.[32]

During James II's reign, Griffith remained at the core of the Congregational movement—his prominence recognized even by the Catholic monarch. The link between Griffith and James II was probably Stephen Lobb, minister of the Nonconformist church at Fetter Lane, London, who was friendly with both men. In May 1688 the king ordered the clergy in the Church of England to read his Declaration of Indulgence from the pulpit. When the Archbishop of Canterbury and six bishops petitioned the king against this order, they were arraigned for seditious libel. Griffith, John Howe, and William Bates defended the prelates on this issue, but were nevertheless part of a contingent of seven Congregational and Baptist ministers invited to meet with James in mid-October. Seeking their support, the king insisted that the queen, Mary of Modena, was indeed the mother of the infant Prince of Wales. To this, one of the ministers replied, "The nation knows not so much," but Griffith and the others agreed to pray for the king and to be peaceful and obedient subjects. As a last-ditch appeal for Nonconformist support, the meeting was a failure, but it underscores once again the place Griffith enjoyed at the heart of the Congregational movement. During the course of the Revolution Griffith, Baxter, Bates, and John Howe worked to maintain a united front among Nonconformists, even as three deans—Simon Patrick, Edward Stillingfleet, and John Tillotson—led the unsuccessful movement within the established church to achieve a better rapport with the Nonconformists.[33]

Some time after 1684 Griffith moved his congregation from Plasterers' Hall to Girdlers' Hall in Basinghall Street. Although he had been a very popular preacher as a young man, his congregation now dwindled in size. He may have been the Mr. Griffith who received a

---

[32]*CSPD, 1682*, 610; *CSPD, 1683 (II)*, 72; *Calamy Revised*, 237. For Goodenough, see *BDBR, s.v.*

[33]Calamy, *Life*, 1:375, 410; Douglas R. Lacey, *Dissent and Parliamentary Politics in England, 1661-1689* (New Brunswick NJ, 1969) 219-20; Roger Thomas, "Comprehension and Indulgence," in *From Uniformity to Unity 1662-1962*, ed. Geoffrey F. Nuttall and Owen Chadwick (London, 1962) 239-40. Lobb died at Griffith's house in 1699. Calamy, *Life*, 1:410.

pass on 18 April 1690 to travel to Caernarvonshire and then return to London. That summer he was one of the fourteen Congregational and Presbyterian ministers selected to manage the Common Fund. With men such as Cokayne, Mead, Barker, Isaac Chauncy, John Faldo, and Nathaniel Mather—his Congregational colleagues—he was responsible for insuring that the Fund fulfilled its objective of relieving clerical poverty and providing assistance for future ministers' education. At the outset the fund had to gather data from around the country to identify the most pressing areas of need. Griffith was later a "messenger" to the meeting that founded the Congregational Fund Board on 17 December 1695.[34]

At least twice in the 1690s Griffith had occasion to assert his evangelical but moderate theological creed. In 1690 Samuel Crisp published the collected works of his Antinomian father, Dr. Tobias Crisp (d. 1643). Because eight of the fifty-two sermons had never been previously published, Samuel included a signed testimony from twelve London ministers concerning their authenticity. In addition to six Presbyterians and one Baptist, the signatories included the Congregationalists Griffith, Cokayne, Nathaniel and Increase Mather, and Isaac Chauncy. Infuriated by this publication and the apparent endorsement by the twelve clerics, Baxter condemned both Crisp's Antinomianism and the ministers in a lecture at Pinners' Hall on 28 January 1690. When Samuel Crisp defended his father in *Christ Made Sin* (1691), Daniel Williams, a disciple of Baxter, countered with *Gospel-Truth Stated and Vindicated* (1692). Replete with a testimonial signed by Presbyterian ministers (16 in the first edition, 49 in the second[35]), it was taken by the Congregationalists as a partisan attack on them.

---

[34]Anon., "A View of the Dissenting Intrest in London of the Presbyterian & Independent Denominations from the Year 1695 to the 25 of December 1731," Dr. Williams's Library, MS RNC 38.18, fol. 76; Calamy, *Non. Mem.*, 1: 107; *CSPD*, 1689-90, 560; R. Tudur Jones, *Congregationalism in England 1662-1962* (London, 1962) 111; Roger Thomas, "Parties in Nonconformity," in *The English Presbyterians: From Elizabethan Puritanism to Modern Unitarianism* (London, 1968) 101; *TCHS*, 5: 135.

[35]Among the subscribers to the first edition were John Reynolds, William Bates, and John Howe. Included among the new subscribers to the second edition were Calamy's grandson Edmund, Matthew Sylvester, who edited Baxter's autobiography, and Daniel Burgess.

Six Congregationalists, including Griffith, Isaac Chauncy, and Robert Trail signed a "Paper of Objections" castigating Williams. He in turn replied to their criticism in the third edition of his book, which prompted Trail to attack him in *A Vindication of the Protestant Doctrine Concerning Justification, and of Its Preachers and Professors, from the Unjust Charge of Antinomianism* (1692). "These debates," said Calamy's grandson, "filled the town with noise and heat. . . ." The dispute was a major factor in undermining the union that Presbyterians and Congregationalists such as Griffith had been seeking.[36]

Although Griffith opposed Williams's attack on Crisp, he was not himself an Antinomian. Indeed, in 1699 he joined with four other Congregational ministers—Mead, Richard Taylor, John Nesbitt, and Stephen Lobb—in attacking both Antinomians and uneducated preachers in *A Declaration of the Congregational Ministers in and about London Against Antinomian Errours and Ignorant . . . Persons Intruding Themselves into the Ministry.*

Having preached into his early eighties, Griffith died early in 1702; his will (dated 15 June 1698) was proved on 17 April 1702. According to the will his personalty was valued at approximately £1600. He bequeathed £10 to the poor of his congregation. By his wife, Elizabeth, he had four sons—Richard, Henry, George (baptized on 21 September 1656), and Charles (d. 1670)—and three daughters—Elizabeth, Anne (d. 1670), and Anne. Anne and Charles were buried in Bunhill Fields. During the course of his ministry he had befriended such prominent Congregationalists as John Owen, Thomas Goodwin, Philip Nye, and Joseph Caryl. On his visits to the City Bunyan must have called on him, and from time to time he worked closely with such Presbyterians as William Bates and Thomas Watson. His correspondence with Philip Lord Wharton and his wife extended over more than three decades (1662-1695). He was on close enough terms with Lord Wharton to receive a gift of venison from him in 1681 and the use of his coach for a journey to Wooburn. Griffith was also a correspondent of the educational reformer and ecumenical advocate John

---

[36]Peter Toon, *The Emergence of Hyper-Calvinism in English Nonconformity 1689-1765* (London, 1967) 49-50, 66, 68; Jones, *Congregationalism in England*, 115-16; Thomas, "Parties in Nonconformity," 117-19; Calamy, *Life*, 1:324.

Dury.[37] For a time in the 1650s he was close to those who governed the country, preaching frequently to Oliver Cromwell and Parliament. His apparent friendship with Richard Cromwell made him suspect with the Restoration state into the early 1670s.

Above all, Griffith provided the Congregationalists with continuity of leadership from the revolutionary years of the late 1640s and 1650s through the decades of persecution to the years of toleration and potential union with the Presbyterians. Owen, the most prominent of the Congregationalists, had died in 1683, Goodwin and Brooks in 1680, Caryl in 1673, Nye in 1672, and Bridge in 1670. Of the leading Congregationalists in the period after the Glorious Revolution, only Griffith had played a major role in pre-Restoration Independency. To his guiding hand must go a good share of the responsibility for the survival of the principles and institutions of Congregationalism.

---

[37]Prerogative Court of Canterbury, Wills, 17 April 1702; *Calamy Revised*, 237. There are seven letters from Griffith to Lord Wharton and one to Lady Wharton in the Bodleian (Rawlinson MSS 50-52). His letter to Dury is in Dr. Williams's Library (Baxter MSS 6, fol. 87). He also wrote (in 1658) to Henry Cromwell; British Library, Lansdowne MS 823, fol. 43.

chapter 4

One "of the Chiefest Captains of the Anabaptists": John Simpson, the Struggles of a Fifth Monarchist

In sharp contrast to George Griffith, whose adherence to the Congregationalist tradition remained constant and whose relative moderation made possible cooperative activities with the Presbyterians, John Simpson's career was turbulent. An Independent of Antinomian persuasion in the early 1640s, he became convinced of the validity of believer's baptism later in the decade, yet his congregation remained open to Independents and Baptists alike. Throughout the early 1650s he was one of the leading Fifth Monarchists and thus an object of attack by prominent Independents, but when he recanted his extreme millenarian tenets, he was in turn castigated by the Fifth Monarchists in his own congregation. Occasionally reputed to be mad by some of his opponents, Simpson was in fact a troubled man—though hardly insane. The key to his career was probably his unwavering conviction of the potency of divine grace and its free, nonlegalistic operation in the world. Even as a Fifth Monarchist he rejected the tendency of others in the movement to espouse a literal, "legalistic" interpretation of Scripture. His understanding of free grace was more in the tradition of John Saltmarsh, who played down the idea of a covenant between God and man in order to stress the unfettered nature of divine grace. Neither was Simpson committed to any sense of denominational loyalty, as some of his contemporaries clearly were, but like Henry Jessey and John Bunyan he embraced saints as saints, wherever he found them. This tendency to eschew narrow group loyalties sometimes created difficulties for him, especially among the Fifth Monarchists, but it also makes him representative of those whose overriding sense of spiritual communion led them to de-emphasize the traditional stress on polity and sacraments. Simpson vacillated in his attitude toward the government, but he remained constant in his devotion to the principle of broad Christian fellowship as well as his conviction of the imminent return of Christ. Because of the warmth and zeal with which he espoused these convictions, he provoked substantial hostility during his career.

Born about 1615 in the parish of St. Dunstan's in the East, London, Simpson was the son of Fabian Simpson. He matriculated at Exeter College, Oxford, at age sixteen on 2 December 1631 and graduated B.A. (30 April 1635) and M.A. (18 January 1638). He was probably the John Simpson reported living in the parish of St. Botolph's, Aldgate, London, in 1638. On 22 March 1642, while the attention of the political nation was focused on the militia controversy, Simpson, who seems already to have adopted Antinomian tenets, was appointed lecturer at St. Dunstan's—where John Childerley (d. 1645) was rector—by the House of Commons. A month later, on 29 April, he also received the lectureship at St. Botolph's, Aldgate, where he assumed the ministerial duties as well when the royalist incumbent, the curate Thomas Swadlin, fled the parish. Simpson's radical preaching, however, was so controversial that complaints were made to the House of Commons. On 9 October 1643 the House ordered that Simpson be discharged from his lectureship at St. Botolph's and not be permitted to preach anywhere without its approval. The parishioners were instructed to find another lecturer.[1]

[1] *Al. Oxon., s.v.*; T. C. Dale, *The Inhabitants of London in 1638*, 2 vols. (London, 1931) 2:213; Shaw, 2:301-302; A. G. Matthews, *Walker Revised* (Oxford, 1948) 44, 59; *TBHS* 3:123; *CJ*, 3:268. Simpson must not be confused with the John Simpson who was Rector of Mount Bures, Essex, beginning in 1616. This Simpson was charged with a variety of offenses in March 1644 before the Essex County Committee, including preaching the same sermons over and over again and permitting Sunday games. Matthews, *Walker Revised*, 163.

Simpson's preaching got him into trouble again in 1644. On the afternoon of 4 February, Cornelius Burgess was scheduled to preach in St. Paul's at the invitation of the Lord Mayor, but Simpson "came in a disorderly Way, and claimed the Pulpit to be provided for him to preach; but he was prevented by the Officers, who locked up the Church Doors. . . ." Uttering "unfitting Speeches," Simpson retaliated by trying to preach in the outdoor pulpit at Paul's Cross, but again the church officials barred him, excusing their action on the grounds that Simpson's preaching was conducive to riotous behavior. The entire episode was reported to the Westminster Assembly of Divines, of which Burgess was a member. At the Assembly's request Philip Herbert, Earl of Pembroke and a lay delegate, gave an account of Simpson's actions to the House of Lords on the 5th, but action was postponed pending further details. The same day the House of Commons ordered that Simpson "the *Antinomian* . . . be sent for as a Delinquent, by the Serjeant at Arms. . . ." Neither House, however, effectively silenced Simpson.[2]

When Stephen Marshall complained to the Commons on 9 August 1644 of the pervasiveness of the Anabaptists and Antinomians, he specifically took note of Simpson. In a previous sermon at which a divine took notes, Simpson had reputedly proclaimed that "Jesus Christ is in Hogs and Dogs, or Sheep; yea, that the same Spirit that ruleth in the Children of God, ruleth in the Children of Disobedience. . . ." Resolving to send for Simpson, the House referred Marshall's complaint against him to the Committee for Plundered Ministers with instructions to examine him and, if necessary, imprison him. He was suspended from preaching until 28 October 1646.[3]

It was probably in 1644 or 1645 that Simpson and the Particular Baptist Hanserd Knollys were confronted by a group of orthodox ministers angered by their Antinomian leanings. At the church of St. Christopher le Stocks in the City, Knollys had proclaimed that all liturgies, including the Book of Common Prayer, were idolatrous. He and Simpson were thereupon "in a Brotherly way dealt with by some

---

[2]*LJ*, 6:409; *CJ*, 3:389.

[3]*CJ*, 3:584, 585; Whitelocke, 2:81.

Ministers" at Edmund Calamy's house. After some discussion Knollys and Simpson, "the Antinomian, set their hands to a Paper drawn up of some Propositions, concerning the Moral Law and the Ten Commandments. . . ." According to Thomas Edwards, however, complaints were subsequently made to Calamy and his colleagues that both men were preaching "against those points they had subscribed."[4]

By 1647 Simpson was associating with Henry Jessey, pastor of a mixed communion church of Baptists and Independents. Simpson, who was Jessey's closest friend among the London ministers from 1647 to 1661, may have owed his conversion to Baptist principles to Jessey or to Knollys, who baptized Jessey in June 1645. Jessey and Simpson were jointly involved in the provision of pastoral care for the spiritually troubled Sarah Wight, whose recovery from severe depression Jessey detailed in *The Exceeding Riches of Grace Advanced . . . in . . . Sarah Wight* (1647).[5]

In November Simpson and Jessey became involved in a loose coalition of Independents and Baptists who tried to dissociate their campaign for religious liberty from the broader Leveller program that entailed substantial political, social, and legal reforms. Undoubtedly afraid that their own cause would be jeopardized by Leveller demands, especially following the condemnation of the Agreement of the People by the House of Commons on 9 November, the coalition issued *A Declaration by Congregational Societies in and about the City of London, as Well of Those Commonly Called Anabaptists, as Others* on the 22nd. The names of the group are known from a signed declaration they issued in 1651, acknowledging the 1647 declaration to have been theirs as well. In addition to Simpson and Jessey, the group included Simpson's close friend of the next decade, Christopher Feake, as well as the Particular Baptists Hanserd Knollys and William Kiffin, and the Independents William Greenhill and Thomas Brooks. In their declaration they repudiated the idea of political parity and instead espoused the importance of placing power in the hands of the godly, who would use it to ensure the propagation of the gospel. Although the Levellers

---

[4]*Gangraena*, 129.

[5]B. R. White, "Henry Jessey in the Great Rebellion," in *Reformation, Conformity and Dissent*, ed. R. Buick Knox (London, 1977) 142, 145.

were ignorant of the authors' identity, they correctly surmised that the declaration was an implicit criticism of their own position, and therefore defended themselves in a petition issued the following day. Simpson, then, played an important role in undermining substantive links between the Particular and mixed communion Baptists on the one hand and the Levellers on the other.[6]

In the same year that Simpson helped write the declaration, he succeeded Walter Cradock as the teacher or pastor of the gathered church that met at Allhallows the Great, Thames Street. One of the favorite congregations of religious radicals, the Allhallows church practiced mixed communion under Simpson, who nevertheless baptized approximately two hundred adults between 1650 and 1653. The congregation attracted a variety of officers from the army, but the most colorful member was Anna Trapnel, who joined about 1650 and who knew Simpson well. The Allhallows congregation, in fact, provided a commendatory epistle to her tract, *Legacy for Saints* (1654), signed in Simpson's absence by an elder and a deacon.[7]

Simpson expounded his Antinomian tenets both in print and in disputations between 1648 and 1650. *The Perfection of Justification Maintained Against the Pharisee* (London, 1648) was a collection of sermons published in response to charges by fifty-two London clergymen that he was an Antinomian. In his answer he developed the theme of the imputation of Christ's righteousness to the elect, for whom it is the sole basis of their justification in the sight of God. From God's perspective, moreover, such justification occurred in eternity, not at a particular moment in human history. The real danger to the gospel, he asserted, was the Arminian challenge to the doctrine of free grace as well as the growing acceptance of the notion that good works are important as preparation to receive grace. Simpson appended to this work a poem by the Welsh Independent Morgan Llwyd entitled "The Order of Christs Remote Poore and Despicable Churches in Wales." It echoed Simpson's belief that Christians must "wellcome saincts as saincts."

---

[6]Tolmie, 169-70.

[7]Ibid., 109; RCC, 346; Anna Trapnel, *The Cry of a Stone* (London, 1654) 3; Trapnel, *Legacy for Saints* (London, 1654), epistle.

104 / RICHARD L. GREAVES

Simpson became involved in several debates with the Arminian Independent John Goodwin in 1650. On 31 December of the preceding year Goodwin had debated with the Welsh evangelist Vavasor Powell the question of whether God intended that all of Adam's posterity would be saved by Christ's death. Goodwin had wanted the debate because Powell had reportedly referred to his doctrine as unsound. When Powell was bested in the debate, followers of Simpson pressed him to take Powell's place. On 14 January Goodwin and Simpson debated at Allhallows whether the decrees of election and reprobation pertained to particular persons or to the categories of believers and nonbelievers. With William Ames and John Griffith as the moderators, Simpson contended that the decrees were applicable to individuals rather than categories of persons. Four weeks later, on 11 February, the two men again debated, probably at Allhallows, with James Cranford and John Griffith as the moderators. On this occasion the subject was "whether the Heathen who want the ministry of the Gospel have not Sufficiency of means to believe unto Salvation?" Simpson insisted they did not. The debates were held in the presence of numerous ministers and a very large crowd of lay observers. Two accounts of the debates were subsequently published: *Truths Conflict with Error: Or Universal Redemption Controverted in Three Publike Disputations,* by John Weekes, published on 28 March 1650 and *A Right Use Made by a Stander-by at the Two Disputations . . . Concerning the Poynts of Generall Redemption* by John Graunt in 1650 ("1649").[8] The debates seem to have left a residue of bitterness between the contenders and their respective supporters. A friend of the Leveller William Walwyn was approvingly described as "very religious after the way of Mr[.] Simpson of All-hallowe's Thames-street, and no admirer of Mr[.] John Goodwin. . . ."[9]

The execution of Charles I on 30 January 1649 and the establishment of the republic intensified millenarian expectations. Many of those who anticipated the imminent establishment of the kingdom of Christ looked to millenarian preachers such as Simpson for advice. In 1650, for instance, the English forces in Scotland were in correspon-

---

[8] I am indebted to Dr. Ellen More for providing helpful information about John Goodwin.

[9] *The Leveller Tracts 1647-1653,* ed. William Haller and Godfrey Davies (New York, 1944) 377.

SAINTS AND REBELS / 105

dence with Simpson and Feake. Simpson himself had military experience and served for a time as a major in the New Model Army. He was with Major-General Thomas Harrison at the battle of Worcester on 3 September 1651. The Public Record Office has an order from the Council of State directing ordnance officers to deliver six barrels of gunpowder and match to Major Simpson "for the use of volunteers under Major-Gen. Harrison."[10]

In the republic, demand for Simpson's services grew in London. He was appointed Rector of St. Botolph's, Bishopsgate, by the Committee for Plundered Ministers on 17 March 1652 to succeed the sequestered Nehemiah Rogers. "By election of the people," Simpson also continued as lecturer at St. Botolph's, Aldgate, throughout the 1650s, as well as at Allhallows the Great, where Jessey and Feake also lectured. The rector at Allhallows was the Independent Robert Bragge.[11]

As the nominee of Thomas Harrison, one of the most powerful political zealots, Simpson preached a fast sermon to the Rump on 13 March 1651. Members also heard sermons the same day from the prominent Independent John Owen and the Presbyterian polemicist John Ley (or Leigh). Simpson, who was "exceeding home in his application," "set up the spirit of God against humane learning, against that order of men who challenge to themselves the prerogative of dispensing it; he said the word Chemarim, used in Zephany [Zeph. 1:4], did properly signify black coats [clergy]. . . . He further said, he believed the Lord had more eminently blessed the preaching of the gospel by the soldiers of the army, than he had done the endeavours of the ministers, in many years together." The attack was representative of the views on higher education and the formal ministry held by such radical critics as John Webster, William Dell, and the Quakers. Following Simpson's sermon, the House erupted into a stormy two-hour debate, in which he was implicitly rebuked and Harrison casti-

---

[10]Anon., *A Declaration of Several of the Churches of Christ* (London, 1654) 9; *CSPD, 1651*, 533; *CSPD, 1652-53*, 549.

[11]*CSPD, 1655*, 226; Matthews, *Walker Revised*, 56; Capp, *FMM*, 58-59, 262. For Bragge, see *Calamy Revised, s.v.*

gated for sponsoring him. A motion to give Simpson the customary vote of thanks for his sermon was defeated.[12]

In the same year Independents and Baptists mounted a campaign aimed at placing the government in the hands of the godly. As part of this effort, Simpson, Feake, Jessey, Kiffin, Knollys, Harrison, Brooks, Greenhill, and the other authors of the 1647 declaration again banded together to issue A Declaration of Divers Elders and Brethren of Congregationall Societies (1651). Although they explicitly acknowledged the duty of all people, including saints, to submit to civil authority—whether infidel or Christian—Simpson and his coauthors also expressed their hope that the franchise would be given to all "visible saints," including those who were Presbyterians by choice and not compulsion. Other religious radicals proposed a more extreme course in which only visible saints would enjoy the franchise and would exercise it by selecting members for a godly sanhedrin in lieu of the traditional Parliament. One advocate of this view, a certain D. T., specifically pointed to the churches of Simpson, Jessey, Feake, Kiffin, John Goodwin, Thomas Goodwin, and Sidrach Simpson as having congregations that should exercise political power.[13]

The time for action seemed ripe after Cromwell defeated Charles II and the Scots at Worcester on 3 September 1651. A delegation of the godly, which probably included Simpson as well as Feake, urged Cromwell to get on with the task of reformation, especially through Parliament. When Cromwell offered them insufficient encouragement during the course of two interviews, they resolved instead to meet at Allhallows in December to plot their own course. Simpson, Feake, and Jessey, who regularly lectured at Allhallows, undoubtedly exercised a prominent role in formulating the "General Heads of Prayer," a charter of the group's objectives: (1) removing anything that hindered the coming of Christ's kingdom; (2) ousting ungodly ministers and magistrates from their positions; (3) healing divisions among the saints; (4) persuading the army and Parliament to honor their prom-

---

[12]Nickolls, OLPS, 82-83; Richard L. Greaves, The Puritan Revolution and Educational Thought: Background for Reform (New Brunswick NJ, 1969) ch. 6; CJ, 6:549.

[13]A Declaration of Divers Elders and Brethren of Congregationall Societies (London, 1651) 3, 5, 8; A Model of a New Representative (n. p., 1651); A Cry for a Right Improvement of All Our Mercies (London, 1651); D. T., Certain Qveries (London, 1651) 8.

ises; (5) negotiating with the Dutch without harming the cause of Christ in either country. Thus was born the Fifth Monarchy movement. An attempt to win the backing of the government, the army, and the Independent leaders in a conference at Charles Fleetwood's house failed, however, when the Fifth Monarchists were repudiated by Owen, Philip Nye, Thomas Goodwin, and Sidrach Simpson—the Independent spokesmen. Instead of healing the divisions among the saints, the establishment of the Fifth Monarchy movement exacerbated them. Some contact among the radicals, however, continued. On 31 January 1652, for example, John Lilburne wrote to the Fifth Monarchists Simpson and Feake as well as to the Particular Baptist William Kiffin asking them to pray for him in their meetings and to care for his wife and children during his exile.[14]

Following the defection of a number of prominent persons from the Fifth Monarchy movement in the first half of 1652, Feake and his colleagues set about to reorganize the remaining adherents, probably in the early summer. Invitations were sent to six London churches asking them to dispatch delegates to meetings at London House and then in Blackfriars, which claimed to be independent of City jurisdiction on the basis of medieval rights of sanctuary. The meeting place in Blackfriars was probably the church of St. Anne, where Feake was lecturer. Feake and Simpson provided the leadership, with the support of George Cokayne, the Independent minister of St. Pancras, Soper Lane. One of those who attended the meetings was John Rogers, recently returned from Dublin where he had been sent to preach by the Council of State in 1651, and soon to become one of the most outspoken proponents of Fifth Monarchist ideology. Such army officers as Major William Packer and Captain John Spencer were also involved. The Welsh evangelist Vavasor Powell, who was with Simpson at Allhallows in 1653, must have visited the Fifth Monarchist meetings in Blackfriars.[15]

---

[14]Brown, 19-20; Capp, *FMM*, 58-59; Pauline Gregg, *Free-born John: A Biography of John Lilburne* (London, 1961) 311. The Presbyterians failed to exercise any control over the Allhallows church. The moderator of the third classis reported to the London Synod on 29 April 1652 that this church had a minister but no elders. *TBHS* 3: 124.

[15]Brown, 21-22; Capp, *FMM*, 59-60; *TBHS* 3: 124.

Fifth Monarchist meetings were sometimes stormy. On 22 November 1652 William Erbery, a Seeker openly hostile to external forms in Christianity, visited a meeting at London House, near St. Paul's. Feake's sermon on the subject of prayer ("short breathings of . . . present desires to God") met with Erbery's approval, but then Simpson mounted the pulpit. Rather than offer a prayer he began to preach "or *prophesie,* as he terms it, and thinks it so; so do not I," insisted Erbery. "Neither do I think, that when prayers were made for *Peter* by the Church, that they spent their time in Preaching." Erbery was incensed that before Simpson even announced his text, he launched into a "large Preface; and, (as if he had stood on the Stool of Repentance) he *confesseth his faults* before us all." Simpson used his preface to make three specific points:

> First, he *professed himself a fool,* for the rising of his heart against that which another held forth not according to his apprehension.
> Secondly, he said that *he was a fool* again, for that *rigidness* of spirit, to stick to his own, or to *oppose the light that might shine in another,* i. e. *the Lord in them.*
> He shewed further how God had *judged that rigidness in Prelacy and Presbytery,* and would also in the *Independents or Dippers;* so he calleth the Baptized Churches. . . .

The last point had a particular bearing on the purpose of the meeting—to unite the Independents and the Baptists and further the propagation of the gospel. To Erbery the dream of such unity was futile until that apocalyptic time when "wrath be poured forth on all their Forms. . . ." Only when the legal institutions had been crushed could the Spirit achieve unity by gathering up "all the Saints and men in God."[16]

When Erbery could take no more of Simpson's "low and Legal" sermon, he interrupted the preacher to request a sermon on prayer in the Spirit. In the confusion that erupted, Erbery compared Simpson's "common" prayers to the prelates' Book of Common Prayer and charged him with legalistic preaching. Colonel William Packer sprang to Simpson's defense, accusing Erbery of having a "Ranting Spirit." Er-

---

[16]William Erbery, *The Testimony of William Erbery, Left upon Record* (London, 1658) 44, 47; Erbery, *The Bishop of London* (1653), passim.

bery responded by calling Packer a liar. Erbery was finally forced to leave, but he got the last word by providing his version of the encounter in *The Testimony of William Erbery, Left upon Record.*[17]

When Cromwell forcibly dissolved the Rump in April 1653, Simpson and Feake were initially hopeful. "The pulpitt men of Blackfriers predicate alowd the Generall's wisdome for grubbing up the wicked Parliament, not leaving a rotten roote thereof." Disillusion quickly set in at Blackfriars as Cromwell's intentions were questioned. On 16 and 23 May preachers at Blackfriars claimed to have revealed knowledge that God intended to bestow the English monarchy on a new line, apparently King Jesus. Harrison himself preached in mid-May that England would soon have a monarch "after Gods owne heart, and a King anointed with the Spiritt." To such prophecies Cromwell responded by banning "Harrisons gathered Churches at Blackfryers" and trying to silence Feake.[18]

The summer and fall of 1653 was a time of particular tension among the saints, who experienced mixed emotions of anticipation and frustration as they watched Cromwell maneuver. The internal divisiveness was manifest in part when the Welsh prophet Arise Evans castigated Feake and Simpson. In an attempt to keep the godly united, Simpson and Jessey visited some thirty churches in Essex, Suffolk, and Norfolk during the summer. While on this tour Simpson may have gone as far north as Northumberland, for the records of Thomas Tillam's Baptist church at Hexham reveal a visit from "Capt. Sympson and Capt. Mason" on 16 August. Their trip was "by order, from London and Newcastle churches," the latter being that of Thomas Gower and Paul Hobson. As a result of this visit, Simpson and Mason, "hearing of our constitution and condition, sweetly and lovingly owned us as their brethren. . . ."[19]

If John Simpson was indeed the visitor to Hexham on 16 August, he had to hurry south after that, for on the 20th Commander Peter

---

[17]Erbery, *Testimony*, 46-47; Erbery, *Bishop of London*, passim.

[18]D. A. Johnson and D. G. Vaisey, eds., *Staffordshire and the Great Rebellion* (Stafford, 1964) 73; Capp, *FMM*, 65-66.

[19]Christopher Hill, *Change and Continuity in Seventeenth-Century England* (Cambridge, 1975) 64; White, "Henry Jessey," 140-41; RCC, 293-94.

Pett of Aldborough, Suffolk, informed the Admiralty Committee that he had arranged quarters for Simpson and Jessey with a Mrs. Bence. This enabled them to preach on 25 August at a service of thanksgiving on board Robert Blake's flagship, the *General*, anchored off Aldborough. The service, commemorating victories over the Dutch fleet, underscored Fifth Monarchist support for the war, which they viewed as a means to hasten the arrival of the millennium. The invitation to preach on Blake's flagship and the interest shown by the navy commissioners in their movements suggest the respect enjoyed by Simpson and Jessey in government circles. Following their visit to the *General*, where their service received the "great attention of the seamen," Simpson and Jessey continued their tour by visiting churches in the Yarmouth area.[20]

After the conclusion of their trip, Jessey's church at Swan Alley, Coleman Street, wrote to the Hexham church on 2 October to report the return of Simpson and Jessey. They had visited some ten churches in each of the counties of Essex, Suffolk, and Norfolk in order "to understand their way and order, and to further love, amongst all that love the Lord Jesus in sincerity, and communion with them." The two men had been warmly received, though the churches—"sound in the faith, and holy in life"—differed over such matters as baptism, the laying on of hands, the blessing of infants, and the singing of psalms and hymns. Such a description suggests that Simpson and Jessey visited Particular Baptist, General Baptist, Independent, and possibly open communion churches.[21]

Several weeks before Jessey's church sent this letter to Hexham, the congregations of Simpson (at Blackfriars), Jessey, and Knollys had written to the same church "about nearer communion and provoking to pray for the pouring forth of the Spirit, for furnishing ministry, magistracy, &c." No answer had been received for this appeal for closer relations by the time Jessey's church wrote again on 2 October. In the same period the Western Association of eight Particular Baptist churches located in Gloucester, Hereford, Monmouth, and Worcester was also trying to establish communion with the Hexham congrega-

[20]*CSPD*, 1653-54, 104, 481, 485.
[21]*RCC*, 346-47.

tion. The journey of Simpson and Jessey was thus part of a broader movement in 1653 to bring the gathered churches into a closer union, probably because of the eschatological expectations so widespread at this time.[22]

Among the Fifth Monarchists the hope of summer was followed by the bitter disillusionment of the autumn. As the radicals in the Barebones were frustrated in their drive to attain sweeping legal and religious reforms, anger with Cromwell mounted. In November three or four preachers at Blackfriars charged that he was "the man of sin, the old dragon, and many other scripture ill names. . . ." Simpson was probably among those summoned with Feake to appear before Cromwell on the 30th to answer for such diatribes. Unmoved by Cromwell's assertion that they were impugning the government, Feake and his colleagues were further outraged when Cromwell—spurred on by the moderates—ordered the dissolution of the Barebones on 12 December. On the 19th, three days after Cromwell took the oath as Lord Protector, Feake and Powell publicly denounced him as a "perjured villaine." Powell predicted the imminent collapse of the government and wondered aloud if God would have Cromwell or Christ rule England.[23]

Although Cromwell banned further meetings at Blackfriars and briefly imprisoned Powell and Feake, he treated Simpson more leniently. According to a report from the Venetian secretary in England, Simpson "is considered mad and has therefore been pardoned, but if he persists in his abuse of the present government he and all his imitators may expect severe punishment." Feake and Powell were summoned before the Council but released on the 21st. If Simpson escaped because the government really suspected he was insane, they were probably led to this conclusion by the extremity of his views rather than feigned behavior on his part. Feake too complained that people thought him mad, but retorted, "Paul himself complains, that he was cried down for a madman, and yet the cause that he was engaged in

---

[22]Ibid., 345-46; *TBHS*, 5:22. At one point during the decade 1646-1656, a John Simpson paid £50 for bishop's lands for the use of William Simpson, minister of Lythe, Yorkshire. Shaw, *History*, 2:563. This is probably not the John Simpson who is our subject.

[23]Thurloe, *SP*, 1:621; Capp, *FMM*, 73, 101.

was the cause of Christ. . . ." Simpson, Feake, and Powell were all judged "Mad men" by Alexander de Samand's master, who prohibited the young man from attending their services. In all likelihood, such slanderous attributions stemmed from the radical nature of Fifth Monarchist ideology. Men who aspired to reshape English government and influence English politicians would hardly do so by feigning insanity.[24]

Despite their brush with the law, the Fifth Monarchist leaders would not be silenced. For his part Simpson prophesied that the Protectorate would fall within six months. The accuracy of his vision, he proclaimed, was attested by his correct prediction of the dissolution of both the Rump and the Barebones Parliaments. To his latest outbursts the government responded with force. A warrant for Powell's arrest was issued on 10 January, but he eluded the authorities and escaped to Wales. A warrant for the arrest of Simpson and Feake was issued on the 25th, the same day that the Council of State appointed a special committee, which included Sir Charles Wolseley and Colonel William Sydenham, to examine the accusations against them. They appeared before the Council the following day. On the 28th the committee recommended that they be imprisoned in Windsor Castle in order to preserve the country's peace, and a warrant to this effect was issued. Their imprisonment came under the provisions of an ordinance that made it treasonous to assert that the Protector's authority was usurped, illegal, or tyrannical. With apparent relief, one of John Thurloe's correspondents reported the apprehension of Simpson and Feake, "two of the chiefest captains of the anabaptists, who did preach most scornfully against the present government." Their incarceration, observed the Venetian secretary on 28 February, was "for expressing themselves in favour of the royal cause and speaking to the disparagement of the present government." "The royal cause" was not that of Charles II but King Jesus, and the monarchy they espoused was not that of tradition, but a new and godly institution. In contrast, Richard Bradshaw, the English ambassador at Hamburg, expressed sorrow at

[24]Capp, *FMM*, 86-87, 101; *CSP Venetian, 1653-54*, 169; Thurloe, *SP*, 5:759. Hill's suggestion that madness was a cover-up for the expression of dangerous ideas does not seem applicable to the leading Fifth Monarchists. *The World Turned Upside Down* (New York, 1972) 227.

the imprisonment of Feake and Simpson, finding them overzealous and unable to see the hand of providence in the establishment of the Protectorate. "They cannot deny," he insisted, "but that the power and authoritie is still in the hands of God's choyce instruments. . . ."[25]

While Simpson languished in prison, his congregation at Allhallows lost some of its zeal. Marchamont Nedham, the government's publicist, informed the Lord Protector on 7 February that Allhallows was "a dull assembly" without Simpson and Feake, "for they were the men that carried it on with heat." Nevertheless he thought the meetings should be suppressed because they adversely affected Cromwell's reputation among foreign visitors. "The congregation," to which Jessey, John Spencer, and Highland were preaching, "is crowded, the humours boiling, and as much scum comes off as ever, but more warily."[26]

From Windsor, Simpson penned a series of letters to his flock at Allhallows, hoping to keep their enthusiasm alive. A February letter reminded them that when the Spirit returns to the saints, the churches of Christ will become the schools of the prophets, and the "universities as now they stand upon an Antichristian foundation must be tumbled down, Antichrist hath set up those Cages of unclean Birds, that they who go thither may learn to sing the whores songs. . . ." Continuing to echo the general theme of his controversial 1651 sermon to the Rump, Simpson then turned to the ministry, which he insisted must likewise perish because it "stands upon a Popish foot and Antichrists foundation, yea the best of Ministers must be thrown down, so far as they stand upon an Antichristian Bottom, though God will own what is of his own Spirit in them. . . ." He lashed out against tithes, setting before the godly of Allhallows the merits of voluntary maintenance for ministers. Ironically, however, he had accepted tithes in his position at St. Botolph's, Bishopsgate.[27]

---

[25]*CSP Venetian*, 1653-54, 169, 186-87; P. G. Rogers, *The Fifth Monarchy Men* (London, 1966) 42; *CSPD*, 1653-54, 368, 371, 449; Whitelocke, 4:81; Thurloe, *SP*, 2:67, 88.

[26]*CSPD*, 1653-54, 393. For Jessey, Spencer, and Highland see *BDBR*, *s.vv.*

[27]John Simpson, Letters, ad cal. *The Old Leaven Purged Out. Or, the Apostacy of This Day Further Opened* (n.p., 1658) 4-5, 13, 17.

114 / RICHARD L. GREAVES

The zealousness that once stirred his followers as he thundered from the pulpit now poured forth in Simpson's letters. The saints must, he implored, "help Christ to the throne of *England*." God would "bring down Tyrants, and Persecutors, new, and old." Refusing to be penitent, Simpson confidently rejoiced that he had espoused the message of the Fifth Monarchy. As for Cromwell, Simpson explained that God himself had pressed him to take his life in his hands by dealing plainly with the Lord Protector in showing him the error of his ways. "Within a few years, not to say moneths, I shall be found, without *Cromwells* timely repentance, as true a Prophet unto him, as I was to the long sitting *Parliament*." It was only a little more than two months later that Simpson had a dramatic vision of Cromwell's fall. The "great O" ran towards a crown, sat in a chair of state, sprouted horns, and then "was shamefully tumbled from his *Pomp*, and *Glory*." In contrast to the retribution he prophesied for Cromwell, Simpson found spiritual solace in his confinement: "I have thorow mercy a whole week together tasted the sweetness of God in close Imprisonment. . . ."[28]

The months at Windsor provided Simpson with time to reflect on his beliefs, which resulted in the publication that year of his most important work, *The Great Joy of Saints*. Despite his earlier adherence to Antinomian principles, Simpson followed other Fifth Monarchists in recognizing the significance of the Mosaic law. The Old Testament, after all, was crucial for the development of Fifth Monarchist millennial theory, and it would not do to suppress its teachings as the Antinomians and Ranters did. He also argued in this work for the extension of toleration even to Familists, recognizing that external force can produce no more than outward conformity. Continuing his longtime concern for unifying the godly, he was critical of saints who moved from congregation to congregation in search of a "true" church with "the true practise of all Ordinances." In *The Great Joy* Simpson continued his practice of prophesying by recording his vision of the day when the "wicked, ungodly, and unbelieving men shall be raised as slaves, and vassals, and be brought forth in chaines and fetters, before the dreadfull tribunall." By contrast the saints would appear as sovereigns.[29]

---

[28]Ibid., 6, 9, 13, 18-19.

[29]Simpson, *The Great Joy of Saints* (London, 1654), pt. 1:25-27, 118; pt. 2:47, 248, 273.

Simpson's incarceration created problems for the state. On 26 April the Council of State had to authorize some of his parishioners at St. Botolph's, Bishopsgate, to receive the income from his benefice in order to hire a replacement and support his wife and children. The Council was frankly concerned that his church had been without a minister or was "uncertainly supplied," hence the following day eight parishioners were ordered to find a clergyman approved by the Commissioners for the Approbation of Ministers. The man so selected was Daniel Nicholls.[30]

The Council of State was also worried that "great numbers of people, some of whom are disaffected," flocked to Windsor everyday to see Simpson and Feake. Some of them, the Council complained, "are disaffected, and . . . take the opportunity of such assembling to vent their own discontents, leavening others thereby," while others "hold secret conferences" with Simpson and Feake as well as correspond with them. The Council, therefore, ordered the governor of the castle to prohibit them from all public speaking and to keep them close prisoners. John Rogers, who would shortly be arrested himself (on 26 July), called on Cromwell not only to release Simpson and Feake, "the Lord's prisoners," but to allow them to reveal God's vision to him. For its own reasons, the government issued a warrant for Simpson's release on 4 July, following this nine days later with a restriction prohibiting him from preaching within five miles of London. More conservative voices must have been raised, however, for on the 17th the prohibition was extended to an area ten miles around London, and he was barred from the City altogether.[31]

In the months that followed, Simpson apparently remained quiet, even to the point of accepting his exile from London. There was even a report on 10 August that he "now owns and prayes for the present Powers." He presumably kept in contact with his London followers and, therefore, would have known of their participation in the preparation of a Fifth Monarchist manifesto, which coincided with the convening of the first Protectorate Parliament in September 1654. En-

---

[30]*CSPD, 1654*, 120, 124.

[31]Ibid., 188-89, 253, 256, 438; Rogers, *Fifth Monarchy Men*, 45; Whitelocke, 4: 125. The order of 17 July contains this provision: "The observation hereof committed to Capt. Thos. Harrison, Governor of Upnor Castle, Kent."

titled *A Declaration of Several of the Churches of Christ*, the manifesto accused the government of complicity with Antichrist because it had embraced the material wealth of the old monarchy and aristocracy. The purpose of the *Declaration* was to "ease and exonerate our selves in the sense we have of our duty herein, and be withdrawn (to the eye of all) from partaking in the crying sins and Apostacie of the Times. . . ." The 150 signatories represented the congregations of Simpson, Feake, Rogers, Jessey, Knollys, Praisegod Barebones, and others. Whether Simpson sanctioned the manifesto is not known, but it is clear that some of his followers had begun to have doubts about his continued loyalty to Fifth Monarchist principles.[32]

Despite being banned from London, Simpson returned to the City in December 1654, hoping to counter the growing doubts about his loyalty. On the 18th he preached at Allhallows on Psalm 102: 19-21. "Hee declared his sufferings for Christ, that it was in declareing against the sinnes of men, and though hee was accused for treason, yett he never spake against any man but it was from the law of God or of the land, and therefore was not guiltye." Now, however, he was defying the order of banishment in the name of liberty. He had also heard rumors that he welcomed the exile and had no desire to return to his church, "and that it was given out from the Court that hee might come to London if he was bound to show his readyness to serve Christ and his Church, though he ventured his life in it." Although Simpson declared from the pulpit "his sameness to what he ever was; and that he never in the least doubted of the goodness of his cause, in bearing witness against the last publique things, as a publique sinne against former vowes," he did not fully convince at least some of his hearers. One anonymous millenarian subsequently remarked that Simpson "I apprehend not to be fully enlightned about the kingdome of Christ. . . ." He also predicted that Simpson's return to the City would bring "further tryalls upon the spirits of the Church in some tyme."[33]

---

[32]*Severall Proceedings*, 255 (10-17 August 1654); *TBHS* 3: 136, 147 (the text of the *Declaration* is reprinted on 129-47).

[33]*Clarke Papers*, 2: xxxv; 3: 13-14.

After Simpson had preached a second sermon, Cromwell requested that he confer with him "as a brother and a christian," bringing with him three or four members of his church. When Simpson presented the invitation to his congregation, they voted that he should confer with the Lord Protector. Accompanied by five of his people, Simpson spent an entire day at Whitehall. There were two sessions, lasting from 9:00 A.M. to 12:00 P.M. and from 3:00 P.M. to 7:00 P.M., broken only by the Protector's previously scheduled lunch with an ambassador. Although he provided food for them, they refused to eat, preferring instead to think through more of the issues they wished to raise with Cromwell. One of their chief concerns was the issue of tithes, which they understood Cromwell had previously told Jessey he would abolish. To this the Protector responded that he "wist not whether he had said so or no. . . ." Furthermore, he insisted that he alone had no authority to terminate tithes, and that his Council in any case opposed such action. When Simpson accused Cromwell of having broken his promise to uphold the laws by imprisoning himself and Feake, the Protector retorted that unless he had done so, the two men would have been tried under the Treason Ordinance, with the likely penalty of death. Cromwell became irate when Simpson accused him, as Protector, of having violated the March 1649 act making it treason to promote anyone to the name or power of a king. "Well said, Simpson, thou art plain indeed; not only to tell me I have broken my vowes, but that I am in plain termes A Traitor." Simpson's delegation also faulted Cromwell for using the Triers to deny liberty to the saints, but Cromwell defended himself by arguing that the Triers only barred knaves from the ministry, not the godly. Finally, Cromwell dismissed Simpson and his co-believers, exhorting them "to carry soberly, as that should be best for them." For their part, Simpson's delegation was dissatisfied with Cromwell's responses. [34]

Despite the Protector's inability to sway Simpson in a personal confrontation, Cromwell continued in 1655 with his face-to-face meetings. The failure of his West Indian expedition in the winter of 1654-1655—the capture of Jamaica notwithstanding—was interpreted by the Fifth Monarchists to be a further sign of God's disap-

---

[34]Ibid., 2: xxxvi-xxxvii.

proval of the Protectorate. When they stepped up their criticism of the government, Fleetwood summoned various radicals, including Simpson and Jessey, in the hope of changing their minds, but he was unsuccessful. Cromwell himself was involved again on 15 February, when he met with four prominent Fifth Monarchists who were suspected of plotting against the government and spreading treasonous publications. The four—Harrison, John Carew, Hugh Courtney, and Nathaniel Rich—agreed to confer with Cromwell only if Simpson, John Pendarves (a Baptist minister and a Fifth Monarchist), and a Mr. Bankes were present. Cromwell granted their request, and Simpson was there to hear the four tell the Lord Protector that it was lawful for Christians to take up arms against his government. They also denounced his Parliament because its power derived from the people rather than God. Cromwell himself, Carew charged, had taken the crown from the head of Christ and placed it on his own. Although the four were thereupon imprisoned, Simpson was not detained. Perhaps Cromwell intended this as an object lesson for him.[35]

Trouble developed that summer in the parish of St. Botolph's, Bishopsgate. Dissatisfaction with Daniel Nicholls had already been voiced the preceding October by "the chiefest of the parish," who regarded him as too young and physically weak. At that time they had hoped to find another replacement for Simpson. Taking note of a new petition to this effect on 4 July 1655, the Council of State terminated Nicholls's appointment the following day and revoked the original grant of the living to Simpson (17 March 1652). According to the petition, most of the parishioners desired the services of Samuel Lee, an Independent. On 24 July, however, Cromwell received a petition from another group of St. Botolph's parishioners, thanking him for the "means of Grace which we have enjoyed under John Simpson, and since his restraint, under Dan. Nicholls, whereby many have been turned from Satan to God. . . ." These petitioners had hoped to continue with Simpson as their pastor, for he was "growing daily more fixed in declaring to us the Gospel of Christ," but they were troubled because "some few" of the parishioners had successfully persuaded the Council of State to remove both Simpson and Nicholls and

[35]*Old Leaven,* 4; anon., *Some Considerations by Way of Proposal* (London, 1658) 2, 7; Thurloe, *SP,* 4:650; Brown, 93-94; *Clarke Papers,* 2:242-46.

to appoint Lee, "who shows no wish to come." They begged instead for Cromwell to allow Simpson or Nicholls to continue at St. Botolph's. Cromwell, however, intervened personally with Lee and persuaded him to accept the living, where he remained until 1659.[36]

Neither the imprisonment of the other Fifth Monarchists nor the loss of his benefice intimidated Simpson. Cromwell tried again in October 1655 to dissuade Simpson, Jessey, and others from their hostility to the government, but he got no more than a promise that they would meet with him again. Colonel Jerome Sankey, a Particular Baptist who supported the Protectorate, informed Henry Cromwell in Ireland that attempts to win the support of Simpson and Jessey were unsuccessful.[37]

In November Vavasor Powell, who had maintained a barrage of criticism against the Protectorate, prepared a petition to Cromwell protesting wickedness in high places, accusing him of betraying the godly cause, and protesting against tithes and high taxes. There was hostility as well to imprisonment without due cause, to the continuation of customs and honors of the monarchical era, to the preferment of favorites and relatives, and to the existence of too many officers in the army. Cromwell was admonished to "lie down in the dust, and acknowledge your iniquity," especially for forgetting the Engagement against monarchical government. "You have caused great searching of heart, and divisions among many of God's people by a sudden, strange, and unexpected alteration of government. . . ." Affixed to the petition, entitled *A Word for God*, were in excess of 300 signatures, though Simpson's was not one. Major-General James Berry spoke with Powell about the petition, extracting a statement of regret about the way it had been used. In Berry's judgment the government was overreacting to the petition, and he personally expressed hope that Powell and his colleagues would give him their help and advice in the future.[38]

---

[36]*CSPD, 1654*, 124; *CSPD, 1655*, 226, 254. For Lee see *BDBR, s.v.*

[37]White, "Henry Jessey," 149; *BQ*, 25: 105-106.

[38]Thurloe, *SP*, 4: 359, 380-84; A. H. Dodd, "A Remonstrance from Wales, 1655," *Bulletin of the Board of Celtic Studies* 17 (1956-1958): 279-92.

The government's alarm over *A Word for God* stemmed not only
from its being printed, but from Simpson and Cornet Wentworth
Day's reading of it from the pulpit of Allhallows on 3 December to a
group of approximately 500 people. The petition referred to "the severall Remonstrances of the Army, charging his Highnesse with the
breach thereof, and calling him a perjured person and apostate etc."
Simpson and Day, fumed Thurloe, "rayled . . . in such scurrillous language, that all this towne ringes of it. The best termes they gave us at
Whitehall were, the theeves and robbers at Whitehall, and the great
theife Oliver Cromwell, the tyrant and usurper; which expressions
they used above 20 tymes, *cum multis aliis*, stirringe up the people to
action against the government." Based on the petition, Thurloe was
convinced that the Fifth Monarchists wanted to recall the "old" Parliament. They appeal, he informed Henry Cromwell, "to the gener-
ality of the people for justice and righteousnes, comend parlaments
chosen by the people (the thinge they most of all hate) or doe any
other thinge, rather then misse of their end of bringinge things to
trouble and confusion. . . ."[39]

For his part in reading *A Word for God* at Allhallows, Cornet Day
was arrested, but Simpson narrowly escaped and went into hiding.
Warrants for the apprehension of both were issued on 12 December.
Simpson periodically emerged to preach but then quickly retreated
underground. On Christmas day Thurloe grumbled to Henry Cromwell that Simpson "preaches like any Bedlam, but takes his opportunities to doe it, that he may, after he hath done, escape beinge
apprehended, and soe hides hymselfe." Accusations of madness came
from others as well. Major-General Edward Whalley, an Independent
in religion, professed not to be surprised at the "mad . . . zeale" of
Simpson and Day, for "they have long bin possest with it." From Edinburgh Lord Broghill observed to Thurloe that the Allhallows's preachers were "still mad" and had to be punished or the government was
tacitly confessing to the truth of their message. "It has greived many
an honnest hart, that they have bin suffered soe longe; and 'twould
satisfy them, if they were tollerated noe longer. I feare," he warned
Thurloe, that "indulgency will rather heighten their evell, then win

---

[39]*Clarke Papers*, 3: 62; *CSPD*, *1655-56*, 576; Thurloe, *SP*, 4: 321, 373-74.

them from it." Whalley too was unhappy with the toleration of the Fifth Monarchists and openly marveled at Cromwell's patience in dealing with Simpson. In contrast, Henry Cromwell supported a policy of "tenderness" towards them as long as they were kept from exercising power, for he was convinced that they would not tolerate others. He suspected, however, that they enjoyed influential backing, or Simpson and Day would not have been so bold. "Howe longe have the Anabapt[ists] and they bin at odds? from whence comes John Sympson?"[40]

In the midst of this controversy Simpson was attacked again by Arise Evans. In *A Reflection of a Pamphlet Lately Published by One Aspinwall*, which appeared on 10 December 1655, Evans denounced Simpson, Feake, and other Fifth Monarchists as a "murmuring people" with the interests of Satan. Their pantheon of demigods, he asserted, comprised Simpson, Feake, Powell, Harrison, and Rogers.

Finally the government apprehended Simpson in January 1656. According to Edmund Ludlow, Simpson was imprisoned because he, along with Feake and Rogers, had "publickly declared against his [Cromwell's] usurpation both by printing and preaching. . . ." A somewhat different version was reported to the exiled Sir Edward Nicholas by a Colonel R. W., who had heard that Cromwell had to double his guards at Christmas out of fear of an Anabaptist plot. The conspirators allegedly had sought the intentions of the army officers. "Some say (but it is thought a fable) that they have lately tampered with his barber to make short work of him, but they certainly hope to destroy him by prayer, which (as they say) was the way they raised him. Simpson, with one or two other fierce Levites, and a cornet of Harrison's regiment, are made prisoners on this account."[41]

The incarceration, however, was brief, for Simpson was freed the following month. Either the return to prison or, as Dr. B. R. White suggests, the influence of Jessey prompted Simpson to moderate his opinions. In a letter to Henry Cromwell dated 19 February, Thurloe reported that Simpson was now preaching that Christ would return in person prior to the commencement of the millennium. "This he

---

[40]*Clarke Papers*, 3:62; Thurloe, *SP*, 4:308, 321, 343, 348.

[41]*The Memoirs of Edmund Ludlow*, ed. C. H. Firth, 2 vols. (Oxford, 1894) 1:380.

preached yesterday openly, and afterwards at a more private meetinge he told them, that he knew, that they had an intention both heere and in the countrye to take armes, but for his part he sayd, he was utterly against it, and would declare hymselfe soe." At this, some in the audience openly baited him until the meeting broke up in confusion.[42]

Simpson's defection from the Fifth Monarchists led to a major rupture in the Allhallows congregation. A group of seventy-two Fifth Monarchist members prepared a substantive indictment of the government and the army, which were charged with apostasy and the promulgation of antichristian laws. The New Model was specifically accused of treasonous conduct in violating the March 1649 act prohibiting government by a single person, and of oppression for imprisoning saints such as Simpson and Harrison. When the document containing the charges was presented to the congregation on 1 June 1656, Simpson and his supporters succeeded in delaying a debate, which could only have further exacerbated tensions. In the interval Simpson appealed for help to various leaders of Independent and Baptist churches in London, including Jessey, Knollys, Cokayne, and Praisegod Barebones. Pressed by the Fifth Monarchists, however, they agreed not to intervene until the Allhallows congregation had debated the issues. After the resulting disputations failed to resolve the differences, the Fifth Monarchist group turned for support to such outside leaders of the movement as Henry Danvers, John Clarke, and John Canne, as well as non-Fifth Monarchists such as Barebones. Simpson, however, refused to allow their participation in the dispute. Because the Fifth Monarchists in the congregation reiterated their charges in a letter, Simpson responded by renewing his appeal for outside assistance. When a delegation came in January 1657, the Fifth Monarchists persuaded them to leave on the grounds that they lacked an invitation from the entire congregation. In the spring the Fifth Monarchists formulated a statement of secession, which outside Fifth Monarchists approved, and the formal breach occurred on 1 September. The majority, however, remained with Simpson.[43]

---

[42]White, "Henry Jessey," 153; Thurloe, SP, 4: 545.

[43]Old Leaven, passim; Capp, FMM, 276-78. The Fifth Monarchists in the Allhallows congregation were also angry because Simpson had changed his mind and now recognized the legitimacy of the Triers. Old Leaven, pt. 2: 2.

While these divisive events were transpiring, the gulf between Simpson and the Fifth Monarchists widened. There was a particularly stormy meeting at Allhallows on 5 January 1657 when Feake addressed the congregation for three hours. Before he spoke, a representative from Simpson's church and another from Kiffin's offered prayer, deploring the divisions among the churches. In his address, however, Feake argued that more disunity was necessary: "When the churches are gathering corruption, and striking in with the anti-christian powers of the world, and complying with the interest of Babylon, 'tis high time then," he contended, "to rouze, and rattle them. . . ." Livid over his brief arrest the previous day, Feake denounced the Protectorate, claiming it was "as Babylonish as ever, and there is as much of Babylon in the civil state, and the lawyers, and the old popish laws, and the clergy-state, as ever." After Feake accused the army of supporting popery as much as Charles I and Laud had done, he recounted his persecution at the hands of the Cromwellian government. "And if I be mad (as men say) know it is for your sakes, for the saints sakes that I am so." At the conclusion of his diatribe Feake asked the audience to comment on malicious gossip spread about him. Ignoring the proposed topic of discussion, Jessey rose to denounce Feake's call to rend the churches further for the sake of Christ. Kiffin and Simpson reiterated Jessey's view as well as protested Feake's use of the terms Babylonish and antichristian to describe the Protectorate. In the resulting confusion Kiffin was denounced as a courtier and Simpson as an apostate because he had once preached "the same things in the same place. . . ."[44]

Simpson further alienated some of the Fifth Monarchists by opposing their observance of the Saturday sabbath. The tendency of Fifth Monarchists to interpret the Old Testament literally led a few, such as John Spittlehouse, to adopt the Jewish sabbath, but like most Christians Simpson regarded this practice as abrogated with the cessation of the Jewish ceremonial law. When Simpson preached against the Saturday sabbath on 14 December 1656, he provoked retorts by Spittlehouse in *A Manifestation of Sundry Gross Absurdities* (1656) and *A Return to Some Expressions* (1656).

---

[44]Thurloe, *SP*, 5:755-59.

While Simpson was feuding with the Fifth Monarchists, he became embroiled in a bitter dispute with Zachary Crofton, the Presbyterian Curate of St. Botolph's, Aldgate, who was described by a later author as "an upright man, but of a warm and hasty temper: an acute, learned and solid divine. . . ." At Crofton's appointment to this living in 1655, Simpson himself had been a candidate for the post, and the two never got along. Simpson had no sympathy for Crofton's practice of paedobaptism alone or his emphasis on catechizing. When Crofton wrote a tract entitled *Catechizing God's Ordinance* (1656), Simpson warned the parishioners that memorizing a catechism was "not to worship God; [you may] as well buy your children rattles or hobby horses."[45]

Early in 1657, when Simpson was caught up in the controversy at Allhallows, Crofton tried to oust him from the lectureship at St. Botolph's, which he hoped to assume himself. On 10 February more than sixty "well-affected" parishioners successfully petitioned Cromwell to permit Simpson to lecture on Sunday and once during the week. "Having divers years enjoyed the labours of John Simpson as lecturer, and finding his ministry a blessing to us, and of great advantage towards the maintenance of our numerous poor, we beg that he may be allowed to lecture one part of the Lord's day, and one day in the week." Crofton chafed under the order but was forced to acquiesce. When, however, Cromwell was reinstalled as Lord Protector under the terms of the Humble Petition and Advice on 26 June, Crofton saw an opportunity to renew his attack against Simpson. In a letter to Simpson dated 31 July, Crofton informed him: "If the order by colour of which you invaded my church, did give you . . . any power so to doe, the late revolution hath made it voide and nulle. . . ." Cromwell had sworn to uphold the law, hence Crofton insisted that he would "reenioyc mine owne interest . . . as I am legall incumbent of the place." If Simpson objected, Crofton challenged him to take his case to court.[46]

The following Sunday Crofton, as he had promised, disrupted Simpson's lecture. Following Simpson's appeal to the Council of State

---

[45]Calamy, *Non. Mem.*, 1: 103 (quoted); J. A. Dodd, "Troubles in a City Parish Under the Protectorate," *EHR* 10 (January 1895): 43-44.

[46]*CSPD, 1656-57*, 272 (quoted), 281; *CSPD, 1657-58*, 48 (quoted); Dodd, "Troubles in a City Parish," 45.

on 4 August, Crofton was ordered to desist, and the Committee for Ejecting Scandalous Ministers was instructed to examine Crofton for his contempt of the Council's order (dated 10 February) permitting Simpson to lecture at St. Botolph's. On the next Sunday Crofton, supported by Middlesex constables, refused to vacate the pulpit after the morning service and would not recognize the Council's order because it had mistakenly been addressed to "Mr. Grafton." Such behavior, Simpson's friends asserted, "caused much disturbance, hazarding bloodshed." Simpson's supporters thereupon enlisted the help of various Common Councilmen, churchwardens, and others, who protested to the Council of State on the 13th about Crofton's conduct. The next day the Council reaffirmed Simpson's right to lecture, and Cromwell himself approved the order. Crofton protested in vain that he had been willing to yield the pulpit to Simpson at 3:00 P.M. on the 4th, and that as the lawful incumbent he had a right to lecture in his own church. For a time the feud between the two men became so embittered that both preached simultaneously—Crofton from the pulpit and Simpson from the gallery opposite him. Such antics, fumed one of Crofton's supporters, led "to the great disturbance and scandal of Christian people."[47]

Embittered, Crofton refused to accept the inevitable. Not only did he use the pulpit to protest Simpson's right to lecture at St. Botolph's, but he wrote a tract entitled *Right Re-entred* (1657) recounting his side of the controversy. In September Crofton tried without success to force Simpson to debate with him on the topic of baptism. Wearying of the harassment, Simpson and his supporters petitioned the Council of State on 22 October for Crofton's removal on the grounds that he preached sedition. The Council in turn referred the matter to the Commissioners for the Ejection of Scandalous Ministers, who examined Crofton on 2 December. Eleven formal charges were laid against Crofton by Simpson's group, including accusations that he had consulted Satan, used offensive language about Cromwell, excessively beaten a maidservant, refused to obey the Council's order respecting Simpson's right to preach, and refused to allow thanksgiving services for Cromwell's victories at Dunbar and Worcester. The

[47]*CSPD*, 1657-58, 50, 62, 64-65; Dodd, "Troubles in a City Parish," 44-46, 54 (quoted).

commissioners apparently chose not to resolve the case, and both men continued—uneasily—to share the pulpit at St. Botolph's.[48]

In September 1657 the Council of State had tried to resolve the controversy by finding Simpson an alternate site for his congregation. On the 24th the Council ordered that waste land at the west end of St. Paul's be given to his congregation. The land appropriated the following February contained the ruins of the Convocation House and the adjoining cloisters near St. Paul's. The House itself "lies on a heap, roof and floor fallen down, windows broken, iron and lead embezzled, the whole building ruinous and very dangerous, and the waste ground spread with soft stone and rubbish." Because of renewed problems with Crofton, petitioners of St. Botolph's, Bishopsgate, asked the Council on 16 March 1658 to permit Simpson to preach once each Sunday. On this occasion the Council referred the petition to a committee consisting of Richard Cromwell, Philip Skippon, Charles Fleetwood, Sir Charles Wolseley, Lord Walter Strickland, and Sir Gilbert Pickering, the Lord Chamberlain. The fate of the petition is unrecorded.[49]

Simpson's name also came before the Council in connection with an unsuccessful attempt to merge the small parishes of St. Bennet's, Paul's Wharf, and St. Peter's, Paul's Wharf. Because St. Bennet's was a poor parish and wanted to retain its minister, John Jackson, despite having only £50 p.a. to support him, its parishioners favored union. Two churchwardens and some of the parishioners at St. Peter's petitioned Cromwell on 11 May 1658 to oppose the merger, noting that this would not only inconvenience them but prejudice Cromwell's rights as patron. Because their minister, Edward Marbury, had died, they hoped to procure the services of Simpson, "a pious and painful preacher." Because each living was worth only £50 p.a., the Trustees for the Maintenance of Ministers approved the union. The Presbyterians, hoping to block the spread of Simpson's influence, favored the merger, with Jackson receiving testimonies of support from Calamy, Simeon Ashe, William Jenkins, and Bartholomew Beale. The Council

[48]Dodd, "Troubles in a City Parish," 46-49.

[49]CSPD, 1657-58, 109, 280-81, 330.

of State, however, referred the matter to the Commissioners for Ejecting Scandalous Ministers, and ultimately the union attempt failed.[50]
    During this period Simpson's congregation became one of the
gathered churches in London with links to the Bedford congregation
to which John Bunyan belonged and would subsequently become the
minister. In May 1658 the Bedford church provided a letter of recommendation to Simpson's congregation on behalf of a sister Fryer,
who had moved to London. Others followed. Later that year a Bedford
member who wished to transfer to another congregation for question-
able reasons was encouraged to seek the advice of Simpson, Jessey,
and Rogers. When the Bedford church searched for an assistant to its
minister, John Burton, in 1659, the elders and deacons sent letters to
Simpson, Jessey, and Cokayne "for their assistance and fartherance in
our inquiring out such an able godly man as may be suitable for our
help."[51]
    After Cromwell died on 3 September 1658, Simpson's troubles
with Crofton intensified again. In 1657 the latter had refused Simpson
the right to preach at a service of commemoration for the first battle
of Newbury (1643). The survivors who lived in the parish of St. Botolph's appealed to the Council of State. Every year on 20 September,
they claimed, they held a service to thank God for their deliverance,
but in the previous year Crofton's objections had forced them to use
a neighboring church. This year they hoped Richard Cromwell would
insist that Crofton allow Simpson to conduct the service. The Council's action is not recorded. The parishioners again went to the Council on 20 January 1659, successfully seeking permission for Simpson
to preach funeral sermons with the approval of a deputy Common
Councilman and the ward council. Although he had recently raised
nearly £20 for the poor, Crofton tried to stop him from preaching sermons for deceased benefactors. The parishioners complained: "the
perverse carriage of Zachary Crofton . . . will admit none of the ministers appointed to preach the funeral sermons of deceased benefac-

[50]*CSPD*, 1658-59, 13-14.

[51]*The Minutes of the First Independent Church (Now Bunyan Meeting) at Bedford 1656-1766*,
ed. H. G. Tibbutt (Bedfordshire Historical Record Society, 1976) 30, 31, 34
(quoted), 37.

tors, as at other churches, amongst whose poor the said charity has been distributed."[52]

The return of the Rump Parliament in the spring of 1659 boded well for Simpson. Parish wardens and "several well-affected Inhabitants" of St. Botolph's, Bishopsgate, petitioned Parliament for his return as rector, though Samuel Lee had been serving in that capacity since July 1655 at Cromwell's request.[53] When the committee that examined the matter reported to the House on 29 August, there was a debate, but Simpson's supporters won and the benefice was restored to him. The same year his final work, *The Herbal of Divinity*, was published.[54]

As the Restoration approached, Simpson faced perhaps the most difficult period in his career. After General Monck arrived in London, Simpson, Powell, Kiffin, and other radicals were denounced as fanatics. On Easter Sunday (22 April 1660) the royal arms were displayed in Simpson's church at Allhallows, "which being privately done was a great eye-sore to his people when they came to church and saw it." Simpson personally must have been upset by the Restoration, for as late as October of that year he defended the regicides in a sermon at Bishopsgate. "Though the unjust judges now condemned the saints to death, they were justified before God, and had acted conscientiously."[55]

On 31 March 1661, Simpson participated in a major ecumenical event in London. "Very great Congregations" of Presbyterians, Independents, Baptists, and Fifth Monarchists met, so much so that one observer thought "the major part of [the] Citty of London were there." At Allhallows the Great, Simpson followed Thomas Palmer into the pulpit, after the latter had warned his audience that they must prepare to suffer, knowing that their deaths were but a prelude to their resurrection. Reinforcing that theme, Simpson exhorted the people to

---

[52]*CSPD*, *1658-59*, 138, 258.

[53]According to *Ath. Oxon.*, 4:345, he was ejected by the Rump, but A. G. Matthews (*Calamy Revised*, 321) says he resigned.

[54]*CJ*, 7:770.

[55]*BQ* 6:216; *The Diary of Samuel Pepys*, ed. Henry B. Wheatley, 9 vols. (London, 1910-1918) 1:108; *CSPD* *1660-61*, 320 (quoted).

demonstrate their faith in the promises of God by suffering for his sake. That evening the saints moved to St. Antholin's, where the preacher called on them to perish rather than pollute their consciences "with the superstition & prophanenesse of these tymes." One informant noted that the meetings were especially frequented by former Cromwellian naval officers.[56]

In the summer and fall of 1661, Simpson preached on a regular basis at Allhallows[57] with such radicals as Jessey, Knollys, Kiffin, Anthony Palmer, and Laurence Wise. He had regular services on Mondays and Tuesdays, and preached on fast days as well. According to a government informant, "those that preach there are bred to it at a conventicle in Anchor Lane, where two pulpits are put up for prophesying. A brief was read last Sunday, where the King's name was muttered over, and those of archbishops and bishops omitted." The kernel of Simpson's message was the need to battle evil principalities and powers: The saints, he cried, must be ready to fight to the end against the forces of evil, knowing that the godly would ultimately triumph and rule as judges with Jesus Christ. For views such as this, he appeared on an August list of eighteen suspected plotters, among whom were the Particular Baptists Edward Harrison, William Kiffin, and Henry Jessey, as well as various ex-Cromwellian officers. The following month his name appeared at the top of a list of nineteen preachers—including Anthony Palmer, Laurence Wise, and Kiffin—who allegedly seduced the people. Preaching from the book of Revelation at Allhallows on 26 September, Simpson promised that the people of God would overcome their enemies, though they must not be afraid but must overturn those things that are contrary to the divine will.[58]

In October 1661 Sir Edward Nicholas, a secretary of state, received extracts of sermons preached at Allhallows by Simpson, Kiffin, Wise, (Stephen?) Ford, and others. The government kept closer watch on these proceedings, and on 2 November information on "seditious" sermons by Simpson, Palmer, and a Mr. Carter was reported

---

[56]PRO SP 29/34/2.

[57]Robert Bragge continued as rector at Allhallows until his ejection in 1662, following which his followers met with him at Pewterers' Hall. *Calamy Revised, s.v.*

[58]*CSPD, 1661-62,* 87 (quoted); PRO SP 29/40/101; 29/41/56; 29/42/36.

to Sir Edward Broughton, Keeper of the Gatehouse. In a sermon on Daniel 2:35, Simpson talked of a stone that would crush all earthly powers, so that the enemies of the saints "had Best have a care how they medell with any of his [God's] peopell" lest this stone "Crush them." Expounding on Revelation 3:20, he insisted that the godly must be willing to lose their property and go to prison for their faith, and in a sermon on the ensuing verse he called on the saints to "fight it out to the Last." Anglicans were castigated for their conformity, and the faithful were cautioned to have nothing to do with them. No wonder Simpson was condemned as one of the "Chief Ringleaders" in London who fomented dissatisfaction. In one of the last sermons before his arrest, Simpson preached at Allhallows on 31 October, warning that the end of the ungodly was nigh: "They shall be overtorne[d] not by might nor power but by the sperett of the saints mad[e] perfect. Babylon shall fall and Anti Christ shall be throne out[,] itt is your hour Christians[,] doe not feare. . . ."[59]

A warrant was issued on 29 November to Broughton to take Simpson into custody for seditious and dangerous speech. The government also seized notes from sermons by Simpson, (Stephen?) Ford, and (John?) James "chiefly bearing upon the protection shown by God towards his people, when persecuted by ungodly enemies." After Simpson took the oath of supremacy, the nonresistance oath, and the oath abjuring the Solemn League and Covenant, he was released the next year. To have refused the oaths, he wearily pleaded, would have been a sin against God, his congregation, his family, and himself.[60]

Although his submission disappointed his followers, Simpson might have recovered his nerve and resumed his fiery sermons as he had in the past. This time, however, death intervened in June 1662. At Simpson's funeral on the 26th, the unnamed preacher extolled Simpson as one who "loved no man upon the account of opinion, but upon the account of union with Christ. . . ." He endeavored to instruct every member of his congregation in this principle, according

[59]*CSPD*, *1661-62*, 97, 111; PRO SP 29/43/57; 29/43/107; 29/44/4; 29/44/137.

[60]*CSPD*, *1661-62*, 133, 162 (quoted); Capp, *FMM*, 182, 204; *Kingdomes Intelligencer*, 49 (25 Nov.-2 Dec. 1661) 744; *Mercurius Publicus*, 49 (28 Nov.-5 Dec. 1661) 752.

to the elegist. "To my best remembrance," the preacher wrote, "I never saw nor enjoyed more of the presence and glory of God in any Assembly (setting the Ministry of Mr. [William] Bridge of Yarmouth aside) than I have done in your Assemblies." Simpson was praised for having put behind him the vanities of his youth, replacing them with a devotion to the ministry as well as to his wife and children. As a pastor he was a strong proponent of "closet devotion," family worship, and public worship. Simpson's Antinomian tenets had offended many, the funeral orator acknowledged, but in reality he preached often on the apostolic cautions against sin. Free grace did not mean licentiousness. The zealousness with which Simpson approached his ministerial responsibility is reflected in his refusal of remuneration for his sermons, especially at funerals. When payment was forced upon him for preaching funeral sermons, he donated the money to the indigent. Yet Simpson had to be defended in his own funeral sermon from charges that his submission to the government was a denial of the principles for which he had stood. In death—as in life—Simpson was the center of controversy. He was buried the following day, 27 June 1662.[61]

In his masterful study of the Fifth Monarchy Movement, B. S. Capp succinctly characterizes Simpson as "a major figure, but unstable and [he] lost the confidence of many saints."[62] Those godly who were disappointed in him could not object to the constancy of his belief in the gathered church or in his willingness to embrace the elitist notion that the godly must rule the world. Moreover the egalitarianism that was part of the Fifth Monarchists' view of themselves was if anything enhanced by Simpson's steadfast adherence to the extension of the hand of fellowship to all the godly. He wavered, however, in one critical area—his view of the political establishment. Although his incarceration in Windsor Castle apparently did not tame him for long, it may have left him with permanent emotional scars. That experience, coupled with some words of counsel from Henry Jessey, seems to have been the reason for Simpson's repudiation of militant

---

[61]Mather Papers, CMHS, 4th ser., 8 (1868): 197; Capp. FMM, 204; anon., The Failing & Perishing of Good Men a Matter of Great & Sore Lamentation ([London], 1663), epistle and 1 passim, especially 18-20, 27. The funeral sermon may have been given by Simpson's friend, George Cokayne. For Cokayne see BDBR, s.v.

[62]Capp, FMM, 262.

millenarianism following a brief return to prison early in 1656. Yet at the Restoration he was still sufficiently radical to preach in justification of the regicides as God's servants. Faced once again with the rigors of prison, however, his spirit of defiance—once so strong—left him and he took the obligatory oaths mandated by the Restoration state. Undoubtedly weary from nearly two decades of struggle, Simpson lacked the strength—or perhaps the conviction—to continue his opposition underground. Had he not died in the early summer of 1662, he might have been forced into the underground after St. Bartholomew's Day.

chapter 5

One "of the Most Dangerous Fellows in the North": Paul Hobson and the Quest for Godly Government

Particular Baptists figured prominently in the militant and millenarian activities of the 1640s and 1650s: serving in the New Model Army, enthusing about the prospects of the Barebones Parliament, and struggling to achieve godly rule in England. At the Restoration many forsook their militant activism and suffered passively under the repression of the Clarendon Code, but others became involved in the radical underground, which repeatedly hatched plots to undermine the restored monarchy and the ecclesiastical establishment.

Paul Hobson, a Particular Baptist who served in the parliamentary forces and then in a variety of positions during the Commonwealth and Protectorate, was accused by Charles II's government of being a leader in the underground. For this he spent years in the Tower of London and Chepstow Castle until his health was impaired, finally winning release only on the condition that he go into exile. He did not, however, die as a Baptist martyr, but rather as a person suspected—perhaps unfairly—of turning king's evidence to save his life. Moreover, this man of forthright conviction was allegedly involved at the

end of his life in a sex scandal with other Baptists the very year he was
released from prison.

Hobson's origins are apparently lost in obscurity, though Thomas
Edwards says that he was a tailor from Buckinghamshire. Hobson first
appears in London in the late 1630s, when he was a barber surgeon.
He joined the Separatist church founded in 1639 by the feltmaker John
Green and the coachman John Spencer at Crutched Friars in London.
Because of his Separatist convictions, Hobson refused to subscribe to
the Solemn League and Covenant in 1643. By that time he had joined
the parliamentary army, where he served in Thomas Fairfax's regiment
of foot. On 13 May 1644 he participated in a court-martial at Farn-
ham, Surrey. His own career was further advanced due to Cromwell's
decision, made after the fall of York, to appoint sectarian officers in
the army of the Eastern Association. As part of this program, Hobson
was placed in command of the troop of Captain Clement Armiger,
who had been discharged for refusing to support religious toleration.[1]

Sometime in the early 1640s, Hobson adopted the tenets of the
Particular (Calvinistic) Baptists, and by 1644 he had become, with
Thomas Gower, a leader of one of the seven Particular Baptist
churches in London. Its members apparently had seceded from the
Separatist congregation of Green and Spencer. Hobson, as a leader of
his church, was one of fifteen signatories of *The Confession of Faith* published by those churches in 1644. Accused as heretics by their critics,
who erroneously charged them "with holding Free-will, Falling away
from grace, denying Originall sinne, disclaiming of Magistracy, . . .
[and] doing acts unseemly in the dispensing the Ordinance of Baptism," Hobson and his colleagues intended the confession as a public
apologia. In light of Hobson's active role in the parliamentary forces,
it is fitting that the confession not only deplored "Prelaticall Hier-
archy" but praised the Long Parliament for its role in overthrowing *jure
divino* episcopacy. The confession also carried the warning that if the
Long Parliament refused toleration to the Baptists, the latter would
continue to worship as they deemed appropriate, "not daring to give

---

[1] *Gangraena*, 121-22; Crosby, 3:26; ; W. T. Whitley, "The Rev. Colonel Paul
Hobson," BQ 9:307; Champlin Burrage, *The Early English Dissenters in the Light of Recent
Research (1550-1641)*, 2 vols. (Cambridge, 1912) 2:304-305; TBHS 1:235; Clive
Holmes, *The Eastern Association in the English Civil War* (Cambridge, 1974) 199.

place to suspend our practice. . . ."[2] Among the other signatories of the confession were such prominent Baptist leaders as William Kiffin, Thomas Patient, John Spilsbury, and Samuel Richardson. A second edition of the confession, published in January 1646, was signed by representatives of eight churches, including that of Hobson and Gower.[3]

Already Hobson was becoming notorious in conservative and moderate circles. In December 1644 the divines of Sion College, London, issued a sweeping denunciation of Hobson and such assorted radicals as John Milton, Roger Williams, the Arminian Independent John Goodwin, the Socinian John Biddle, and the Antinomian John Saltmarsh. Although the Presbyterian chronicler of the sectaries, Thomas Edwards, had never met Hobson, he regarded the conventicles of Hobson, William Erbery, Henry Denne, Thomas Lamb, and Clement Writer as "the nurseries of all Errours and Heresies, very Pesthouses," and warned people not to attend their meetings.[4]

Hobson now engaged in a flurry of literary activity, publishing three religious tracts in 1645, including *A Discoverie of Truth*. *The Fallacy of Infants Baptisme Discovered* (1645), in which he refuted the views of the paedobaptists, was timed to coincide with a debate scheduled to take place in London between Edmund Calamy on one side and various Baptists on the other. Hobson and an unnamed colleague were arranging for Baptists from the surrounding counties as well as the City to be present for the disputation. The Lord Mayor, apparently fearing the debate would lead to riotous behavior, banned it. An indication of Hobson's views on this subject is found in *The Fallacy*, in which a principal theme is that in paedobaptism people "make the old Testament expound the new, whereas the new should expound the old; Christ should, and doth expound Moses." Moreover, just as believers only are admitted to the Lord's supper, so none but believers should be baptized. There is, he averred, a "oneness that is between the ground that

---

[2]*Baptist Confessions of Faith*, ed. William L. Lumpkin (Philadelphia, 1959) 153-56, 170.

[3]Tolmie, 58.

[4]Christopher Hill, *Milton and the English Revolution* (Harmondsworth, 1979) 225-26; *Gangraena*, 205, 210.

. . . [Christ] layes down for men to be baptized, & the ground he layes down for men to break Bread." In *Christ the Effect Not the Cause of the Love of God* (1645), a collection of sermons, Hobson called for the gospel to be preached to all persons, notwithstanding the validity of the external decrees of predestination. In these sermons he also attacked the Anselmic theory of the atonement based on the concept that God required Christ to provide him with sufficient "satisfaction" to atone for the sins of the elect. Edwards was outraged by Hobson's argument that Christ did not purchase salvation for the elect, but was himself purchased by divine love in order to reconcile the elect to God.[5]

Although Hobson continued to associate with his London congregation until at least 1646, he took advantage of his military travels to spread the Baptist message as far afield as Yarmouth, Bristol, Exeter, Kingsbridge in Devon, and Newport Pagnell in Buckinghamshire. According to Edwards, by 1646 Hobson had been a preacher "a great while." His books, along with those of Tobias Crisp, John Saltmarsh, and Walter Cradock, were responsible according to Richard Baxter for the spread of Antinomian tenets in the army. When in London Hobson preached on Wednesday afternoons at Chequer Alley, Finsbury Fields, probably in the church of the Particular Baptist Hanserd Knollys. Such afternoon sermons reflect the continuation of the Puritan tradition of weekday lectures to bolster the faith of the godly and increase their understanding of the Christian faith. Preaching to Separatist congregations as well as to military units wherever he went, Hobson allegedly spoke "much against Duties and of Revelations, what God had revealed to him. . . ." He also denounced, says Baptist historian Thomas Crosby, "the *presbyterian establishment*, their ministry, and *childrens baptism*. . . ." Hobson's spiritual experience, according to Edwards, reflected a pronounced revulsion against formal religious

---

[5]Paul Hobson, *The Fallacy of Infants Baptisme Discovered* (London, 1645), passim (13 quoted); *Gangraena*, 88, 123. Theodore Sippell is probably correct in attributing to Hobson an anonymous letter published by Thomas Edwards (*Gangraena*, 89-91). According to the unnamed London minister who gave it to Edwards, the letter came from "a great Sectary" in the Bath area. Hobson, in fact, was traveling in the west in this period. The letter reflects Hobson's known Antinomian views and his rejection of the Anselmic doctrine of the atonement. The letter is reprinted at the conclusion to this chapter. Sippell, *William Dell's Programm einer "lutherischen" Gemeinschaftsbewegung* (Tübingen, 1911) 82, n. 1.

observances: "I was once," said Hobson, "as legal as any of you can be, I durst never a morning but pray, nor never a night before I went to Bed but pray; I durst not eat a bit of Bread but I gave thankes; I daily prayed and wept for my sinnes, so that I had almost wept out my Eyes with sorrow for sin: But I am perswaded when I used all these duties, I had not one jot of God in me." Instead Hobson's formula for spiritual peace was an almost mystical experience of Christ and the belief that Christians were indeed freed from the Mosaic law. [6]

For establishing conventicles and preaching in contravention of a parliamentary ordinance, Hobson and Captain Richard Beaumont were arrested at Newport Pagnell in June 1645 by Sir Samuel Luke, the governor of the parliamentary garrison. They were also accused of being absent from a public thanksgiving service for the victory at Naseby. Although "this day was ordered for a Thanksgiving . . . these men whose spiritts it seemes were in a higher spheare then ordinary, withdrew themselves with a company of ignorant women, and a yong boy . . . and seven men more to Lathbury, where . . . they exercizd their guifts." Luke had permitted them to preach in the week preceding the day of thanksgiving, but their offense on this occasion was too much for him to ignore, especially since Captain Beaumont had reportedly said that he now thought it inappropriate to continue fighting in the parliamentary cause. When Hobson and Beaumont retaliated with charges of physical abuse at the hands of Luke's officers, Luke sent them and his officers to Sir Thomas Fairfax. Rather than disciplining Hobson and Beaumont, Fairfax was instead sympathetic, pointing out to Luke that they had been discharged from their commands at their own request. Fairfax, moreover, was incensed by the harsh treatment allegedly accorded the two men by Luke's ensign and marshal. Insisting that Hobson and Beaumont were gentlemen who had carried themselves with courage and fidelity in the parliamentary cause, Fairfax demanded reparations for them. Luke, angered by the tolerant attitude at headquarters, complained to Colonel Charles Fleetwood: "Now that these two men Hobson and Beaumont . . . should come countenanced with your authority to preach the working of miracles, and declare the unlawfulness of fighting in this cause is

---

[6]*Gangraena*, 121-23; *TBHS* 4: 130; *Rel. Bax.*, pt. 1: 111; Tolmie, 60; Crosby, 3: 27.

no less strange to me, than their [harsh] usage here seems strange to you."[7]

Although Luke's officers were cashiered for their conduct, he rearrested Hobson and Beaumont and sent them to a parliamentary committee for investigation. His letter to the Independent Richard Knightley, M.P. for Northampton, explained: "This day [24 June] they came again to this towne with this Passe from Col. Fleetewood, and sending for them to know the occasion of their comeing, they questioned mee to my face whether my committment of them was legall or illegall. . . ." Considering them to be Anabaptists, Luke wanted Parliament to punish them inasmuch as their beliefs "cannot consist with Magistracy or Government. . . ." Hobson himself threatened to appeal to his friends in the House of Commons, asserting that they would "make this businesse *the leading case of the Kingdome for all the godly party*; adding, that if *the godly and well affected party were thus persecuted, they should be forced to make a worse breach then that was yet, when they had done with the Kings party*; and saying, *when they had made an end of the war with the Cavaliers, they should be forced to raise a new Army to fight with them.*" Hobson's friends did in fact see to it that the parliamentary committee responsible for examining his case discharged him. Released again, the undaunted Hobson preached the following Sunday at Moorfields in London. He warned that if the godly could not preach, they would cause a bigger breach within the parliamentary camp than that previously made between the royalists and their parliamentary foes. Thereafter he preached regularly at Moorfields on Sundays and weekdays, as well as continuing his Wednesday afternoon lectures at Chequer Alley, Finsbury Fields.[8]

Shortly after his discharge by the parliamentary committee, Hobson was summoned to Bristol by an unnamed colonel. According to the hostile account of Edwards, the purpose was "to doe some service there, (as if he had not done mischeif enough in *London*). . . ." Bristol, which had fallen to Prince Rupert in July 1643, was retaken by Crom-

---

[7]British Library, Egerton MS 786, fols. 25, 45, 47; *The Letter Books 1644-45 of Sir Samuel Luke: Parliamentary Governor of Newport Pagnell*, ed. H. G. Tibbutt (London, 1963) 322-23, 328-29, 582-83; *Original Letters, Illustrative of English History*, ed. Sir Henry Ellis, 3rd ser. (London, 1846) 4:254-55, 262-66.

[8]*Letter Books of Luke*, 586, 622; *Gangraena*, 122-23 (quoted); Crosby, 1:226.

well and Fairfax in September 1645. In the aftermath of the recon-
quest, according to one of Edwards's correspondents, the only
persons "imployed in any service, or put into any place, or lookt upon
with any respect," were those who were adherents of "the New Light
and New way. . . ." The records of the open communion church in
Bristol indicate that this was a time of considerable confusion and "little Order," in which "every meeting almost was filled with Disputes
and debates, . . ." many of them occasioned by the behavior of members during the period of royalist occupation. Hobson's presence was
probably needed to help stabilize the situation in the town, though
there is nothing to link him to the turmoil in Bristol's open communion congregation. Nor is there any evidence to indicate how long
Hobson remained in Bristol, but in June 1646 he was in Exeter and was
working in general throughout Devon. He apparently had ties to the
Particular Baptist church at Dartmouth. [9]

   In addition to his preaching, Hobson continued to write. His *Prac-
ticall Divinity: Or a Helpe Through the Blessing of God to Lead Men More to Look
Within Themselves*, published in 1646, was an exposition on the life of
saints and their rapture in the love of Christ. The strong emphasis on
the nearly mystical sense of union with Christ, which Hobson shared
with William Erbery, was reflected again the following year in *A Gar-
den Inclosed, and Wisdom Justified Only of Her Children*.

   In June 1646 it was reported that Hobson had "saluted the Army
with a farewell Sermon, and is sent as an Emissary to Exeter, to raise
a party there." He returned to military duty the following year, suc-
ceeding William Master as major in the regiment of Colonel Robert
Lilburne. He served under Lieutenant-Colonel Henry Lilburne and
was assisted by Captains Abraham Holmes and Richard Deane and
Lieutenants Nathaniel Strange, John Mason, and John Turner. Of
these officers, at least Robert Lilburne, Holmes, Deane, Strange, and
Mason were Baptists. Hobson's most important assignment was to approach the king that June with respect to a negotiated settlement. In
the course of this task he contacted the royalist Sir Lewis Dyve, who

---

   [9]*Gangraena*, 123-24; *The Records of a Church of Christ in Bristol, 1640-1687*, ed. Roger
Hayden (Bristol Record Society, 1974) 98-99; Allan Brockett, *Nonconformity in Exeter
1650-1875* (Manchester, 1962) 14; Joseph Ivimey, *A History of the English Baptists* (London, 1811) 2: 133-34.

was then in the Tower with Hobson's friend, the Leveller John Lilburne. Hobson, however, did not support the Levellers later that year when they attempted to win the backing of the New Model Army. When troops in Colonel Robert Lilburne's regiment defied their officers—including Hobson—by proclaiming support for the Levellers in November at Ware, Hertfordshire, Hobson and his fellow officers issued a *Remonstrance Sent from Colonell Lilburnes Regiment*, asserting their loyalty to Fairfax and warning of the threat of such divisive acts to the country. Among the officers who signed with Hobson were Captains Deane and Holmes and Lieutenants Strange, Turner, and Mason.[10] Hobson's action was instrumental in helping to undermine the vitality of the Leveller movement. The cause of religious reform, in his judgment, could not be jeopardized by the sweeping Leveller demands for a broader franchise and social and legal reforms.

At the outbreak of the second Civil War, Hobson was dispatched to Exeter. Subsequently he was with Lilburne's regiment at Newcastle in August 1648, where he was appointed deputy governor. Following the defection of Henry Lilburne to Charles I, Hobson became lieutenant-colonel of the regiment. He and Major John Cobbett, Captain Samuel Clark, and Captain Robert Hutton signed a letter accompanying an address to General Fairfax in October 1648 that protested the attempt to reach an accommodation with Charles I at Newport. In December 1649 Hobson was appointed a commissioner in both county Durham and the city of Newcastle for the assessment of funds to support the military. He performed the same service again in November 1650 and (for Durham alone) in December 1652.[11]

The attempt of conservatives and moderates to discredit the radical revolution of 1648-1649 included the publication of a pamphlet intended to blacken the reputation of Hobson and his men. The colorful title is self-explanatory: *Newes from Powles, or the New Reformation of the Army: With a True Relation of a Cowlt That Was Foaled in the Cathedrall*

[10]*Calamy Revised*, 269; Firth & Davies, 2:456; BQ, 1:236, 288; *The Tower of London Letter-Book of Sir Lewis Dyve, 1646-47*, ed. H. G. Tibbutt, *Publications of the Bedfordshire Historical Record Society* 38 (1958): 58-59; Tolmie, 167-68.

[11]BQ, 1:288; 9:307; Firth & Davies, 2:459; Firth & Rait, 2:297, 305, 465, 474, 661.

Church of St. Paul in London, and How It Was Publiquely Baptized by Paul Hobsons Souldiers (1649).

At Newcastle Hobson became embroiled in the witchcraft controversy that erupted in 1649. When the Common Council determined to squelch witchcraft in March, a witchpricker from Scotland was hired to test accused witches. Most of the thirty women examined by the witchpricker were found guilty. Although Hobson exposed the witchpricker as a fraud, at least fifteen women were executed.[12]

Hobson was probably involved in founding a Particular Baptist church at Newcastle between 1649 and 1651, making it one of the oldest Baptist churches in northern England. According to the records of the Baptist church at Hexham, the Newcastle congregation was the "only church in this county which was in the profession of the faith before us." Gower became the church's pastor and Hobson an elder.[13]

In the meantime Hobson remained on active military duty. In January 1650 he had difficulty trying to apprehend a group of Cavaliers, who joined forces with some moss-troopers, disarmed the men sent to arrest them, and seized the arrest warrants, forcing Hobson to dispatch a larger contingent before he could restore order. From Newcastle he reported on 16 May 1650 to William Clarke, recently the secretary to the Council of the Army, concerning events in Scotland. Charles II reached an accommodation with the Covenanters that spring at Breda and the situation in the north looked grim. "We are well and very safe," Hobson assured Clarke, "but much admire at the army's not marching," especially since the king and the Scots have become allies. He was pleased, however, that "the old malignants" were offended by Charles's concessions to the Scots, "there being two or three come from hence who was in the last party that was routed with Montrose [at Carbisdale on 27 April] and declare to the malignants their sad usage by the Scotch presbyterians. . . ." In the judgment of the Royalists, Charles had betrayed the monarchy as much as any En-

---

[12]Roger Howell, Jr., *Newcastle upon Tyne and the Puritan Revolution: A Study of the Civil War in North England* (Oxford, 1967) 232-33; Samuel Parker, *History of His Own Time* (London, 1727) 10-11, 55-60.

[13]*RCC*, 352; Howell, *Newcastle upon Tyne*, 248-49.

glish sectary. Nevertheless Hobson found it difficult to trust the embittered Cavaliers any more than the Scots, "they both thirsting for the blood of the honest party in England." In a postscript he expressed a longing to Clarke that the godly in both countries would better understand each other, and that the Scottish Presbyterians would recognize the danger of fighting for a man whose triumph would lead to their destruction. The Scottish clergy, he complained, "pray exceedingly for the King's safe arrival in Scotland and stir up the people in all places to affect his Majesty as a man brought in to the Kirk and therefore of necessity to God."[14]

Hobson's regiment was divided in August 1650. He remained in Newcastle, however, where he was responsible to Sir Arthur Haselrig, Lilburne's replacement as regimental commander. After Cromwell routed the Scots at Dunbar in September, Hobson was assigned the responsibility of conveying prisoners to Durham. Perhaps as many as 1,600 died *en route*, and of the 3,000 who reached Durham, another 1,600 perished, mostly due to insufficient food. Possibly in revulsion against such massive human suffering, Hobson resigned from the army later that year and settled at Sacriston, near Chester-le-Street, Durham, where he lived as a gentleman. Two years later, in February 1653, the government appointed him to the Commission for Propagating the Gospel in the Northern Counties, the latter being a direct manifestation of the Puritan and sectarian concern to spread the gospel to "the dark corners of the land."[15]

The years that followed were filled with religious controversy, much of it revolving around Hobson and the Baptist evangelist Thomas Tillam, who came in 1651 to Hexham, Northumberland, twelve miles from Newcastle. He had been sent with the blessing of the Commission for Propagating the Gospel in the Northern Counties by the Baptist church of Hanserd Knollys in London. As this congregation later explained, "when our brother went out from us, we judged, from that little knowledge we had of him whilst he was with us, that the Lord had enriched him with some spiritual gifts, the

---

[14]Whitelocke, 3: 137; HMC 51, *Leyborne-Popham*, 73-74.

[15]Firth & Davies, 2: 460; H. J. McLachlan, *Socinianism in Seventeenth Century England* (Oxford, 1951) 220.

which might be useful and successful through the blessing of God in other places abroad." In Hexham Tillam fulfilled the duties of a lectureship founded by the London Mercers' Company some twenty years earlier. Within seven months he had established a Baptist church at Hexham, and in March 1653 that congregation asked Knollys's Coleman Street church for permission to make Tillam its regular minister: "Our hearts' desires after him are, for a nearer and closer interest in him, if, by the will of God, this grace may be ministered unto us by you."[16]

By 1653, however, relations between the Hexham Baptists and the church of Hobson and Gower in Newcastle had already begun to sour. This was due in part to Gower's belief—apparently shared by Hobson—that ministers must not be fully dependent on their congregations for financial support, whereas Tillam insisted that the ministry was a full-time task. A letter of 15 March 1653 from Edmund Hickeringill, a member of the Hexham church and that congregation's messenger to Scotland, expressed hope to the church that there would shortly be "a good correspondence and union twixt the saints at Newcastle and yourselves, that fellow members of the same body might not disown each other, having one Lord, one faith, one baptism." Hickeringill went on to observe that Captain James Turner, a member and later the pastor of the Baptist church at Newcastle, had already accepted the principle of "living upon the gospel when maintenance is freely given," and Hickeringill hoped that Gower would soon do likewise. Hobson and Gower also opposed Tillam's practice of the laying on of hands and the blessing of infants. The differences between the two churches were serious enough to prompt the Newcastle Baptists to complain about Tillam to the Coleman Street congregation. The latter responded to the Hexham church on 24 March, leaving the decision to make Tillam their minister in Hexham's hands. They also noted that they had written to Tillam about the charges made against him by the Newcastle Baptists, asking for his response. "Till then," they urged, "let brotherly love continue."[17]

---

[16]*RCC*, 304, 313-17 (314 quoted), 320 (quoted).

[17]Ibid., 295, 318 (quoted), 319-21 (321 quoted); Fergus G. Little and Edmund F. Walker, *The Story of the Northern Baptists* (Newcastle upon Tyne, 1945) 8. Hicker-

While this dispute was festering, another controversy erupted. In June 1653 Hobson introduced Tillam to a man pretending to be the Jew Joseph ben Israel of Mantua. He had learned of Hobson, with whom he stayed a month in Newcastle, while still abroad. The impostor was in reality a Scottish Catholic named Thomas Ramsay who was determined to discredit the Protestants. After persuading Tillam that he had been convinced of the doctrine of the Trinity by studying Plato, he was baptized by Tillam. A suspicious group of Newcastle ministers, sensing an opportunity to discredit the Baptists, unmasked Ramsay by confronting him with the master of the ship that had conveyed him under the alias Thomas Horsley from Hamburg to England. While seasick, Ramsay had made some admissions to the ship's captain, and his real identity was confirmed when a letter to his father was intercepted. The Independent Samuel Hammond, Vicar of Newcastle, Thomas Weld, a Puritan minister from Gateshead, and Cuthbert Sydenham and William Durant, both lecturers in Newcastle, exposed the affair to the public in *A False Jew* (London, 1653). Two other accounts were published anonymously: *The Converted Jew or the Substance of the Declaration and Confession by Joseph ben Israel* (Gateshead, 1653) and *The Counterfeit Jew* (Newcastle, 1653). Tillam defended himself in *Banners of Love Displaied over the Church of Christ* (London, 1654).[18]

The fiasco over the false Jew may have temporarily brought the feuding Baptists of Newcastle and Hexham closer together, for in November Hobson witnessed a marriage in Tillam's house. The following month, however, the dispute flared again. The Newcastle church formulated twelve articles against Tillam, "wherein," the Hexham Baptists asserted, "manifestly appeared a subtle design to break or divide the church of Hexham." Although Tillam responded promptly with the full support of his congregation, Gower complained without success to the Coleman Street church in London. According to the

---

ingill became a member of the Baptist church at Leith, from which he was excommunicated in May 1653. After a brief period as a Quaker, he became a Deist in July 1653, and finally an Anglican in 1660. See *BDBR, s.v.* Can the Captain *James* Turner associated with the Newcastle Baptist church be the same man as the Lieutenant *John* Turner who served with Hobson in Lilburne's regiment?

[18]*RCC*, 292; *DNB, s.v.* Thomas Ramsay; Howell, *Newcastle upon Tyne*, 250-51.

Hexham records, "God blasted all his endeavours, and wonderfully preserved the integrity of his despised servant [Tillam], giving him still a large room in the hearts of his people of that society." The bitterness spread further afield when Henry Haggar, a General Baptist leader in the Stafford area, accused Hobson that year of being out of fellowship with other Baptists. Hobson was also challenged by the Quakers in this period; about 1654 they converted six members of the Newcastle Baptist church.[19]

In 1654 Tillam and his followers retaliated against Hobson by giving credence to hearsay charges about him peddled by Samuel Hammond. Tillam then wrote to the Newcastle church repeating the accusations. On 28 May Gower and other Newcastle Baptists responded, pointing out that Hammond had "prejudicial thoughts" against Tillam as well as Hobson, and that his accusations had been secondhand and related to the period in Hobson's life before his conversion. "Therefore," the Baptists said, "we judge it no sufficient ground to hinder his [Hobson's] joining with us, knowing that God hath been pleased . . . to make him with shame to be more ready to accuse himself, and acknowledge his own evil committed in those days of wantonness, than any can be to accuse him." The Hexham church replied rather feebly on 3 August that Tillam had only conveyed the charges against Hobson "to be a monitor to you" and to enable the Newcastle congregation to ascertain the veracity of the charges. To this Gower and his flock responded on the 27th that the Hexham answer was insufficient and evasive. The Newcastle church, they reported, had sent Tillam's accusations and their response to the Coleman Street church in London in order to resolve the dispute "and also deal with your brother Tillam for his several evils there charged against him." In an undated reply, the Hexham church indicated displeasure at the appeal to London, insisted that all charges against Tillam were unfounded, and bemoaned the differences between the two churches. The final recorded letter in the dispute came from Newcastle. In it Gower and his friends objected that Tillam had made Hammond's charges against Hobson public. Moreover, whereas Tillam "did demand of us a rule for admonishing our brother Hobson be-

[19]*RCC*, 294 (quoted), 300, 353; Henry Haggar, *The Foundation of the Font Discovered* (London, 1653) 111.

fore he informed us [of the accusations], we think he had the same rule, and it was as orderly for him so far to own him [Hobson], as to desire him to preach to the church at Hexham." Gower also took this occasion to insist that the main barrier to union between the churches was the determination of the Hexham congregation to cling to the worldly principle of full-time support for its minister ("the unrighteous wages of Balaam").[20]

The feud continued in 1655 as a consequence of the publication of Hobson's *Fourteen Queries and Ten Absurdities About the Extent of Christ's Death*, which attacked the Arminian doctrine of unlimited atonement and the General Baptist practice of the laying on of hands. "This opinion of freewill, with the rest therein exprest, doth increase so much in these northern parts, and it comes with such a face of rationality, that many poor precious hearts who are weak in the faith are apt to stumble, and in an especial manner some about Hull, where I was an eye and ear witness not long since of the sad disaster that is befallen the church of Christ there upon that account." Although he was not a General Baptist, Tillam favored the laying on of hands and consequently criticized Hobson in *The Fourth Principle of Christian Religion* (1655). This, however, was too much for the Coleman Street church to accept, and it disowned Tillam for advocating this practice. The pressures on the Hexham church were now so intense that the congregation split into pro- and anti-Tillam factions. Probably because of the schism, Tillam left Hexham about 1656. Throughout the entire controversy the real victors were Hammond and his associates, who resented Tillam's success in spreading Baptist tenets in the north. Hobson, Gower, and their supporters in Newcastle had unwittingly been used to drive Tillam from the region. This perhaps was a major factor in the subsequent decline of the Hexham church after the Restoration. According to the church records, "after this, the church here began sadly to decline their duties, break off their meetings, and forget their Rock. Whereupon miserable effects ensued to be their portion, so that most of them returned to folly."[21]

---

[20]*RCC*, 355-57 (356 quoted), 359-61 (360 quoted), 362-65 (362 quoted), 367-72 (371, 372 quoted).

[21]Hobson, *Fourteen Queries and Ten Absurdities* (London, 1655), epistle; *RCC*, 295-97 (297 quoted); Howell, *Newcastle upon Tyne*, 253.

In the meantime Hobson had once again assumed an active role in national affairs. Interpreting Cromwell's summoning of the Barebones Parliament as a sign of the imminent second coming of Christ, Hobson, with John Joplin (or Jopling) and others, signed a congratulatory address to Cromwell from the people of county Durham on 28 April 1653. Cromwell was also hoping to receive similar pledges of support from Baptist congregations at Hexham, Derby, Burton, Dublin, and Horton (near Bradford). The dissolution of the Barebones in December made Hobson so irate that he demanded the excommunication of church members who signed addresses of loyalty to the Lord Protector. His case against the Protectorate was presented to the army in eight arguments, which he subsequently expanded to eighteen for general publication. The heart of his case claimed that God's people had broken the covenant by accepting the Protectorate. His arguments received a stormy reception, for a correspondent of Cromwell's secretary, John Thurloe, informed the government in February 1654 that "manie of the rebaptized judgment meet at Newcastle about Paule Hobson's 8 diabolical reasons, sensureing all that signed the adresses to his highness to be incomunicable in the ordinances of God, hatch'd in his fraudulent head. . . . It is thought all the dissenting brothers will agree this day to publish something to the world, about cleareing themselves from suspicion."[22]

Despite his hostility to the Protectorate, Hobson was appointed a Fellow of Eton College in 1654. Apparently because of an interest in education, he was named by Cromwell to be a visitor of the new college at Durham in 1657. At this time he was described as a gentleman of Seggerston-Hugh, though he continued to preach. In 1655 the Quakers John Wilkinson and John Story informed Margaret Fell that Hobson was "declaring many filthy things to render the Truth odious" in Wiltshire. According to Laurence Clarkson, who was influenced by Hobson to become a Baptist but subsequently became a Seeker and then a Ranter, Hobson "brake forth [in his sermons] with such expressions of the in-comes and out-goes of God, that my soul much desired such a gift of preaching. . . ." Hobson 's emphasis on grace was sufficiently pronounced to prompt Richard Baxter to label him an An-

---

[22]Nickolls, *OLPS*, 91, 134; *BQ* 9: 307-308; Brown, 73, 77; Thurloe, *SP*, 3: 138. Cf. British Library, Additional MS 4159, fols. 195 ff.

tinomian, an appellation he also used for John Bunyan. In 1658 William Grigge, in *The Quakers Jesus*, associated Hobson with the Socinians John Biddle and Paul Best, though a modern Unitarian specialist has concluded that Hobson himself was no Socinian. Hobson did, however, tend to view Christ as a natural son of God, and the Holy Spirit as divine activity in the world rather than the third person of the Trinity.[23]

By the summer of 1657 Hobson was once again actively involved with the army as a lieutenant-colonel. Soldiers on Holy Island, Northumberland, formally asked the government to have Hobson pay them. The same year an incident occurred involving his wife, which reflected his status at Whitehall. On Sunday, 25 August, his wife Hester was riding with a Mr. Collier to attend church services at Sunderland when she was stopped by George Lilburne, J. P., who seized her horse and fined her 20s. for violating the sabbath. When she complained to the Council of State, its members recommended that Cromwell remove Lilburne from his post.[24]

In the turmoil that followed Cromwell's death and the inability of his son Richard to govern effectively, Hobson was appointed a militia commissioner for county Durham by Parliament in July 1659. Subsequently he worked closely with Gower, Colonel Robert Lilburne, and John Joplin in supporting Lambert's futile attempt to block General Monck's efforts to restore the monarchy. At the Restoration Hobson, who lost his fellowship at Eton, settled in London where he joined the Particular Baptist church of William Kiffin. Disillusioned by the Restoration, Hobson left the same year for the Netherlands. There he served as an agent for Tillam in a utopian scheme to establish a godly society on old monastic lands in the Palatinate procured from the Margrave of Brandenburg. Eventually several hundred families from the Durham area migrated to this community. Hobson was in London again the following year, where he associated with "N. S.", presumably

[23]*Calamy Revised*, 269; Burton, 2:536; Story and Wilkinson to Fell, Friends House (London), Swarthmore MSS, I, fol. 35, cited in BQ, 26:349; B. R. White, *Hanserd Knollys and Radical Dissent in the 17th Century* (London, 1977) 13, 26; Clarkson, cited in A. L. Morton, *The World of the Ranters: Religious Radicalism in the English Revolution* (London, 1970) 116; McLachlan, *Socinianism*, 222-24.

[24]*CSPD*, 1657-58, 72, 78-80, 101.

Nathaniel Strange, a Particular Baptist and a Fifth Monarchist who had once served in Robert Lilburne's regiment with Hobson. Now estranged from the Baptists in London, Hobson soon questioned the validity of Strange's church, including its "gospel ordinances."[25]

Returning to Durham, Hobson was arrested by the Bishop of Durham in August 1661, following the unsuccessful insurrection of the more radical Fifth Monarchists under Thomas Venner. On that occasion Hobson was described as "an Agent for a German Prince to carry away Manufactur[e]s," an illusion to his involvement in Tillam's Palatinate scheme. He remained in prison only briefly, and when the deputy lieutenants wanted to interrogate him in November, he fled with Joplin back to London. There he continued to correspond with the Baptists in Durham. He was briefly imprisoned again in the spring of 1662. On 7 November 1662, the Bishop of Durham, Hobson's implacable enemy, formally asked Sir Gilbert Gerard to apprehend Hobson and Gower, who were staying at Thomas Lomes's house in Lothbury, London, because they were "two of the most dangerous fellowes in all the North, who at this day holds intelligence with most of the disaffected persons in the [suspected] designe . . ." (i.e., the Tong Plot to assassinate the king and establish a godly republic). To prevent them from learning that their lodgings had been discovered, and that their secret messages to the north had been intercepted, they were to be seized speedily and secretly. A warrant for their arrest was issued the same day. Ten days later Hobson was released on a bond of £1000, pledging his good behavior and his appearance before a secretary of state when summoned. He identified himself at this point as an M.D. of Bishopsgate, London. On the 20th, the Bishop of Durham sent extracts from Hobson's correspondence to Whitehall, hoping in vain that he would not be released.[26]

Those letters, however, fail to demonstrate that Hobson was, as the deputy lieutenants thought, "a very dangerous & disaffected person. . . ." To Joplin, who believed that "now the beast doth not only roar but rage," Hobson wrote on 30 October:

---

[25]Firth & Rait, 2: 1323; *CSPD*, 1659-60, 294-95; BQ, 9: 308.

[26]PRO SP 29/40/42; 29/62/71; 29/63/2; 29/63/34.1; *CSPD*, 1661-62, 62, 549, 559, 564; James Walker, "The Yorkshire Plot, 1663," *Yorkshire Archaeological Journal* 31 (1934): 351.

Tis not for me to write any thing to move thy mind after any deliverance, but what is locked up in the will of God. Live there quietly, & you will read it, and live in it before it's seen: 'tis a time to try all our confidence[,] comforts, principles[,] practise.

The despair Hobson felt was revealed in a letter written the same day to John Hall: "My straights are so great that I know not which way to turn my selfe: for I am forced to be as private as I can." Five days later he assured Joplin that his friends were well, "though the devils reig."[27]

Although the government suspected Hobson of seditious undertakings well before 1663, it was apparently not until that time that he became embroiled in treasonous activity. He was in London with Gower since at least March of that year, when he was under surveillance by agents of his old nemesis, the Bishop of Durham. With Gower, Joplin, the inveterate revolutionary Thomas Blood and others, Hobson was involved in the 1663 Yorkshire Plot. According to Captain Robert Atkinson—himself arrested for his alleged role in the plot—Hobson, Joplin, Dr. Edward Richardson, and Lieutenant-Colonel John Mason were its masterminds.[28]

In theory the plotters initially intended no physical harm to Charles II or Queen Catherine, and no political assassinations. Their goals included forcing the king to honor the promises made in the 1660 Declaration of Breda, including the provision of liberty of conscience to all Protestants. The plotters wanted "a Gospel magistracy and ministry" and the abolition of the excise and hearth taxes. Their plans envisaged the overthrow of their principal political enemies, the Dukes of Albemarle and Buckingham. The Earl of Manchester, Sir Thomas Fairfax, and Sir John Lawson allegedly had been informed of the plot but disowned it, whereas Lord Wharton was supposedly privy to it. Those prominent advocates of the Good Old Cause, John Lambert and the regicide William Goffe, were reportedly to raise London on 12 October. The plotters believed they had important support from many in the Life Guards and Albemarle's own regiment, as

---

[27]PRO SP 29/63/34; 29/63/34.1.

[28]PRO SP 29/70/58; 29/93/11; 29/99/30.1; CSPD, 1663-64, 91-92, 352.

well as disaffected persons in the fleet, in Scotland, and overseas. In the north alone, there were supposedly 2,000 horse and dragoons in Durham and Westmorland, plus additional sympathetic men in the trained bands. If the king refused to grant liberty of conscience, the rebels were prepared to demand the recall of the Long Parliament.[29]

Hobson's role in all this allegedly entailed heading a committee in London that corresponded with the plotters in the north. It was Hobson's responsibility to give the signal for the Northern rebels to rise in groups of forty or fifty, to seize the gentry with their horses and weapons, and to capture York Castle. Subsequent testimony revealed that he did in fact communicate with Joplin in code, and that Joplin deciphered his information and communicated it to the plotters. Hobson's wife participated by helping to pass along a draft of the rebels' declaration in late June, though Hobson learned that a copy of it was supposedly in the king's hands a mere three hours after a messenger had given it to Hobson's wife. Hobson nevertheless urged the messenger to press ahead with the rising, arguing that success was possible if they acted by 10 August. The government in any case had learned of the plotting from Major Joshua Greathead and Colonel Smithson, and ordered York secured with troops of horse and foot. By royal command the Duke of Buckingham was dispatched in early August to the West Riding to exercise his responsibilities as lord lieutenant. Although Hobson reportedly sent word to his cohorts in the north to raise a troop of cavalry to overwhelm the duke on his northward march and then advance on London, Buckingham arrived safely in Yorkshire and took command of the militia. According to Sir John Reresby, who preceded Buckingham north, "the partys concern'd in the carrying on of this design were some officers of the late Parliament army, and some dissatisfyed persons upon account of looseing their Crown and Church lands by the Kings return, and dissenters in point of religion." Between 5 and 7 August, the authorities arrested and briefly held nearly a hundred persons on the pretext of attending illegal meetings.[30]

[29]CSPD, 1663-64, 91-92, 352.

[30]Ibid., 263, 279-80, 296, 329-30, 331-32, 485, 540, 571; PRO SP 29/93/9; 29/97/63; Sir John Reresby, Memoirs of Sir John Reresby, ed. Andrew Browning (Glasgow, 1936) 47. Smithson had been a major in the regiment of Robert Lilburne. See Firth & Davies, 264, 266, 273-76.

A warrant for Hobson's arrest on charges of sedition and treason was issued on 19 August, the day after authorities intercepted his letter to Joplin in the north. Hobson was apprehended the next day and committed to the Tower of London. There his wife was allowed to visit him in the presence of a jailer, but he was not given the liberty of the Tower until 21 October. Confined to his cell before that time he found that his health began to fail, and by early December he was ill. In the meantime the government tried to unravel the tale of his involvement, including his use of the aliases Dr. Smith and Dr. Love. He was personally interrogated in October by a secretary of state, the Privy Council, and the king himself (in private). By 26 November, some of Hobson's fellow radicals were convinced that he had informed on them in return for leniency, but Captain Atkinson was probably telling the truth when he confessed that Hobson "played double, and did (indeed) advance the designe by all means possible," even while pretending to keep the king informed. Whether Hobson revealed anything to Charles is largely immaterial so far as the plot was concerned. The government had been well aware of the proposed insurrection set for 12 October, and the attempted risings at Farnley Wood near Leeds, at Woodham Moor in Durham, and at Kaber Rigg in Westmorland were exercises in futility.[31]

Some of Hobson's time in prison was spent writing, including some correspondence with Joplin and Captain John Atkinson, "the stockinger." From this period also comes his apologetic, autobiographical tract, *Innocency, Though Under a Cloud, Cleared* (1664). He also wrote a hymn of twenty-one verses, including these lines extolling spiritual freedom:

> Now I true Liberty doe know,
>   To Christ I'le praises sing,
> For He thro' Death will bring me home
>   No more to sigh and sin;
> I wish this news abroad may spread,
>   That all my foes may see,

---

[31]PRO SP 29/81/32; 29/84/64; 29/90/112; *CSPD, 1663-64*, 244, 245, 247, 263, 292, 309, 352 (quoted), 367, 521; *BQ*, 9:309; Reresby, *Memoirs*, 48-49. Cf. Walker, "The Yorkshire Plot, 1663," 348-59.

And Saints with understanding read
And know my Liberty.

On 26 January 1664, Hobson and his fellow prisoner, Captain John Gregory, appealed to Sir Joseph Williamson for permission to go into exile overseas before they died in the Tower. The request was denied, but the government neither put Hobson on trial nor called on him to testify against the other accused plotters—perhaps suggesting that he had struck a deal with the king. On 31 March a warrant was issued to have Hobson transferred to Chepstow Castle in Monmouthshire, the result perhaps of petitions from Gregory and Hobson to Charles II to be sent to Jamaica. From Chepstow Hobson petitioned Sir Henry Bennet, a secretary of state, on 18 August 1664 to be sent into exile, protesting that he had no prisoner's allowance. Still insisting upon his innocence, he admitted to nothing "except miscarrying himself before the King and his honour [Bennet] at Whitehall, for which he is very sorry." A similar petition was directed to Charles the following month. On 12 January 1665, a warrant was issued directing that Hobson be returned to the Tower of London. By now the king had apparently indicated that he thought exile was appropriate, for Hobson again petitioned the king, alluding to this fact.[32]

Release came at last on 28 April 1665, with the stipulation that Hobson go into exile in the Carolinas. Scandal, however, ensued. Following the renewal of his association with Kiffin's Devonshire Square church, Hobson allegedly became involved with two women and another man in wanton conduct. There is insufficient evidence to determine the validity of the accusation. His family had apparently gone to live in the diocese of Durham, for in his will dated 12 March 1664, he had urged his wife Hester "to goe and live with my said Children in the Bishopricke of Durham keeping possession for me and my children." He had a son (Paul) and four daughters (Hester, Lydia, Sara, and Reubenah). Hobson may have died in England; his will was proved on 13 June 1666. He left property at Sacriston. His London congregation, which had met in Bishopsgate, apparently did not survive his imprisonment, for there was no mention of it in a list of Non-

---

[32]BQ, 9:309 (quoted); CSPD, 1663-64, 453, 536, 537, 545, 574, 670 (quoted); CSPD, 1664-65, 22, 169, 186.

conformist congregations in London raided in 1670. Hobson's reputation did, however, survive him. As late as 1692 the Presbyterian Daniel Williams—now remembered as the founder of Dr. Williams's Library—reminded his readers that Hobson, John Saltmarsh, Henry Denne, and John Eaton were Antinomians who had to be repudiated by the Westminster Assembly of Divines.[33]

Hobson's career is one of remarkable consistency. The only change of consequence in his religious views occurred in the early 1640s when he embraced the tenet of believer's baptism in addition to the separatist principles he already espoused. Because of his military career he was responsible for helping spread Particular Baptist ideas across much of England, ranging from Newcastle to Bristol, though his major work was in the northeast. With Gower and Tillam he must be regarded as one of the most influential Baptists in county Durham during the seventeenth century. He was also steadfastly loyal to the military, standing with General Fairfax against the Levellers. In this regard he is representative of the Particular Baptists in general who, as Professor Tolmie has demonstrated, refused to support the Levellers in their critical attempt to win extensive backing from the New Model Army. Hobson was not a Cromwellian who embraced the Protectorate, even though his hostility was not sufficiently pronounced to cause him to reject various appointments offered by the Protectoral regime. Hobson's overriding goal was the establishment, primarily in a millenarian context, of a godly government and the spread of the Particular Baptist movement.

---

[33]*Calamy Revised*, 269; BQ 9:251, 308-10; Prerogative Court of Canterbury, Wills, 13 June 1666; W. T. Whitley, *The Baptists of London 1612-1928* (London, [1928]) 104; Daniel Williams, *Gospel-Truth Stated and Vindicated* (2nd ed., London, 1692), sig. A2ᵛ.

An Anonymous Letter, Possibly from Paul Hobson, to Friends in London, c. 1645

Dearly beloved in the Lord Iesus, My dearest respects and unexpressable love remembred to you, longing to see your face in the flesh, that we might be comforted together in the discovery of what the Lord hath made known to us of that great mystery, *God manifest in the flesh:* In which is discovered His everlasting love to the Sons of men, which he hath been alwayes discovering in all Ages, since the beginning of the World to this day, but darkly, vailedly, hiddenly as it were; so that all those several wayes of Gods dealing with the Sons of men, have been still so many pledges of his love, so that God hath not bin discovering divers things to the Sons of men, but one thing at several times in divers manners. Therefore I behold but one thing in all the Scriptures, under divers Administrations: So I understand the two Covenants to be but two Administrations of one thing; and that which makes the Scriptures Law or Gospel, is our understanding of them in either of those two considerations: So that Christ Iesus came to witnesse and declare this love of God to us, not to procure it for us: For if God had at any time any displeasure to us, he had been changeable, seeing before the world began, he saw us lovely in his Son. Now I conceive Christs coming, was more like a Conqueror to destroy the enmity in our nature, and for to convince us of the Love of God to us, by destroying in our nature, that we thought stood between God and us, according to that of the Apostle, *Heb. 2. For as much as the Children were partakers of flesh and blood, he likewise took part of the same,* To what end? *To destroy him who had the power of death:* Who is that? *The Devil:* Why so? *To deliver them who through fear of death were all their life time subject to bondage:* So that we being in bondage, his coming was to deliver us, not to procure the Love of God to us, or satisfie him, as some say: He was as I may so say, a most glorious publisher of the Gospel, as he himself saith, *He was sent to Preach the Gospel, to heal the broken hearted, to Preach deliverance to the Captives, to set at liberty them that are bruised,* Luke 14. 18, 19. All that which Christ here saith to be the end of his coming, is not a word mentioned of any thing done by him in way of satisfying God. Again, *Ioh. 18. 37.* Iesus saith to *Pilate, To this end was I born, and for this cause came I into the world,* namely, *to bear witnesse to the truth.* Oh me thinks how ignorant to this day is the world of the end of Christs coming! which makes them so dark in the understanding what Christ is: people look upon him so to be God, as not at all to be man: whereas I am of the minde, he was very man of the same nature with us: for otherwise it would be no encouragement to us, to go to the Father upon the same ground that Christ is entred, if he was of a more holier nature then us; but in this appears Gods Love to us, that he would take one of us in the same condition, to convince us of what he is to us, and hath made us to be in him: That now we are to stand still and behold the glory of God come forth, and brought to light by the appearing of our Lord Iesus Christ, who hath abolished death, and brought life and immortality to light: Therefore he saith, I will declare thy name to my brethren. O then let us behold Christ Iesus in all that he is to be the representation of God to us, in which same glory, God hath and ever will behold

us; which the more we behold, we shall see our selves changed into the same
Image from glory to glory. Me thinks the beholding of Christ to be holy in the
flesh, is a dishonour to God, in that we should conceive holinesse out of God,
which is to make another God. Again it would be a dishonour to Christ, in that
he would be but fleshly: And again, a discomfort to the Saints, in that he should
be of a more holier nature then they, as being no ground for them to come near
with boldnes to God: Again, it is to make the body of Christ a Monster, the head
of one nature, the body of another. Now to conceive all fulnesse of holinesse in
God, and that Christ is and ever was, and the Saints in him, beheld holy, righteous, and unblameable, as they are and ever were, beheld in the Spirit in union
with God, having their being in him: and so its said, the fulnesse of God dwelt
in Christ, and ye are compleat in him, one God and Father of all, who is above
all, through all, and in you all.

This Letter was given me by a Reverend Minister of the City, who told me it was a Letter
sent out of the West from about Bath, by a great Sectary in those parts.
[Gangraena, 89-91]

chapter 6

Gentleman Revolutionary:
Henry Danvers
and the Radical Underground*

Despite his aristocratic background and inheritance of the family estate, Henry Danvers was one of the most consistent radicals in seventeenth-century England. Because of his social status and political leanings, he was appointed to a variety of civil and military posts in the 1640s and 1650s, the most significant of which was the governorship of Stafford. Like Paul Hobson, he had great expectations of the Barebones Parliament—in which he sat—but after its dissolution he bitterly opposed the Protectorate. Like John Simpson, he was a Fifth Monarchist, but when Simpson recanted his views Danvers was one of those to whom the remaining radicals in Simpson's congregation looked for assistance. Danvers's own religious pilgrimage was modest in scope, extending from the Independents to the General Baptists and ultimately to the Particular Baptists. His published views on believer's baptism were at the heart of a lively pamphlet war involving such noted Nonconformists as Richard Baxter and John Bun-

*Portions of this chapter were previously published in the _Baptist Quarterly_ 29 (January 1981): 32-43.

yan in the 1670s. From the outset of the Restoration he was firmly committed to activity in the radical underground, successfully eluding repeated efforts by government agents to apprehend him. He had ties to such influential figures as Algernon Sidney, for whom he served as an election manager, and the Duke of Monmouth, for whom he failed to raise London in 1685, thus earning the opprobrium of the Whig historian Thomas Macaulay. More than most, Danvers's career vividly illustrates the tenacity with which some Nonconformists espoused the Good Old Cause from the 1640s well into the 1680s.

The second son of William and Elizabeth Danvers of Swithland Hall, near Mountsorrel and Loughborough, Leicestershire, Henry Danvers was born about 1619. His father was a cousin of Sir John Coke of Melbourne Hall, Derbyshire. Both men supported the parliamentary cause in the 1640s, and at the onset of the Civil War there was an abortive plan for Coke to move to Swithland for his safety. One of Coke's sons-in-law was Sir Edward Hartopp, father of Sir John Hartopp, with whom Henry Danvers was subsequently associated. Danvers himself eventually married Coke's daughter Anne after her first husband, Henry Sacheverell, died in 1662. By this time Anne's sister Mary, whose first husband was Sir Edward Hartopp (d. 1658), was married to Charles Fleetwood, the former Cromwellian major-general. From his father Danvers inherited the family estate, worth about £300-£400 p.a. in 1656, though he had to put it into trust at the Restoration in order to protect it from "the persecutors of his time."[1]

Danvers may have studied at Trinity College, Oxford, for the title page of the Congregational Library copy of his 1663 tract, *The Mystery of Magistracy Unvailed*, contains an annotation suggesting as much. A young man of approximately twenty-three when the Civil War erupted, he supported the parliamentary cause and ultimately became a colonel in its forces. With future associates such as Thomas Harrison and Hugh Courtney, he engaged in discussions of the Agreement of the People, the proposed Leveller constitution, in 1647-1648. He was present at a meeting of the General Council of the Army at Whitehall on 14 December 1648 when a lengthy debate occurred on the question "whether to have any reserve to except religious thinges,

¹Geoffrey F. Nuttall, "Henry Danvers, His Wife and the 'Heavenly Line'," *BQ* 29 (January 1982): 217; Capp, *FMM*, 248; Crosby, 3:97; *BQ*, 25:366.

or only to give power in naturall and civil thinges [to the civil government], and to say nothing of religion?" There is, however, no indication that Danvers spoke in the debate, though he probably would have supported the position on religious toleration espoused by the Levellers and the sectarian officers, judging by arguments he published the following March.[2]

Danvers's position in the shire and his commitment to the parliamentary cause were responsible for his service on the Staffordshire County Committee from 1647 to 1652. He was also a justice of the peace, in which capacity he was "well beloved among the people" and "noted for one, that would take no bribes." Four times in all in 1649, 1650, and 1652 he was appointed a commissioner in Leicestershire for the general assessment, which raised funds to support troops in England and Ireland. On 15 and 16 June 1649 the Council of State directed Major Danvers and others to make certain Belvoir Castle had been demolished in order to prevent its use by Royalists. "You cannot," the Council said, "but have still a sense of what the country suffered while Belvoir Castle was kept a garrison by the enemy," hence Danvers, Colonel Rossiter, William Hartopp, and William Bury were ordered to certify its destruction. Perhaps it was in this connection that the Council of State commissioned him as a major in the Leicestershire militia on 5 March 1650, although two months later on 14 May, he also received a commission as colonel in the Staffordshire militia.[3]

During his tenure as Governor of Stafford (1650-1652), Danvers was continuously concerned with matters of security. In June 1650 he submitted a proposal to the Council of State for the improvement of Stafford's defense, and in return received £100 from the Ordnance Committee for the garrison. This was supplemented with an additional £50 in October. On 15 March 1651 the Council directed Major-General Harrison to have Danvers detain two military officers, Colonel Bowyer and Captain Snead, as well as other dangerous persons who posed a threat to public peace. On the 27th, the day after the Council had discussed a report from Danvers on Stafford's security, it

---

[2]*DNB, s.v.,*; Capp, *FMM*, 248; Brown, 22; *Clarke Papers*, 2:71 (quoted), 282.

[3]Capp, *FMM*, 248; Crosby, 3:97 (quoted); Firth & Rait, 2:37, 301, 470, 667; *CSPD*, 1649-50, 187, 189-90 (quoted); *CSPD*, 1650, 211, 223, 505, 506, 580, 595.

took up the problem of three men it had ordered Danvers to arrest. Two were military officers—Colonel Philip Jackson and Captain Henry Stone—but the third was John Swynfen, a Presbyterian M.P. who had been ejected from the Rump Parliament at Pride's Purge. In 1647-1648 Swynfen had favored a negotiated settlement with the king, and the Council was now clearly worried about his intentions. "Having considered the dangers of your parts," the Council informed Danvers, "and the designs now on foot there, and particularly upon the garrison of Stafford . . .," it ordered the three prisoners sent to Denbigh Castle. On 5 April, however, the Council after reconsidering ordered Danvers to discharge them on recognizances of £1000 each in addition to sureties. Due to its royalist designs, Stafford increasingly became a town "of very great concernment." In April the Council provided Danvers with £200 for its defense to be used as Harrison determined. The Council also went on record as approving Danvers's mobilization of the militia. [4]

As the country prepared for the invasion of Charles II and the Scots in the summer of 1651, Danvers readied his forces. On 15 August the Council of State expressed its satisfaction with his preparations as well as his "forward march with them [his troops], as also of the good affection in your country, in so generally appearing for the common defence and their own, against the invasion. We doubt not but, by this your readiness, your forces will have a share in the merit of this service, and this general manifestation of affection will be a discouragement to any further attempts against the peace of the commonwealth." The Council then ordered Danvers to dispatch any troops he could spare to Cheshire and to await orders from Lambert or Harrison. Based on Danvers's report of the state of his forces, the Council determined on 2 September that he and the Governor of Chester should supply the Governor of Shropshire with three hundred pikes to arm his garrison. [5]

In the aftermath of Charles's defeat at Worcester on 3 September, the Council requested that Cromwell provide Danvers with a com-

---

[4]*CSPD, 1650,* 211, 223, 580; *CSPD, 1651,* 86, 112, 114 (quoted), 132, 133; *BDBR, s.v.* John Swynfen.

[5]*CSPD, 1651,* 319, 331, 332 (quoted), 339, 398.

mission to try those in Staffordshire who had aided the invading army. On the 13th the Council ordered Danvers to send a group of royalist prisoners to London to stand trial for treason. Included among them were Thomas Wentworth, Earl of Cleveland, who had fought at Worcester but briefly escaped; Colonel Thomas Blague, who fled with Charles from Worcester to Boscobel in Shropshire; and Major David Galbreith. Prisoners of lesser importance were to be sent to Bristol for "disposal abroad." Although the king was in Hampshire in mid-October, the Council, suspecting he was still in the Midlands, directed that Captain John Ley conduct a search for him there as well as for George Villiers, Duke of Buckingham, and their supporters. Any prisoners were to be taken to Danvers for examination. As the royalist threat subsided, the Council no longer found it necessary to maintain such frequent contact with Danvers, though in June 1652 he was ordered to provide 400 muskets, 300 pikes, and 350 collars of bandoliers for troops preparing to serve in Ireland.[6]

Danvers had been an Independent, but while he was governor of Stafford he was rebaptized and joined the General Baptist congregation associated with Henry Haggar. Danvers had already written in favor of religious toleration in *Certain Quaeries Concerning Liberty of Conscience* (March 1649), which was addressed to "the Ministers (so called) of Leicestershire." Yet during his governorship at Stafford he expelled the Presbyterian minister Richard Bell for refusing to subscribe to the Engagement. Danvers's religious convictions were further manifested in 1652 when he signed a petition to the Rump protesting the Independents' scheme for a national ministry. This was Roger Williams's *The Fourth Paper, Presented by Major Butler, to the Honourable Committee of Parliament, for the Propagating the Gospel*. John Owen and his associates were trying to reinstate mandatory church attendance for all excommunicated persons who refused to attend because of issues of conscience. The Independents proposed to permit the existence of congregations outside the established church, but only if they registered with the state and advocated nothing contrary to Christian principles. This, of course, would have banned toleration

<hr>

[6]Ibid., 411, 426, 443-44, 474, 475, 477; *CSPD*, 1651-52, 566. For other business between Danvers and the Council of State, see *CSPD*, 1651, 463, 466, 486; *CSPD*, 1651-52, 73.

162 / RICHARD L. GREAVES

for such groups as Catholics, Jews, and Socinians, the latter because they were deists. Conceived as too restrictive, the proposal was opposed by Danvers as well as by Major William Butler, a Leveller.[7]

On 15 June 1653, some two weeks before the opening of the Barebones Parliament on 4 July, the Council of State ordered lodgings for Danvers in London. While in the City he served as joint-elder of the General Baptist church of Edmund Chillenden, which met at Aldgate. (The church moved to St. Paul's in 1653 and then to Chequer without Aldgate in 1656.) Chillenden himself belonged to the Fifth Monarchy movement and may have been the person who converted Danvers to its tenets. In the Barebones Parliament Danvers sat for Leicester and served on committees dealing with tithes, Scottish affairs, and prisons and poor prisoners. In the Parliament's debates he distinguished himself by advocating religious toleration, hence a list published in 1654 properly recognized him as an opponent of a national ministry. Having been a trustee for the use of sequestered tithes during the Commonwealth (1649-1650), he brought some expertise to the Barebones's committee on tithes, which included such other prominent radicals as Harrison, Courtney, and Arthur Squibb. These men were also adherents of the Fifth Monarchy movement. Despite the efforts of Danvers and his colleagues, the committee reported on 2 December that the majority favored a retention of the tithing system. Although the radicals forced a debate, they lost by two votes, with Danvers serving as teller. The day after the vote the moderates caucused and determined to resign their authority to Cromwell early the following day, an action to which Cromwell acquiesced.[8]

In the years after the dissolution of the Barebones Parliament Danvers's disaffection with the government intensified. He pressed for the

---

[7]A. G. Matthews, *The Congregational Churches of Staffordshire* (London, 1924) 21, 34; BQ, 25:285; Tai Liu, *Discord in Zion* (The Hague, 1973) 111; Michael R. Watts, *The Dissenters* (Oxford, 1978) 140.

[8]*CSPD, 1652-53,* 412; W. T. Whitley, *The Baptists of London 1612-1928* (London, [1928]) 113; Firth & Rait, 2:143-44, 371; Capp, FMM, 178, 245, 248; W. K. Jordan, *The Development of Religious Toleration in England,* 4 vols. (Cambridge MA, 1932-1940) 3:146ff.; Liu, *Discord in Zion,* 93, 168; CJ, 7:285-86; H. A. Glass, *The Barebone Parliament* (London, 1899) 74. As a tithes commissioner Danvers dispensed salaries and augmentations to preaching ministers as determined by Parliament.

SAINTS AND REBELS / 163

churches to protest against the Protectorate, though Chillenden opposed such action. As Chillenden explained to John Thurloe on 31 December 1655, when Cromwell became Protector, Danvers "would have all the churches to have declared ther protest against it, and this moved in a very greate assembly, [but] I did oppose it, and my soe opposinge it made the whole assembly lay it aside. . . ." Undaunted, the following March Danvers urged the saints to rise in rebellion, and the same year he entered into negotiations with the Commonwealthsmen to pursue this aim. He did not, however, join in Thomas Venner's plan for an insurrection to topple Cromwell and establish a divine kingdom governed by a sanhedrin of saints with scripturally sanctioned laws. Harrison, who knew of these plans but refused participation, may have informed and influenced Danvers. In any case Danvers, Harrison, Courtney, the Commonwealthsman John Lawson, Colonel John Okey, and Nathaniel Rich were arrested in April 1657 and briefly imprisoned for suspected complicity.[9]

In the midst of these events Danvers became involved in the schism in John Simpson's congregation at Allhallows the Great. When Simpson retracted his Fifth Monarchy views by February 1656, the Fifth Monarchists in his congregation mounted a campaign to change his mind. That summer they enlisted the assistance of Danvers, Clement Ireton, Arthur Squibb, and others for a debate, but Simpson refused them entry to the church. The following year the Fifth Monarchists in the congregation sought and obtained the permission of Danvers, Squibb, and others to separate from Simpson's church.[10]

Danvers presumably rejoiced with other Fifth Monarchists in April 1659 when Richard Cromwell dissolved his Parliament under pressure from Charles Fleetwood, Harrison, and others. Demands by some Fifth Monarchists for something akin to the Barebones Parliament were turned aside in favor of the restoration of the Rump, which the Fifth Monarchists had been happy enough to see terminated in 1653. With the change in fortunes Danvers was instructed to attend the

[9]Thurloe, *SP*, 4: 365 (quoted), 629; *CSPD*, 1656-57, 351; Cromwell, *WS*, 4: 465; Capp, *FMM*, 118; *Clarke Papers*, 3: 106; *CMHS*, 3rd ser., 1: 184.

[10]Capp, *FMM*, 276-78.

Committee of Safety in July 1659. He was appointed a Militia Commissioner—with such prominent radicals as Sir Arthur Haselrig, Colonel William Purefoy, and Sir John Hartopp, his wife's nephew—for Leicestershire and Staffordshire, and a member of the Staffordshire County Committee (1659-1660). In company with such men as Courtney, Clement Ireton, and Henry Jessey he signed *An Essay Towards Settlement upon a Sure Foundation* in September 1659, which called for religious and legal reforms and the ouster from office of all who had supported the detested Protectorate. In January 1660 he was appointed a commissioner of assessment for the county of Middlesex. Briefly, then, at the end of the 1650s Danvers returned to the sort of local political prominence he had enjoyed almost a decade earlier, but it lasted only until General Monck successfully engineered the restoration of the Stuart monarchy.[11]

At the Restoration Danvers lost his positions but not his militancy. He did take the precaution of placing his estate in the hands of trustees, hoping to ensure its security, though apparently without the success he sought. In 1661 he was reportedly living outside London in the village of Stoke Newington, where Sir John and Lady Hartopp, the daughter of Charles Fleetwood, also lived. Danvers may, in fact, have stayed in their household, and he certainly attended conventicles there. So too did Henry Jessey and Nathaniel Strange, another Baptist, Fifth Monarchist, and former army officer. In late 1660 or early 1661, Danvers met at his brother's house in Soper Lane, near Cheapside, to discuss "prodigyes" with Jessey. About this time Danvers was also allegedly plotting a rising with such disaffected radicals as Clement Ireton and John Okey. In the fall of 1661, Danvers was reportedly staying with his brother, a merchant, in Soper Lane. With other former Cromwellian officers such as William Packer, Thomas Kelscy, and Edward Whalley, he was considered a "Dangerous" person. According to one informant, he had agreed to "head a party" as part of a rising to topple the government, and in this connection was meeting twice weekly with Clement Ireton and others. That year and the next, a series of tracts was published under the general title *Mirabilis Annus*, justifying the cause of the saints and hammering home the ultimate

[11]*CSPD, 1659-60*, 45; Firth & Rait, 2: 1327, 1331, 1373; Capp, *FMM*, 124, 126.

inevitability of divine retribution against their oppressors. Published at least partly by the Fifth Monarchist printer Livewell Chapman, the tracts were thought by the government to have been written by Danvers, Jessey, and the Independent minister George Cokayne. Although Danvers was in hiding, the authorities questioned Jessey in December 1661, but he admitted only to knowing Danvers and having an interest in the material in the inflammatory tracts. According to government agents, a Colonel Danvers was involved in 1662 in the Tong Plot to restore the republic, assassinate Charles II and the Dukes of York and Albemarle, and establish liberty of conscience. This, however, may have been Robert Danvers, a former royalist who had been excluded from the House of Lords in 1660 and had thereafter become embroiled in plots against the government.[12]

While in hiding Henry Danvers wrote his tract, *The Mystery of Magistracy Unvailed* (1663), in which he set forth his political views. Although acknowledging that an act of God was responsible for the restored monarchy, he insisted that Christians openly or secretly resist it as providence provided. The imposition of antichristian sovereigns such as Charles II, he argued, was a curse on the subjects, yet he exhorted the saints to pray for such rulers.[13] These views were probably expressed by Danvers in the conventicles he illegally held in 1663. He was still associated with the Baptist church at Chequer without Aldgate, which became affiliated with the Particular Baptists, and with which John Vernon and Nathaniel Strange were now allied. On 1 February, in fact, Danvers and Vernon preached to a group of the faithful at the "Spread Eagle." In the same year (1663) the almanac writer William Lilly reportedly was preparing a "prognostication" to assist Danvers and his cohorts with their plotting. Danvers

---

[12]Crosby, 3:90ff.; *CSPD*, 1670, 661; PRO SP 29/44/134; 29/45/28; 29/105/37; 29/446/40; Capp, *FMM*, 206, 209, 211; *Mirabilis Annus, or, the Year of Prodigies and Wonders* (1661); *Mirabilis Annus Secundus: Or the Second Year of Prodigies* (1662); *Mirabilis Annus Secundus: Or the Second Part of the Second Years Prodigies* (1662); B. R. White, "Henry Jessey in the Great Rebellion," in *Reformation, Conformity and Dissent*, ed. R. Buick Knox (London, 1977) 152. For Robert Danvers see Richard L. Greaves, "The Tangled Careers of Two Stuart Radicals: Henry and Robert Danvers," *BQ* 29 (January 1981): 40-42.

[13]Henry Danvers, *The Mystery of Magistracy Unvailed* (London, 1663) 20-25, 37.

apparently went into exile in the Netherlands prior to 6 November 1663, and there laid plans with the rebel Colonel Gilby Carr for an insurrection in England. According to informers Danvers had agents in Leicestershire for this purpose, possibly men he had worked with in that county in the early 1650s. Certainly he was associated with Sir John Hartopp, who had a house at Freeby, Leicestershire. On 30 December 1663 the government issued a warrant for the arrest of Danvers, Strange, and the Fifth Monarchist John Skinner.[14]

In January 1664, Danvers was alleged to be involved in a plot to raise forces in the spring of 1664 to fight the Turks and then turn those troops against the English government. He was reportedly visiting his wife in secret at Stoke Newington, disguised in rural garb and "a long beard down to his breast." He also met with Anthony Palmer and other radicals in Soper Lane. The authorities still had not been able to apprehend him by April, and in June he was reportedly conniving with rebels in London and preaching in Leicestershire. With Laurence Wise and Colonel John Gladman, he was also holding conventicles in this period in Moorfields. He was now believed to be plotting to overthrow the Stuarts in late July. His wife subsequently traveled to London to report the latest schemes to Lady Frances Vane, apparently a key contact with revolutionaries in the City. Gladman was arrested in September on charges of trying to raise four hundred men in Staffordshire to support a rebellion in the north. Danvers was probably a party to this planning. In any event, he held a conventicle with Strange, Vernon, Skinner, and Glasse on 26 October at George Cokayne's house. Two weeks later Danvers and Glasse preached at a conventicle in the home of a cheesemonger in Leadenhall Street, and Danvers may have been present the following day (10 November) when Cokayne preached at Danvers's brother's house in Soper Lane. On 4 December Danvers joined Strange to preach once again at the cheesemonger's house, and a fortnight later the two men led a conventicle in Bishopsgate Street. Working now as a team, Danvers and

---

[14]*CSPD, 1663-64*, 327-28, 367, 393; PRO SP 29/71/48; 29/85/48; Whitley, *Baptists of London*, 113; Bernard Capp, *English Almanacs 1500-1800: Astrology and the Popular Press* (Ithaca NY, 1979) 89; G. Lyon Turner, "Williamson's Spy Book," *TCHS* 5 (1912): 315.

Strange preached at conventicles on 1 January in Elbow Lane, and on the 8th of that month in Bread Street.[15]

Although Danvers was finally apprehended in August 1665, he was rescued in Cheapside by a friendly crowd that presumably included numerous Baptists and Fifth Monarchists. In his diary Samuel Pepys recorded the "great Ryott upon Thursday last in Cheapeside, Colonell Danvers, a Delinquent, having been taken, and in his way to the Tower was rescued from the Captain of the Guard and carried away—one only of the Rescuers being taken." On the 30th Danvers was charged with high treason and summoned by proclamation to stand trial. The Sheriff of Leicestershire was ordered to secure his estate in that county pending the trial's outcome. The plot in which he was now alleged to be involved—usually known as the Rathbone Plot—was supposed to occur on 3 September 1665 when Charles would be assassinated, the Tower seized, London put to the torch, a republic established, and property redistributed. A number of schemers, including Colonel John Rathbone, were apprehended and eight executed, though Danvers again eluded his pursuers. On 9 September one of his servants at Maddersall, Staffordshire, claimed ignorance of his whereabouts, though he admitted that he had received money from his master in recent months and books from his brother Charles, a London merchant and Fifth Monarchist. On 22 October government authorities learned that Danvers was still "about" but very wary since his near arrest.[16]

Danvers apparently fled to Ireland, where Colonel Gilby Carr and Colonel Thomas Blood reportedly were plotting to seize Limerick in February 1666. Whether Danvers was present and part of such plans

---

[15]CSPD, 1663-64, 463, 565, 606, 638; PRO SP 29/91/100; 29/99/21.3; 29/103/136; 29/105/37; 29/110/108; CSPD, 1664-65, 246; Whitley, Baptists of London, 115; BDBR, s.v. John Gladman.

[16]PRO SP 29/128/53; 29/133/102; 29/134/51; 29/135/37; The Diary of Samuel Pepys, ed. Robert Latham and William Matthews, 6 (Berkeley, 1972): 184; CSPD, 1664-65, 506, 542, 555; Capp, FMM, 211. Danvers was not mentioned in the account of the plot provided by Sir Roger L'Estrange in A Compendious History (London, 1680) 4-6, though he does comment on "those Fifth Monarchy bigots." Nor is Danvers mentioned in the documents in the Middlesex County Records, ed. J. C. Jeaffreson (London, 1886-1892) 3:376; 4:269-70.

is unknown, though he was linked to a subsequent plot that August involving Blood, the Congregationalist minister Thomas Palmer, and others. The English government also received a report that Danvers was meeting with agents from Holland, who were in contact with the exiled radical Edmund Ludlow, to plan an invasion of England. Perhaps Danvers went with Carr and Blood to Scotland that autumn and took part in the rising of the Covenanters, and was still with Blood when the latter met with Baptists in Westmorland the following spring. In any case a warrant was issued on 2 March 1667 for Danvers's apprehension, instructing that he be brought before either Secretary Arlington if arrested in London or Westminster, or a justice of the peace.[17]

Nothing was heard of Danvers until 28 May 1670, when a new warrant for his arrest was issued. Dr. B. S. Capp suggests that this warrant may have been the result of Danvers's participation in Blood's daring attempt to kidnap and hang the Duke of Ormonde while he was host to William of Orange, but that escapade did not occur until December 1670. The state remained frustrated in its endeavors to apprehend Danvers, and a chagrined Earl of Arran seemed surprised to discover in May 1671 that there were two Colonel Danvers (Henry and Robert), "both dangerous fellows."[18] Henry Danvers did not take advantage of the Declaration of Indulgence in 1672 to apply for a license to preach, undoubtedly because of his fugitive status.

Once again Danvers used his period of hiding to produce another tract, the millenarian *Theopolis, or the City of God* (1672). In it he set forth the postmillennialist view that Christ would not reappear until the conclusion of the thousand years, which would be a time of bliss and health for the saints. In the millennium there would be no church, no ministry, and no ordinances (baptism and the Lord's supper), for Christians would worship by prayer and thanksgiving alone. In company with various other thinkers Danvers anticipated the conversion and return of the Jews to the Holy Land as the prelude to the millen-

[17]W. C. Abbott, *Colonel Thomas Blood, Crown-Stealer, 1618-1680* (New Haven, 1911), passim; Capp, *FMM*, 212; PRO SP 29/187/148; *CSPD, 1666-67*, 64, 427, 463, 537, 545; *CSPD, 1667*, 1-2.

[18]*CSPD, 1670*, 239; *CSPD, 1671*, 283; Capp, *FMM*, 218.

nium, but unlike many millenarians he refrained from making guesses about exact dates.[19]

Still in hiding, Danvers next turned his attention to the subject of baptism in his *Treatise of Baptism* (1673; 2nd ed., 1674; 3rd ed., 1675). Its thesis stated that only the baptism of believers conformed to the ordinance of Christ, and that such baptism was the only means of admission to the church. Just as circumcision was the "visible door of entrance" to the religious community of the Old Testament, so believer's baptism was the only means of entry to the church. According to Danvers, there were seven "spiritual ends" of baptism: (1) Through it the believer had "that represented in a Sign or Figure, and preacht to his Eye . . . which had been preacht to his Ear and Heart by the Word and Spirit of God, respecting the whole Mystery of the Gospel, and his Duty and Obligation therein." (2) The baptismal act was a manifestation of the believer's repentance. (3) It was also a symbol of regeneration, though if the person baptized had not been spiritually converted the symbol was without meaning. (4) Baptism represented the covenant into which the Christian entered with God, especially the believer's responsibility to eschew sin and obey the commands of Christ. (5) Simultaneously baptism was a sign to the Christian that God had forgiven his sins and had bestowed spiritual life on him. (6) It was also a "signal Representation" of the believer's union with Christ "and a *putting* on of Christ figured out by such an Union and Conjunction with the Element, as imports a being born thereof, and . . . being clothed therewith." (7) Finally, as the door to the church, baptism bestowed on the believer the right to participate in all of the ordinances and privileges of the church.[20]

The *Treatise* is particularly interesting because it sparked a broad and heated controversy over the nature of baptism and whether or not it was essential for church membership and communion. John Bunyan argued that it was not in *A Confession of My Faith* (1672). The most im-

---

[19]Henry Danvers, *Theopolis, or the City of God* (London, 1672) 39-46, 72-89. For the general context see Peter Toon, ed., *Puritans, the Millennium and the Future of Israel* (Cambridge, 1970); and Christopher Hill, *The World Turned Upside Down* (New York, 1973) 70-78.

[20]Henry Danvers, *Treatise of Baptism* (2nd ed., London, 1674) 15-16, 18-30, 95 (15 and 25 quoted).

portant point with respect to baptism, he contended, was that "I walk according to my Light with God: otherwise 'tis false; For if a man that seeth it to be his Duty shall despisingly neglect it; or if he that hath no Faith therein shall foolishly take it up; both these are for this the worse, being convicted in themselves for Transgressors." Two traditional Baptists issued rebuttals to Bunyan: Thomas Paul in *Some Serious Reflections* (1673) and John Denne in *Truth Outweighing Error* (1673). Denne regarded Bunyan's position as identical with the Quakers' reliance on the Inner Light, insisting instead that "the question is not, who have Light therein, but who ought to have Light therein?" Bunyan counterattacked in his *Differences in Judgment About Water-Baptism, No Bar to Communion* (1673), to which Danvers responded in "A Postscript" to his *Treatise.* Hoping to overwhelm Bunyan with scriptural citations, Danvers insisted that baptism was "an *Orderly* entring *into the Visible* Church, or Body of Christ, as so fully exprest, I *Cor.* 12. 12. An *Order* faithfully to be observed as a *Fundamental Practice,* Heb. 6. 2. & which must be kept, *Eph.* 2. 21. and duly regarded, I *Cor.* 11. 1, 2. upon the severe penalties threatned, *Mat.* 5. 19. 2 *Joh.* 9. *Act.* 3. 22, 23." He also drew on the analogy of matrimony to buttress his argument against Bunyan: "If it be *prepostrous* and *wicked* for a Man and Woman to cohabite together, and to enjoy the Priviledges of a Marriage-state, without the passing of that publick *Solemnity:* So it is no less *disorderly* upon a *Spiritual* account, for any to claim the Priviledges of a Church, or be admitted to the same till the passing of this Solemnity by them." Bunyan retorted in his *Peaceable Principles and True* (1674) that Danvers was making baptism a wall of separation between the holy who are baptized by water and the holy who are not.[21]

Because Danvers was primarily interested in his *Treatise* in stating the case for believer's baptism, the paedobaptists launched a ferocious assault on his principles. In response to Obadiah Wills's *Infant-Baptisme Asserted* (1674)—to which Richard Baxter contributed a preface—and Richard Blinman's *An Essay Tending to Issue the Controversie* (1674), Dan-

---

[21]John Bunyan, *A Confession of My Faith,* in *The Works of That Eminent Servant of Christ, Mr. John Bunyan,* ed. Samuel Wilson, 2 vols. (London, 1736-37) 2:65; John Denne, *Truth Outweighing Error* (London, 1673) 73 (quoted), 78-79; Danvers, "Postscript" to *Treatise of Baptism,* 45, 52-53; Bunyan, *Peaceable Principles and True,* in *Works,* 2:103 (cf. 109). See Richard L. Greaves, *John Bunyan* (Abingdon, 1969) 135-45.

vers defended adult baptism in the second edition of his *Treatise of Baptism* as well as in his *Innocency and Truth Vindicated* (1675). This in turn provoked a reassertion of the case for paedobaptism in Wills's *Vindiciae vindiciarum* (1675) and Joseph Whiston's *Infant Baptism from Heaven, the Second Part* (1675). Danvers then attacked Wills in *A Rejoynder to Mr. Wills His Vindiciae* (1675). Wills, who had accused Danvers of misquoting and misconstruing the authorities to which he appealed, had also urged Baptists to examine Danvers's work and judge for themselves. In *The Baptists Answer to Mr Obed. Wills His Appeal Against Mr Danvers* (July 1675), Hanserd Knollys, William Kiffin, Daniel Dyke, Thomas Delaune, Henry Forty, and John Gosnold reported that they had studied Wills's allegations and did indeed find some errors by Danvers, which he "ingenuously acknowledges." Generally, however, they found Wills's objections either trivial or satisfactorily refuted by Danvers, and they called on Wills to acknowledge the "great mistakes" he had made. Wills defended himself in *Censura censurae* (1676), to which Delaune responded in his *Just Reproof to Clamorous Cavils of Mr. Obed. Wills* (1676).

If this was not enough, John Tombes, probably the most learned of the Baptists, refuted Wills's *Vindiciae* and Blinman's *Essay* in *A Just Reply to the Books of Mr. Wills and Mr. Blinman* (1675). Blinman, in a *Rejoynder to Mr. Henry D'Anvers* (1675) and Baxter, in *More Proofs of Infants Church Membership* (1675), attacked Danvers. The latter refused to yield, issuing *A Second Reply* (1675) and even *A Third Reply* (1676). In turn Baxter repudiated Danvers's position in a postscript to his *Treatise of Justifying Righteousness* (1676) and his *Review of the State of Christian Infants* (1676). Delaune then attacked Baxter in *Mr. Richard Baxters Review Examined* (1676) as well as Wills and Whiston in *Truth Defended* (1677). Whiston was also attacked by Delaune in a *Brief Survey of Joseph Whiston's Book on Baptism* (1676) and by Edward Hutchinson in his *Treatise Concerning Covenant and Baptism* (1676).[22]

Much of the debate was very tedious and repetitious. Appended to Danvers's *Rejoynder* is an anonymous letter supposedly by a person

---

[22]The controversy also included Benjamin Keach's *Mr. Baxters Arguments for Believers Baptism* (c. 1674), to which Baxter responded in *More Proofs*. Tombes then replied to Baxter in *Some Short Reflections upon Mr. Baxter's Book* (1675). I am indebted to Dr. Geoffrey F. Nuttall for assistance in sorting out this controversy.

of quality—perhaps Danvers himself—which reflects disappointment
at the rancor that characterized the debate:

> When I first read your *treatise of baptism*, I hoped it would have occasioned a
> serious, and full disquisition of that point. But whether, thro' the unhappy
> temper of your opponents, or what else I know not, I have been hitherto dis-
> appointed in my expectation; meeting in their writings with more of heat,
> passion and personal reflections, than of reason, or a sober inquisition after
> truth.

The author was particularly discouraged by the amount of rancor and
malice in the contribution to the debate by Baxter, who "hath had so
great a name for religion and piety."[23]

In the midst of this controversy over baptism, Danvers wrote *A
Treatise of Laying on of Hands* (1674), in which that traditional practice—
now common among the General Baptists—was repudiated as unscriptural. Danvers, who had become a Particular Baptist sometime
after the Restoration, treated the same subject in an appendix to the
second edition of his *Treatise of Baptism*. Here he accused Francis Corn-
well of introducing this practice by insisting on the laying on of hands
when he joined the General Baptist church at White's Alley, Spitalfields, as far back as 1646. Danvers's *Treatise of Laying on of Hands* was
attacked by Benjamin Keach, a London Baptist, in *Laying on of Hands
upon Baptized Believers, as Such, Proved an Ordinance of Christ* (1698).

When the government next noticed Danvers on 27 November
1675, there was some surprise that "a person of his quality and estate"
was preaching on foot throughout the country. At last the authorities
arrested him as he was leaving a conventicle near Aldgate. A contemporary newsletter reported: "Besides his having all along been known
to be disaffected, he was some seven years since ordered to be sent to
the Tower for threatening the Duke of Albemarle, but on the way he
was rescued, and the proclamation against him has until now been ineffectual. Now a fresh information is brought against him. . . ." A warrant of 16 January 1676 directed that he be committed to the Tower
for treason, but he was there only briefly. When his health deterio-
rated the state issued a warrant for his discharge on 28 April 1676, on

---

[23]The letter is reprinted in Crosby, 3:95-96.

payment of £1000 security. According to the Baptist historian Thomas Crosby, his release was due both to the lack of evidence against him and to the influence of his wife with powerful friends at court. He was confined to his house. Apparently undaunted, Danvers was reportedly involved the following year in a fresh plot to assassinate Charles, his brother, and William of Orange, and possibly bring back Richard Cromwell as titular head of state. In addition to Danvers this plot involved William Smith, a crony of Blood (who was now an informant), and the son of the Baptist regicide Daniel Axtel.[24]

No later than 1679 Danvers moved closer to the Whig mainstream and even managed the parliamentary election of Algernon Sidney that year. As the government was increasingly preoccupied with the exclusion controversy, Danvers grew bolder in his pulpit appearances. In December 1681 he was reported ministering to a London conventicle, and by the following year he had a congregation of some six to seven hundred in the City, with a ministerial staff of seven. According to an informant, these people were of the "[Fifth] monerkey Judmentt." They met in the Houndsditch area, near Aldgate. Against the background of the revelations about the Popish Plot, Titus and Samuel Oates visited Danvers at Stoke Newington in January 1682. Danvers made known to them his conviction that those who lost lands at the Restoration must have them restored. Throughout the year he plotted incessantly with this in mind, scheming with members of the Green Ribbon Club, former associates of Blood, and the Fifth Monarchist Walter Thimbleton. In August he huddled with Titus Oates and two shadowy radicals, Radden—associated with Blood in 1666—and Spurway, and the following month there was a report that Baptist bookseller Francis Smith was part of this group. They contemplated kidnapping and possibly executing the king, the Duke of York, and Privy Councillors, thereby encouraging the Duke of Monmouth and the Earl of Shaftesbury to topple the ruling order. These meetings continued in the autumn and spring, and at some point in this period may have merged with the schemes of the Rye House plotters. In any case Danvers was suspected of complicity in that plot, which was un-

---

[24]*CSPD*, 1675-76, 419, 516; *CSPD*, 1676-77, 90; *CSPD*, 1678, 290-91, 299-300; Crosby, 3:97; HMC 19, *Townshend*, 43-44; HMC 25, *LeFleming*, 124 (quoted); Capp, *FMM*, 218-19.

covered on 12 June 1683. Two weeks later Danvers was reportedly associating with the Baptist bookseller John Darby, and at the end of
July there were fears that he, Spurway, and a man named Alexander
were conniving to have Shaftesbury or Monmouth kidnap the king
and force him to sign an Exclusion Bill.[25]

On 16 September 1684 the Privy Council decided to interrogate
Danvers, but when the Councillors learned the following day that his
whereabouts were unknown they opted not to press the search. They
did discover, however, that Danvers had been seen at Algernon Sidney's house. They must have regretted not pursuing the search when
they read Danvers's newest publication in December, *Murther Will
Out*, in which he charged that the imprisoned Earl of Essex did not
commit suicide but was murdered. Regarding this as seditious libel,
the government issued a warrant for his arrest on 30 December for
treasonous activity, and a reward of £100 was posted. Additional warrants were issued on 20 and 26 January, 8 February, and 4 July, in
which he was still listed as residing at Stoke Newington.[26]

The culmination of Danvers's career of scheming came in 1685.
When it became apparent that the Duke of York would succeed
Charles II, Danvers planned an insurrection in London on the day of
the coronation, relying on some five hundred men from Essex and
Hertfordshire who would enter the City under the guise of celebrating
the event. These plans, however, were set aside when he was informed
of the Duke of Monmouth's intention to raise the English. Pledging
his loyalty to Monmouth before the latter's invasion of England, Danvers assured him that "it wou'd be of more Advantage and Importance
to him [to proclaim himself king], than twenty Thousand Men." Yet
the inveterate plotter Robert Ferguson was so suspicious of Danvers's
resolve that he warned one of Monmouth's officers, the sometime
Fifth Monarchist Captain Robert Perrott, that Danvers was unreliable
and cowardly. Monmouth, however, determined to leave the City in

---

[25]M. Dorothy George, "Elections and Electioneering, 1679-81," *EHR* 45 (1930):
565; *BQ*, 1:82, 85-86; Wilson, *HADC*, 1:392-93; *CSPD*, *1680-81*, 613; *CSPD*, *1682*,
237, 358, 405, 495; *CSPD*, *1683 (I)*, 346; *CSPD*, *1683 (II)*, 216; Capp, *FMM*, 82,
220-21.

[26]*CSPD*, *1681-85*, 145, 148, 268, 292; *CSPD*, *1685*, 5, 246; Narcissus Luttrell, *A
Brief Relation of State Affairs*, 6 vols. (Oxford, 1857) 1:324.

the care of Danvers and Thimbleton. In many respects conditions were propitious for Danvers, particularly since many of the troops loyal to James had already marched westward. After Monmouth's landing, Danvers sent word to him that preparations had been made in the City and that he awaited instructions to seize control; but with several thousand men ready to rise, Danvers never acted. According to the famous explanation of Thomas B. Macaulay, "the craven Danvers at first excused his inaction by saying that he would not take up arms till Monmouth was proclaimed King, and when proclaimed King, turned round and declared that good republicans were absolved from all engagements to a leader who had so shamefully broken faith." Macaulay, however, based his judgment on sources strongly biased against Danvers, and it is now reasonably clear that Danvers refused to move until he was certain that Monmouth could break through the king's western defenses and that Cheshire would rise. After the rebellion was suppressed, the government on 27 July gave Danvers twenty days to surrender, but he escaped to the Netherlands. For Danvers and probably most of those who rose in 1685, this was the last blow struck on behalf of the Good Old Cause. Three years later the Glorious Revolution was largely cut of another cloth.[27]

In the Netherlands Danvers must have spent his final years in consternation about the government of James II, but he also had economic interests abroad. He was a major investor in a scheme to employ exiles, many of whom were west country folk experienced in cloth manufacture. With Monmouth's associate Joseph Hilliard and others he was responsible for establishing an English center for the manufacture of cloth at Leewarden in Friesland, and a comparable effort got underway at Luneberg. Danvers did not live to see the Glorious Revolution, which in any case would probably have been too conservative for him to sanction. He probably died late in 1687, for on 2 March 1688 it was noted that he had "died lately" at Utrecht, still outlawed for treason. The pastorship of his church was taken up by Edward Man in 1687.[28]

---

[27]Laurence Echard, *The History of England*, 3 vols. (3rd ed., London, 1720) 1064; T. B. Macaulay, *The History of England*, 5 vols. (New York, 1902) 1:422, 459; C. C. Tench, *The Western Rising* (London, 1969) 88, 148; Capp, *FMM*, 221; Luttrell, *A Brief Relation*, 1:355.

[28]Peter Earle, *Monmouth's Rebels* (New York, 1977) 157, 159; Luttrell, *A Brief Relation*, 1:432; Wilson, *HADC*, 1:396.

Macaulay's assessment that Danvers was "hotheaded, but faint-hearted, constantly urged to the brink of danger by enthusiasm, and constantly stopped on that brink by cowardice," a demagogue and a vile specimen of human nature, is surely too extreme.[29] Danvers was a man captured by his millenarian vision and convinced that the long-awaited thousand years would come only when the saints ushered them in by establishing a godly society. Essentially he was a republican in his political ideology, though he seems to have been willing to tolerate a godly figurehead as a token monarch. His reluctance to raise London for Monmouth may have been due not only to fears that the duke could not pierce the king's western defenses and that Cheshire would not rise, but also to correct suspicions that Monmouth had no intention of governing as a mere puppet of religious sectaries.

Monmouth could never have accepted Danvers's concept of a state governed in accordance with the principles of Mosaic law, with magistrates selected by lot. Danvers did not stop on the brink because of cowardice, but because realistically it was evident that effective action to implement his radical ideology was a wild fantasy. Yet he schemed on. At most Danvers and the men like him who hatched such machinations as the Rathbone and Rye House Plots might have succeeded in assassinating Charles II, the Duke of York, and other notables, but they could never have acquired the political power for the Good Old Cause that perished forever in 1659.

In his better moments Danvers worked with the Exclusionists in an endeavor that at least had some hope of success as well as aims to which many Englishmen could subscribe. Danvers is historically significant in providing a clear contact between Algernon Sidney and the Green Ribbon Club on the one hand and the shadowy world of radical revolutionaries on the other. The government's repeated inability to lay its hands on him and his open preaching to hundreds in London in 1682 are a curious comment on the effectiveness of Stuart rule. Above all, Danvers amply illustrates the extent to which some Nonconformists went in their hostility to Stuart rule as well as the consistency of their espousal of radical ideology.

---

[29]Macaulay, *History of England*, 1:408, 459.

DANVERS'S TIES WITH THE HARTOPPS AND FLEETWOODS

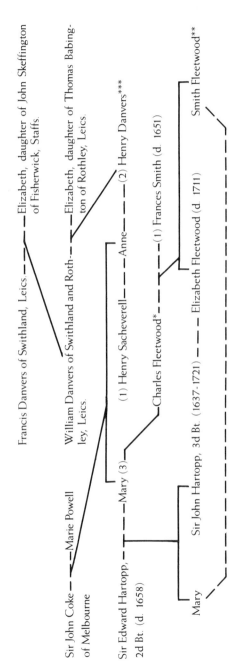

* Fleetwood's second wife was Oliver Cromwell's daughter Bridget (d. 1662), widow of John Ireton (d. 1651).

** In 1666 there was a double wedding of Smith Fleetwood and Mary Hartopp, and Sir John Hartopp and Elizabeth Fleetwood.

*** Danvers's family traces its lineage back to Robert Walleis of Swithland, knight (1270) whose great-granddaughter Margaret wed John Danvers of Shakerston, great-grandson of the earliest known Danvers, Thomas. *The Visitation of the County of Leicester in the Year 1619*, ed. John Fetherston (Harleian Society Publications, vol. 2, 1870) 86-87.

The above chart is intended only to illustrate family links, not to provide a complete genealogy.

chapter 7

"Making the Laws of Christ His Only Rule": Francis Bampfield, Sabbatarian Reformer

Alone among the seven men in this volume, Francis Bampfield was a committed Royalist during the Civil War. In sharp contrast to Henry Danvers and Paul Hobson, he never espoused radical political views, though he too was imprisoned by the Restoration government for his nonconformity. His religious life was a perfect illustration of the classical spiritual pilgrimage, which ranged in his case from fidelity to Anglican principles all the way to the advocacy of Seventh-Day Baptist tenets. Like a number of Fifth Monarchists, Bampfield was attracted to the Saturday sabbath, but he did not share their political ideology. Indeed, his advocacy of sabbatarianism was an outgrowth of his approach to Scripture as the source of all knowledge as well as the boundary and foundation of religious experience. Bampfield is particularly interesting because his biblical studies became the inspiration for a broad-ranging program of reform, the heart of which was educational reform based on a meticulous study of Scripture as the all-encompassing text. In it he believed he found the source of all knowledge, the application of which would extend the frontiers of learning.

In the words of the Nonconformist historian Edmund Calamy, the Bampfields were "an ancient and honourable family" from Devonshire. Born in Devon about 1614-1615, Francis was the third son of John Bampfield, esquire, of Poltimore, Devon, and Elizabeth, daughter of Thomas Drake of Buckland Monachorum. Francis's brother John was created a baronet in 1641 and his brother Thomas served as recorder of Exeter before sitting for that town in the Parliaments of 1654, 1656, and 1659. In the latter he was elected Speaker on 14 April. In the Convention Parliament he again sat for Exeter and is remembered for his motion (which the House dropped) asking the king to marry a Protestant. Francis and Thomas's nephew, Sir Coplestone Bampfield (1636-1691), Sir John's eldest son, actively supported the restoration of Charles II, sat for Tiverton in the Parliament of 1659 and for Devon from 1671 to 1679 and again in 1685. As a justice of the peace in Devon in 1681, he enforced the laws against the Dissenters but was nevertheless ejected from the commission of the peace in James II's reign.[1]

Devoutly religious, Francis Bampfield's parents determined that he would be educated for a career in the church. He later recorded in his autobiography that he never considered another vocation. Educated initially "in the Families of Professors of Religion" and subsequently in a grammar school, he developed a deep love for books as well as a flair for Hebrew. About the age of seventeen he left for Oxford where he became a commoner at Wadham College in 1631, matriculating on 16 May 1634 and graduating B.A. on 4 July 1635. He proceeded M.A. in 1638. Much later he looked back on these years with pronounced bitterness. He had gone to Oxford, he recalled, to acquire a knowledge in the arts and sciences "in that corrupt unscriptural way and manner as then it was, and still is . . . ," but despite his degrees he complained that he obtained little "Scripture-Learning." In retrospect he looked on his years at Oxford as "void space," devoted to the study of pagan philosophy: "The hurt that has been done to my own soul, and the scars that are visibly upon me, by my ill-chosen studies, and misemployed hours heretofore, though in a way of some diligence, do stir up some compassions in me towards others, to indeavour the pre-

---

[1]Calamy, *Non. Mem.*, 2: 149; *DNB*, s.v. Thomas Bampfield; Whitelocke, 4: 342; *DNB*, s.v., Sir Coplestone Bampfield.

venting or curing of the like spreading distemper in their understandings. . . ." That was written in 1677. Four years later he reflected sadly that at Oxford he had enjoyed jesting about Nonconformists. In contrast to Thomas Hobbes's belief that the universities were nurseries of sedition, Bampfield complained bitterly that the "University-Wits had somewhat tainted and sowred him with a bad Ferment, that he was somewhat swoln and prejudiced against the strict Profession of Religion amongst the *Puritan* Party. . . ." Only the religious training he received as a boy, he recalled, preserved his admiration for a holy life.[2]

Bampfield was ordained a deacon by Joseph Hall, Bishop of Exeter, and a presbyter by Robert Skinner, Bishop of Bristol. On 25 July 1639 (or possibly 1640) he was presented to the living at Rampisham in western Dorset. As rector he received tithes worth nearly £100 p.a., which he used to maintain hospitality, relieve the indigent, provide jobs for the unemployed, and purchase Bibles. One of his goals while at Rampisham was not knowingly to allow anyone to beg. Before he left this parish he spent approximately £300 building a new manse. Financially he was able to do this in addition to his active charity because his own needs were met by an annuity of £80 p.a. provided by his father.[3]

Bampfield was collated to a prebendary in Exeter Cathedral on 15 May 1641. A zealous supporter of the king, he doubted whether in good conscience he could pay taxes imposed by Parliament, concerning which he consulted with Dr. Gilbert Ironside, the future Bishop of Bristol. Out of loyalty to Charles I, on 23 May 1645 he brought a horse and arms to the royalist forces at Berry Pomeroy, near Totnes in Devon. Notwithstanding this fact, his father, with the approval of the Dorset Committee, was able to present him to the rectory at Wraxall on 19 January 1647. Bampfield remained loyal to the traditional practices of the Church of England, being the last minister in Dorset to use the Book of Common Prayer in public worship. For his persever-

---

[2]Francis Bampfield, שם אחר. *A Name, an After-one* (London, 1681) 2-3, 36; *Al. Oxon.*, 1:64; *Ath. Oxon.*, 4:126; *Fasti Oxon.*, 1:478, 501 (which gives the date for the M.A. as 7 April 1638, whereas *Al. Oxon.* gives 7 July 1638).

[3]Bampfield, *A Name*, 2, 6, 21; *Calamy Revised, s.v.* The date of presentation to the Rampisham living is given as 1630 in *Al. Oxon.*, 1:64, and 1641 in the *DNB*.

ance he was finally interrupted during a worship service by Round-head troops. According to Richard Baxter, writing as late as 1673, Bampfield and his brother John were "so much against the Parliament's Cause, that to this day, even while he lay in Jail, he most zealously made his followers renounce it." Calamy, however, subsequently claimed that Baxter persuaded Bampfield to endorse the parliamentary cause and take the Engagement in 1653, though Bampfield was opposed to the institution of the Protectorate. In this instance Calamy must have been in error, for Bampfield himself asserted that he never took the Engagement.[4]

The living at Wraxall was a modest one. According to Bampfield, "the small Tithes belonging to the Vicarage were so inconsiderable, that when one whole years Profits were given to the King upon the Benevolence-Act, the Man who was to gather the Profits for the King, had at the years end laid out about five shillings more for decimation and in collecting than he had received. . . ." Bampfield spent the tithes he received at Wraxall as well as his £80 annuity on parish needs, reserving only those funds necessary for the purchase of books and comparable expenses. He even provided £30 to the parish as an augmentation for an assistant.[5]

At this stage of his career Bampfield became convinced of the necessity for further reform in the areas of doctrine, liturgy, and discipline, but his efforts to accomplish these ends, "making the laws of Christ his only rule," led to considerable hostility among the parishioners. His efforts included evening meetings to deal with cases of conscience, which may have been recorded in the "diverse little Books of Diaries of his own Experience." These, however, seem not to have survived. Following the death of William Lyford, Vicar of Sherborne, Dorset, Bampfield was invited by the parishioners to accept the living, but he procrastinated for several years. Not until 28 April 1657 was he formally admitted to this benefice. He was finally persuaded to make the move by the opposition at Wraxall to his attempts to impose

---

[4]*The Minute Books of the Dorset Standing Committee, 23rd Sept., 1646, to 8th May, 1650,* ed. C. H. Mayo (Exeter, 1902) 138; Bampfield, *A Name,* 2; *Ath. Oxon.,* 4: 126; HMC 43, *Fifteenth Report,* Appendix, pt. 7: 85; *Rel. Bax.,* pt. 3: 150; Calamy, *Non. Mem.,* 2: 150, 153; Crosby, 1: 365; Bampfield, *A Just Appeal from the Lower Courts* (London, 1683) 8.

[5]Bampfield, *A Name,* 21.

SAINTS AND REBELS / 183

more effective ecclesiastical discipline. It was probably about this time that others, working on his behalf but not at his instigation, obtained the approval of the Triers for his ministry. Never, however, did he appear before them.[6]

In recounting his spiritual autobiography Bampfield provides no chronological framework for his experience of conversion, but it plausibly may be dated in the late 1650s, probably commencing while he was at Wraxall. Although Bampfield's account is considerably briefer than John Bunyan's *Grace Abounding to the Chief of Sinners* (1666), there are various parallels between the two works, as there are with other versions of this genre from the same period.[7] Like Bunyan, Bampfield was notably influenced by the Apostle Paul, even to the point of structuring his autobiography into parallel sections in which his own life was compared to Paul's. Again like Bunyan, Bampfield recorded that the Holy Spirit worked on him by alternatively terrifying him and then offering divine love. As in Bunyan's experience, Bampfield "lay for many years under a spirit of bondage to Fear, being very often frighted in terrible Dreams, wherein he fell into deep Waters, the Earth sliding away from under him, whilst he endeavoured to climb up to the top of an Hill or Rock for safety, which he was not able to do, falling over Bridges into the Sea, and down from thence into the Gulph and horrible Pit. . . ." The Devil, he asserted, was often at hand, though he escaped Satan's efforts to trap him. From these dreams Bampfield awoke in a cold sweat. For several years these visions kept him in awe and out of sin. Once when he was contemplating evil acts, a powerful voice from heaven struck him like a bolt of thunder: "What if God should strike thee dead and damned upon the place?" The experience motivated Bampfield to go to his chamber, pray, read Scripture, and confess his sins. Bunyan had a similar occurrence while he was playing a game of cat.[8]

---

[6]Calamy, *Non. Mem.*, 2: 149 (quoted); Bampfield, *A Name*, 6 (quoted); *Calamy Revised, s.v.* The date for admission to the Sherborne living is given as 1653 in *Al. Oxon.*, 1:64, and as 1655 in Wilson, *HADC*, 2:587.

[7]See William York Tindall, *John Bunyan, Mechanick Preacher* (New York, 1934) ch. 2.

[8]Bampfield, *A Name*, 3; John Bunyan, *Grace Abounding to the Chief of Sinners*, ed. Roger Sharrock (Oxford, 1962) § 22, p. 10.

Bampfield's religious experience had a touch of the mystical, though like Bunyan's it was grounded in Scripture. As he read the gospels he experienced "sweet Allurings," but yet the tears flowed. He credited the Bible with being the key to his spiritual experience, the essence of which was a personal immediacy with God. He regarded himself as "his own Spiritual Father; . . . he was his own Converter, begotten and born by that Word which he preached to others." In his early career Bunyan too had been spiritually moved as he preached the gospel message to others. As Bampfield was inquiring on one occasion into his spiritual estate, he received a revelation telling him to burn all of his papers, including those containing extracts from other authors, for so much of "Philosophical Learning" was corrupt. The same revelation commanded him to begin religion afresh and obtain everything from Christ and Scripture. This, he was promised, would enable him to be better educated, and nothing of value from his earlier studies would be lost. From 2 Timothy 3:16 he learned that "he must take the whole Scripture along with him, both Old and New Testament to be for him. . . ." The significance attached to the Old Testament subsequently provided him with the foundation for his sabbatarian tenets. He burned his papers and thereafter believed that he received special teachings from the Holy Spirit virtually every week. This he perceived to be the foundation of his ministry: "He ascribes nothing of the Spirituallity of it to his own former Philosophick Studies or self Acquirements or human Instructing, but, it was divine Teaching, and Gifted infusing from Heaven. . . ."[9]   •

According to Bampfield, his call to Sherborne came from thousands in the town itself and "Multitudes" from the surrounding countryside. That choice was made only after a day of fasting. Difficulties arose over his departure from Wraxall, which led to a delay of approximately two years. The case required the arbitration of Presbyterian ministers from other counties as well as the support of both Presbyterian and Independent clergymen in Dorset. When he was at last admitted to the living there was another fast day, which included a service of worship conducted jointly by a Presbyterian and an Independent minister (neither of whom he identified). Some two thou-

---

[9]Bampfield, A Name, 3-4, 8.

sand persons reportedly were present. It was, said Bampfield, "as solemn an Entrance into the taking charge of the People of that Town, as any Pastor that he has heard of in that age. . . ."[10]

According to the historian Edmund Calamy, Bampfield's ministry at Sherborne met with great success, although he did experience difficulty with the Quakers. Anthony Wood's allegation that the people of Sherborne were factious is probably a reference to the parishioners at Wraxall. Bampfield's assistant at Sherborne was Humphrey Philips, who at one time was a chaplain and tutor in the house of Bampfield's father at Poltimore. Philips too was a graduate of Wadham College, Oxford (B.A., 1654; M.A., 1656).[11]

Bampfield apparently played no role in the events of the Restoration. In contrast, his brother Thomas was concerned with the religious settlement and wrote in this regard to Baxter on 26 March 1660, shortly before the Convention Parliament met. In particular Bampfield wanted to know "whether it were not fit by a law declarative to assert the authority of the Scriptures as to doctrine, discipline, and worship in the Church, as to all laws and their execution in the State . . . and, as to private men, their authority and completeness for faith and manners, and to declare all laws contrary to the Scriptures to be void?" Baxter responded on 4 April, affirming the validity of such a law, but despairing that one would be passed in the current political climate. He did, however, send Bampfield the draft of a declaration on religion. [12]

Bampfield continued to minister at Sherborne in 1660, and in addition was restored to his prebend at Exeter Cathedral, from which Parliament had earlier deprived him. Philips, who had left Sherborne to resume his fellowship at Magdalen College, Oxford, was ejected from there in 1660 and returned to assist Bampfield. About 1661 the latter was stricken with an unspecified illness for which the best medical care was ineffectual. When Bampfield turned to the "Ordinance of Anointing the Sick" mentioned in James 5, the local ministers were

---

[10]Ibid., 6-7; Calamy, *Non. Mem.*, 2: 149.

[11]*Ath. Oxon.*, 4: 126; *Calamy Revised, s.v.* Humphrey Philips.

[12]Richard Schlatter, ed., *Richard Baxter & Puritan Politics* (New Brunswick NJ, 1957) 139-45.

critical. Bampfield persisted, however, claiming that a "secret Voice" commanded him to anoint himself after the local pastors had refused to do so. To this anointing he credited his recovery. Trouble loomed on the horizon, however, and the Sunday prior to St. Bartholomew's Day, 1662, he preached his farewell sermon to a "sorrowful congregation." Both he and Philips were ejected from Sherborne, and Bampfield lost his prebend at Exeter Cathedral as well. There was no thought of conformity, for to Bampfield the Book of Common Prayer was an "unclean Constitution of humanely invented Worship. . . ."[13]

On 19 September 1662 Bampfield conducted a worship service in his house for his family and a few neighbors, preaching on 1 Thessalonians 5:6-7. Soldiers interrupted the service, producing a warrant with the names of Bampfield, Philips, and ten others. The two pastors and some twenty-five of their followers were taken to the provost marshal's house and detained for five days—the ministers in one room and the rest in another, which had only one bed. On Saturday evening the entire group was allowed to meet together, but while they were praying the soldiers broke in, called Bampfield a rogue, and "at length . . . laid hands upon him, and forced the rest of the prisoners away." The following day Bampfield received permission to preach to the prisoners, but chaos ensued. Interested townsfolk bribed soldiers to gain entry to the house, only to be expelled. When the owner's wife allowed others to go into the rear yard, her husband threatened them with writs of trespass. As Philips conducted a service that evening, soldiers entered the house and stopped it.[14]

During this brief incarceration friends of the prisoners attempted to bring them food, but the soldiers sometimes seized and "made merry with it." Resourceful visitors smuggled meat to the inmates in their hats. Some visitors were themselves locked up, others thrown down the stairs, and one poor woman was raped by the soldiers. On the following Wednesday, Bampfield and Philips were summoned to appear before four or five deputy lieutenants. Bampfield admitted to

---

[13]Calamy, Cont., 411; Wilson, HADC, 2:587; Calamy Revised, s.v. Humphrey Philips; Bampfield, A Name, 4, 10; Calamy, Non. Mem., 2:149; A. G. Matthews, Walker Revised (Oxford, 1948) 7.

[14]Calamy, Non. Mem., 2:150-51; [Edward Pearse], The Conformist's Fourth Plea for the Nonconformists (London, 1683) 44-45.

conducting an illegal service, but no charges of sedition were made. The men were released after providing sureties and promising to appear at the next assizes.[15]

After their release Bampfield and Philips went to Thomas Bampfield's house at Dunkerton, near Bath, where their preaching began to attract people. Bampfield, however, was arrested again on 23 July 1663 for illegally preaching at Shaftesbury, Dorset, with John Westley, the ejected Vicar of Winterborne Whitchurch, Dorset. Among those imprisoned with them for the same offense were Peter Ince, the ejected Rector of Donhead St. Mary, Wiltshire; Thomas Hallet, the ejected Rector of St. Peter's, Shaftesbury; Josiah Banger, the ejected Vicar of Broadhembury, Devon; and John Sacheverell, the ejected Curate of Wincanton, Somerset. Tried before Judge Archer on the western circuit, each was fined forty marks, but this was reduced to twenty marks and compounded for at a shilling in the pound. Although Westley was released after three months, the others were still in the Dorchester jail a year and a half later when arrangements were made for their freedom on condition that they post bond for good behavior. This, however, Bampfield refused to do, insisting that he "would not be on his good Behaviour (in the Sense of the Law) so much as for an Hour; thinking it would amount to an Acknowledgment of Guilt." Ince and Sacheverell were at first inclined to stand with Bampfield, but friends, Ince's wife, and Bampfield himself persuaded them to post bond. Bampfield told them "that it would add to his Trouble, for them to continue still in Hold, when it was only out of a Deference to him and his Judgment."[16]

While Bampfield remained in the Dorchester jail, his fellow prisoners returned to their preaching as well as to further troubles with the law. Westley was imprisoned three more times, once at Poole, Dorset, for six months. Ince appeared before the Wiltshire Assizes in the autumn of 1665 and at the quarter sessions in June 1676, while Hallet was summoned before the Dorset Assizes in the winter of 1665.

---

[15][Pearse], *Fourth Plea*, 46; Calamy, *Non. Mem.*, 2: 151.

[16]PRO SP 29/98/153; Calamy, *Non. Mem.*, 2: 153-54; *Calamy Revised, s.v.*, John Westley, Peter Ince (quoted), Thomas Hallet, Josiah Banger, John Sacheverell; *BDBR, s.v.* John Westley.

Banger was imprisoned at Exeter in 1669 and later at Ilchester, Somerset. Only Sacheverell escaped further trouble because of his death shortly after his release from Dorchester. Philips appeared before the Dorset Assizes in the winter of 1663, but posted a bond for £40 and had sureties of £20 each from Francis and Thomas Bampfield. Thereafter he served as the latter's chaplain until he was imprisoned at Ilchester for eleven months, following which he visited the Netherlands. Upon his return he preached in Somerset and Wiltshire, for which he was fined and harassed by authorities.[17]

For nearly nine years Bampfield remained in jail, where he organized his own congregation. In the latter part of his incarceration he was preaching as often as sixteen times a week. According to Baxter, Bampfield and other imprisoned clergy preached to visitors from the town once each weekday and twice on Sunday, "till at last the Jaylor was corrected, and an Order made against Jaylors letting in People into the Prisons to hear." During his imprisonment Bampfield refused monetary assistance, preferring to live on his annuity. He petitioned Charles II, possibly in June 1664, disputing the claim that he could not be peaceful if he were released. In addition to abhorring sedition and insurrection, he reminded the king that he had not been "turbulent" during the Civil Wars and that he did not oppose lawful authority. On the other hand he reaffirmed his willingness to be imprisoned for preaching the gospel, particularly inasmuch as he believed that worse punishment would be divinely imposed if he did not preach. He concluded by asking Charles to study Scripture and make it the rule of his kingdom, for "no man has so many prayers, favours, and deliverances, or has so many obligations and advantages for doing good." A warrant dated 13 June 1664 directed that Bampfield be delivered by the Sheriff of Dorset to the commanding officer at Windsor Castle. Whether and for how long the transfer was effected is unclear. The same year the will of George Long (d. Jan. 1665), the ejected Vicar of Bath, designated Francis and Thomas Bampfield as overseers.[18]

---

[17]*Calamy Revised, s.vv.*

[18]Bampfield, *A Name*, 21; *Rel. Bax.*, pt. 1:432; *CSPD*, 1663-64, 612 (quoted); *Calamy Revised, s.v.* George Long.

Bampfield's long imprisonment deepened his spiritual experience, as it had done for Bunyan. As a prisoner Bampfield claimed that he was spiritually comforted and rewarded with "Covenant favours" and that he received "spirit-illuminations." According to his reckoning, about 1664 he discovered that all ministers in the Bible knew the special language of Scripture. Although he already had some knowledge of Greek and Hebrew, he now desired more skill in "the inner knowledg[e] of the *Hebrew* Significations by the Holy Spirits Teachings . . . ," a quest that continued for the rest of his life.[19]

About 1667 Bampfield began having visions in prison. Once, while he was praying on a dark evening, he seemed to be caught up to the heavens where he enjoyed "a clear view of *Christ* in his Glorified Humanity by an Eye of Faith." He compared this experience to that of Paul recorded in 2 Corinthians 12:1-4. In another vision he had "a Self-evidencing view of those Glorious Appearances of Father, Son, and holy Spirit, and distinctness of Communion with each of these in their several subsistences, shining forth in the Face of *Jesus*." According to Bampfield, "this sight covered his Spirit with such a shining Light and bright Glory, that, their faces viewing him, was such an heavenly Manifestation of unveiled Aspects, as dwells with him to this hour. . . ." To Bampfield this amounted to the baptism of the Holy Spirit, a concept that was especially significant to religious radicals in the Stuart age. As a consequence of this vision, he claimed that he was "raised . . . into an higher way of Later-Day-Glory-hymnifying, than his former way of singing by Mens Forms, read out of a Book, could reach unto." Throughout these experiences there is again something of a mystical bent. This is perhaps most evident when Bampfield speaks of his body, soul, and spirit being married to "each of these Three in One *Jehovah*. . . ."[20]

During his long imprisonment Bampfield adopted sabbatarian tenets, a change he dated about 1665. Six or seven years earlier a woman had asked him which day was the proper one for Christian worship, and on that occasion his response was, as he later felt, "a very faint unsatisfactory" one. Now he received two letters posing the same

---

[19]Bampfield, *The Lords Free Prisoner* (London, 1683) 1; *A Name*, 8.

[20]Bampfield, *A Name*, 4, 41.

question from a friend in the country. After a careful examination of pertinent biblical passages, Bampfield became convinced that the Saturday sabbath was mandated by both Scripture and nature (God's rest on the seventh day). At first he began to observe the Saturday sabbath in private, afraid of the furor that would result from an open proclamation of his new belief. But after winning four or five converts in individual discussions with his fellow prisoners, he made his convictions public. When two ministers failed to dissuade him, he conducted his first church service on a Saturday.[21]

One of the ministers who visited Bampfield in prison to try to change his mind about the Saturday sabbath was probably William Benn, the ejected Rector of All Hallows, Dorchester. When Bampfield provided Benn with his reasons for the Saturday sabbath, the latter requested additional biblical corroboration. The essence of Bampfield's position was that "the Seventh day, which is the last day in every Week in the weekly returns of it, is alone that particular, peculiar day in every week, which is the weekly Sabbath day, to be kept holy to Jehova, in obedience to his Command as such, Exod. 20. 8, 9. Deut. 5. 12, 15." Bampfield went on to argue that God himself rested on the seventh day, and that he blessed no day but Saturday as the sabbath. The only biblical commands for sabbath worship, Bampfield insisted, refer to Saturday. Moreover, the law of the sabbath predates the Mosaic law, and Christ himself observed the Saturday sabbath. "And the light of Nature, when cleared up, will tell men, That all labour and motion being in order to rest, and rest being the perfection and end of labour, into which labour, work, and motion doth pass, that therefore the Seventh, which is the last day in every Week, is the fittest and properest day for a religious Rest unto the Creator, for his Worship and Service. . . ."[22]

Benn issued Bampfield's letter and his own response under the title, *The Judgment of Mr. Francis Bampfield, Late Minister of Sherborne in Dorsetshire for the Observation of the Jewish, or Seventh Day Sabboth* (London, 1672). Published originally for Joseph Nevill, it was reissued by Sarah

---

[21] Ibid., 12-14.

[22] Bampfield, in *The Judgment of Mr. Francis Bampfield*, ed. William Benn (London, 1672) 3ʳ-8ʳ (4ʳ⁻ᵛ, 7ʳ⁻ᵛ quoted).

Nevill in 1677. In his short preface Benn accused Bampfield and his friends of being abettors of "the *Jewish* Sect." According to Benn the fourth commandment mandates only the observation of one day in seven on which to worship God; Saturday is not specified. Sunday, however, was the day on which God rested from his greatest work— redemption—as reflected by the resurrection of Christ. Moreover, as mediator Christ had the authority to change the day of worship from Saturday to Sunday, which in fact was done. Bampfield was also attacked for his sabbatarian views by Baxter in *The Divine Appointment of the Lord's Day* (1671). According to Calamy, Bampfield was one of the most admired preachers in western England before he adopted his sabbatarian position. [23]

A warrant for the release of Bampfield, the tanner John Leach, and Joshua Brooke—all arrested for illegal assembly at Shaftesbury in 1663—was issued to Thomas Moore, High Sheriff of Dorset, on 17 May 1672. [24] According to the warrant others had compounded for their fines. Bampfield received the thanks of his prison congregation as they celebrated a fast day prior to his release. On 29 June the government issued him a license to preach under the terms of the Declaration of Indulgence. By order of Lord Clifford, his denomination was listed simply as "a Nonconforming Minister" and the place of his preaching as "general." Clifford probably intervened on Bampfield's behalf in the hope of building stronger political ties with his brothers, one of whom was a baronet and the other the recorder of Exeter. [25]

While imprisoned at Dorchester Bampfield met Damaris Town, whom he called Gnezri-jah. She served as "a common Stewardess and Nurse, to make and bring in Provision of Food, and of other outward Necessaries" for the prisoners. Although she had an elderly mother to support, she dieted and skimped in order to assist imprisoned Non-

---

[23] *The Term Catalogues, 1668-1709 A.D.*, ed. Edward Arber (London, 1903) 1: 197, 269; Benn, *The Judgment*, sig. A2ʳ (quoted), 41-42, 53, 58-59, 61-69; Calamy, *Cont.*, 411.

[24] *CSPD, 1671-72*, 597. The date of release is erroneously cited as 1675 in the *DNB*; Wilson, *HADC*, 2: 588; Crosby, 2: 356; Calamy, *Non. Mem.*, 2: 151.

[25] Bampfield, *A Name*, 7; *CSPD, 1672*, 292; Thomas Richards, *Wales Under the Indulgence (1672-1675)* (London, 1928) 54-55, 110.

conformists. After Bampfield's release he took her on his preaching itineraries as an assistant, finally marrying her on 23 September 1673 in order to prevent a scandal. He was subjected to a barrage of criticism, even by his friends, for marrying beneath his social station. The condemnation actually destroyed the effectiveness of his ministry in some locales. Because of this hostility as well as the need to take a manuscript on the Saturday sabbath to a printer, he went to London. [26]

Bampfield was adamant in asserting his right to marry Damaris Town, though she lacked a dowry. Referring to Samuel Clarke's *Lives*, he cited the example of another imprisoned minister who eventually married the handmaid who assisted him. "As for a Portion, he prizeth Grace at a very low rate, who doth not really in a case of competition, esteem and prefer it above and beyond many Bags of Earthly Treasure. . . ." After all, he reminded his critics, he had no estate and thus no jointure to settle on her, but could bequeath her nothing more than his books and household items. Gnezri-jah's maternal grandfather, Mr. Slado, had been an early proponent of religious reform, had loaned £100 to the Puritan minister John White of Dorchester, and even had "dipped all his Children" at their baptism. After selling his estate in England he bought Irish lands and settled at Limerick, where he patronized lecturers in his home. Two of his daughters married ministers. Gnezri-jah's mother wed Mr. Town, a doctor of divinity who had preferments in Ireland worth £200 p.a. and seven or eight servants. For his zeal against popery, Catholics on one occasion tried to bury him alive. At the outbreak of the Irish Rebellion, Town lost his estate and fled to England, his family scattering into several counties. Bampfield, therefore, found his marriage to Damaris Town wholly justifiable. [27]

It was probably during his period of imprisonment at Dorchester (rather than a later period at Salisbury) that Bampfield and two others became convinced of the validity of believer's baptism. Because of the absence of suitable facilities, they could do no more in prison than resolve to undergo believer's baptism after their release. According to Bampfield's testimony he first tried to do this in London with another

---

[26]Bampfield, *A Name*, 22.

[27]Ibid., 23-24.

man and woman, perhaps his wife Gnezri-jah. The three rowed up the Thames to Battersea and there, on a Saturday morning, began to worship. Before they could baptize themselves in the Thames, they broke up, undoubtedly due to uncertainty over the correct procedure. Bampfield knew how John Smyth had once baptized himself but he was initially reluctant to adopt this method of self-baptism. After traveling to Salisbury, however, he baptized himself at noon in the Avon "as by the Hand of Christ himself . . .," following which he baptized an unnamed companion. [28]

It was probably on this occasion that he was imprisoned at Salisbury for eighteen weeks. To Bampfield this event had apocalyptic significance. According to Revelation 2:10, some of the saints were about to be thrown into prison for ten days, and Bampfield—thinking in terms of a biblical day equaling a year—interpreted this imprisonment as the end of his decade of tribulation. He was discharged without paying a fine. His apocalyptic interpretation suggests the date of this imprisonment as 1673, but he wrote a brief account of it (now lost) entitled *The Open Confessor, and the Free-Prisoner,* to which Crosby assigns a date of 1675. This "sheet," however, must have been written in 1673 or early 1674. [29]

From Salisbury Bampfield returned to London and preached to a group of the godly in his home at Bethnal Green. Dissatisfied with the existing churches, one of which was a Seventh-Day Baptist church under the ministry of John Belcher, these people prevailed upon Bampfield to organize a formal congregation. Baptizing them as believers, he celebrated the Lord's supper with them for the first time in 1674. "We passed," he wrote, "solemnly into a Gospel way of Church-state and Relation, and full Communion, founded on these two great Principles, owning, professing, of Jesus Christ, to be the one and the only Lord over our Consciences, and Law-giver to our Souls; and of the holy Scriptures of Truth, being our one, and our only Rule of Faith, Worship, and Life." The news that another sabbatarian church had been founded was carried to the "Sabbath

[28]Ibid., 14, 16-17.

[29]Bampfield, *The Lords Free Prisoner* (London, 1683) 1; Crosby, 1:368.

Churches" in Wiltshire, Hampshire, Dorset, Gloucestershire, and Berkshire by Bampfield himself.[30]

Early in 1676 Bampfield's congregation was rent by schism, forcing him to organize the remnants into a new church. On 5 March Bampfield and eight men of the new congregation affixed their names to a brief statement reiterating the principles of Christ's sole lordship and the Scripture as the only rule of faith and life. As before, Bampfield continued to live from his annuity, though he expected his followers to tithe. The resulting funds must have been used for charitable purposes. Bampfield had preached to the two other sabbatarian churches in the City, so that inevitably some of them continued to seek him out for spiritual counsel. A real dispute erupted when he admitted a female member of another congregation into his own church, forcing him to defend himself against charges that he was striving for supremacy and was not in harmony with gospel order. Bampfield did, however, try to live peacefully with kindred churches. This spirit is revealed in a letter from his church written on behalf of a member who was traveling in other areas. In it Bampfield asked other churches "that he [brother Warner] may be watched over and made a partaker of the privileges of Christ's house, testifying that he is a brother and faithful and desiring them to receive him . . . in the Lord." The adoption of sabbatarian tenets by Bampfield and his brother Thomas, whom he converted, did lead to a strained relationship with their old friend Humphrey Philips.[31]

In 1677 Bampfield published a major work in two large tomes, the first of which was entitled כל־תושיה. ΠΑΓΓΝΩΣΙΑ ΠΑΝΤΕΧ-ΝΙΑ ΠΑΝΣΟΦΙΑ. All in One. All Useful Sciences and Profitable Arts in One Book of Jehovah Aelohim . . . The First Part. His purpose in writing this treatise was "to hold forth all Sciences and profitable Arts in one Book

---

[30]W. T. Whitley, A History of British Baptists (London, 1923) 134; Bampfield, The Lords Free Prisoner, 1; A Name, 7.

[31]Bampfield, A Name, 21, 27-32, 37; TBHS 3:8-9; CSPD, 1676-77, 543 (quoted); Calamy, Non. Mem., 2:155; Calamy Revised, s.v. Humphrey Philips. In his will Philips stipulated: "My said son shall have all my manuscripts except such parts as contain the History of my life and such parts as my son-in-law shall think fit to publish for the good of the church excepting the part relating to Mr. Bampfield tho' the same be true." Cited in Calamy Revised, s.v. Philips.

of *Jehovah Ælohim*, and to demonstrate the Scripture-way to be the true, the right, the excelling, the only way of perfecting the knowledge of lawful Arts and Sciences, and of the Restauration, and advancement of real Learning. . . ." Bampfield envisioned his task as directing the godly to the Bible where they could attain a clear understanding of the most profound religious mysteries. There "a clear-eyed-Faith may satisfie it self with self-evidencing verities." For him the Bible was a perfect library containing both "saving Knowledge, and profitable Science," and thus contrasted sharply with traditional philosophy, "the vain affectation of humane wisdom. . . ." He denied the possibility of attaining certainty of knowledge through any human endeavor and lamented the fact that the press continued to publish books of "controverted matter."[32]

On this foundation Bampfield proposed to construct a new educational system, its key principle being that "Scripture-knowledge . . . is the sublimest Reason, and the best Learning; the shining emanations of Holy Writ are clearly visible to scriptural Eyes in this age of Light. . . ." Students should be taught nothing contradictory to Scripture. Traditional philosophy was especially dangerous to young scholars according to Bampfield because it awed them with the appearance of authority. Studies must be tailored to the particular abilities of students, thus providing better trained persons for positions in the church and the state. Education must not be monopolized by the few who thrived, as Winstanley likewise charged, on "their rich Trade of over-reaching sophistry. . . ." To implement the spread of knowledge, Bampfield urged the appointment of lecturers in every county to teach biblical subjects in English. This, he believed, "would make popular Judgements, and common Auditors great proficients in Arts, and progressors in Sciences. . . ."[33]

With respect to particular academic subjects, Bampfield argued that all the treasures of knowledge may be found in Scripture, many of whose mysteries are beyond the reach and the rules of philosophy

---

[32]Bampfield, כל־תושיה. ΠΑΓΓΝΩΣΙΑ ΠΑΝΤΕΧΝΙΑ ΠΑΝΣΟΦΙΑ. *All in One* ([London], 1677) 1-2, 6, 18.

[33]Ibid., 4, 8-9 (quoted). For Winstanley's views on education see Richard L. Greaves, "Gerrard Winstanley and Educational Reform in Puritan England," *British Journal of Educational Studies* 17 (June 1969): 166-76.

or traditional learning. The comprehensiveness of biblical knowledge embraces everything from science to music, from geometry to religion; but the highest science is practical Christianity, that is, experimental religion. Because the ultimate aim of education is religious in nature, a greater knowledge of the natural order enables the godly to experience fuller fellowship with God. Such knowledge, however, cannot be acquired unless it is sought in a biblical way. "The vain affectation of Humane Wisdom, which doth thrust upon the credulity of so many a Doctrine of probabilities (concerning the works of Creation and Natural Things) from Anti-Christian and unscriptural Philosophy, but is not according to Christ, and to his Word, is such a deceitful way of false reasoning, as makes a prey of Souls, and is carefully to be avoided, and is but falsly named Science."[34]

Bampfield's educational scheme is rigorously contained within biblical limits. All definitions or descriptions, for example, must be "rectified" by biblical language. Only through Scripture can a full discovery of natural history be made, for in his judgment, the Bible refers to nature as it truly is rather than as it appears to be. The biblical account of creation, for instance, is literally true and must not be interpreted allegorically, philosophically, or mystically. Moreover, only in Scripture can one attain a true understanding of man, which Bampfield calls "*Adam*-Art, or Man Science." The Bible also is the fullest herbal, replete with knowledge about the use of herbs for both eating and healing. Because Scripture is the controlling element in education, Bampfield called for all books, including those in geography as well as philosophy, to be brought into conformity with biblical perceptions. Even maps and globes must be redrawn to harmonize with scriptural geography. When Shem went east, Bampfield argued, he settled America; hence, Asia and America can be "at most but disjoyned by some great River or narrow Channel of the Ocean," and not a large sea between northeastern Asia and northwestern America.[35]

One of the fundamental principles of Bampfield's educational program was that all children study Hebrew, which he deemed the original language. Each country, he proposed, must prepare a biblical

---

[34]Bampfield, *All in One*, 12, 19-41, 45-49, 52 (quoted), 53-57.

[35]Ibid., 10, 42 (quoted), 49-52, 62-65, 106-13, 127-35, 152 (quoted).

lexicon in its native tongue to explain the true meaning of all Hebrew words and phrases relating to the arts and sciences. These words and phrases would be compiled by each profession, so that the best scholars could then gather from Scripture "not only general Rules, but particular Directions . . . [as] a complete Summary, and an exact Directory in that Art and Science." The concern to base scholarship on the Bible was closely associated with Bampfield's concept of the primary goal of learning—the endeavor "to furnish a renewed Understanding, and to advance sanctified Reason, and to raise discerning Grace, for the promoting of the Honour of the LORD, and the holiness and happiness of Souls. . . ." The key to successful learning, he argued, was the assistance of the Holy Spirit so that simple believers, so enlightened into biblical knowledge, could learn more useful things about the natural world in a single year than an unenlightened student could in seven years of traditional academic study.[36]

Bampfield's biblical orientation led him to condemn several common practices, including the traditional interest in astrology, which he judged a black art. He also deplored the use of pagan names for days and months. The proper biblical names for the days of the week in his estimation were "first," "second," "third," and so forth. With respect to months he urged that the nomenclature be altered to "the Head-Moon, or one, or First Moon," and so forth.[37]

Much of *All in One* was devoted to a detailed exposition of the daily works of creation. Bampfield reserved the seventh day for the sequel to *All in One*, which he entitled היום השביעי השבת ΣABBA-TIKH 'HMÉPA . . . *Septima Dies, Dies Desiderabilis, Sabbatum Jehovae. The Seventh-Day-Sabbath the Desirable-Day . . . The Second Part* ([London], 1677). At the outset of this work Bampfield observed that he had experienced a spiritual vision of the natural world, which he wanted others to share, hence he had written *All in One.* Now he wanted to recount his vision of heaven. Just as he was "passing into a Sabbath-enjoyment," however, the Saturday sabbath became controversial, and he bemoaned that he had become a center of debate.[38]

---

[36]Ibid., 9-10, 12.

[37]Ibid., 99-103, 113-26.

[38]Bampfield, היום השביעי השבת ΣABBATIKH 'HMÉPA. . . . *The Seventh-Day Sabbath the Desirable-Day* ([London], 1677) 2-3.

The Seventh-Day-Sabbath develops the themes of Bampfield's 1672 letter to William Benn, buttressing the case for a Saturday sabbath with extensive biblical citations. Bampfield blamed university education for most of the alleged errors regarding the sabbath. Echoing a theme of *All in One*, he asked rhetorically, "How many Millions have been seduced by the *Aristotelian* way of self ratiocination . . . ?" To understand the sabbath properly, he averred, one must approach Scripture with the aid of the Holy Spirit.[39]

The most striking aspect of *The Seventh-Day-Sabbath* is Bampfield's somewhat unorthodox treatment of the covenants. Unlike traditional English Protestant theologians of the period, he rejected the idea that there had ever been a covenant of works in which salvation was possible without divine grace on God's part and justifying faith on man's. Yet he insisted, like many covenant theologians, that the covenant of grace was first made with Noah and then renewed with Abraham. Like strict Calvinists such as John Owen and Thomas Goodwin, Bampfield stressed the promissory nature of the covenant of grace, which he defined as "the LORD'S free promising of Life, of Wisdom, of Righteousness, of Sanctification, of Redemption, of all good things to his people. . . ."[40]

For Bampfield the Old and the New Testaments represented two dispensations of the covenant of grace. All promises of the covenant of grace are the same in both dispensations. The only fundamental difference between the two is that "in the last days, there will be a more clear discovery of this gracious Covenant: a more glorious way of dispensing; a more thorough inabling to the keeping of it." In the new dispensation, unlike the old, the covenant will not be broken. Bampfield also made a distinction between the "superadded" ceremonies of the old dispensation, which belonged to the church of the Israelites, and the more spiritual gospel dispensation. He insisted,

---

[39] Ibid., 52.

[40] Ibid., 92-108 (quote on 94). In his autobiography Bampfield describes the covenant relationship between a believer and his God as a spiritual espousal. *A Name*, 33-34. For strict Calvinist views on the covenant see Richard L. Greaves, *John Bunyan* (Abingdon, 1969) ch. 4; Greaves, ed., *The Miscellaneous Works of John Bunyan* 2 (Oxford, 1976): xxi-xxxii. Professor Michael McGiffert is currently preparing a history of covenant thought.

however, that this distinction did not alter the applicability of the Ten Commandments to both dispensations.[41]

For Bampfield the Ten Commandments were "an absolute and perfect Rule of Life, comprehending all duties whatsoever. . . ." The Mosaic law in general is in fact the covenant of grace embellished with "the Law of Types and of Figures. . . ." This use of typology was fairly common among Bampfield's contemporaries. Like them he argued that these types or figures were "Seals of the assurance of Christ's coming in the fulness of time" to fulfill his promises to the godly. For example, the sacrificial blood of animals in the Old Testament was a type of Christ's blood in the New. The types not only foreshadowed the fulfillment of promises in the new dispensation, but served as a commentary on the entire covenant of grace.[42]

In Bampfield's judgment, the proper observance of the sabbath must be understood in the context of the covenant of grace. Although he accepted Christ as the antitype, he averred that Christ did not abolish the Saturday sabbath but preserved it. The seventh-day sabbath must be observed because "the whole of the Christian Religion for Doctrines, Graces, Duties, Priviledges, and such like parts of that Religion, is one and the same under both the Old and New Testament." He argued, in fact, that the Saturday sabbath is significant precisely because it is a sign to mankind that the privileges of the covenant are the same under both dispensations, old and new. Assertion of a Sunday sabbath, in Bampfield's judgment, undercut the basic continuity of the covenant of grace and was therefore contrary to Scripture.[43]

---

[41]Bampfield, *Seventh-Day Sabbath*, 99, 100 (quoted), 112-13.

[42]Ibid., 96 (quoted), 98, 113 (quoted), 116 (quoted). For the use of typology in this period see Greaves, ed., *The Miscellaneous Works of John Bunyan*, 8 (Oxford, 1979): xliii-1; Joseph A. Galdon, *Typology and Seventeenth-Century Literature* (Paris, 1975); Ursula Brumm, *American Thought and Religious Typology* (New Brunswick NJ, 1970) ch. 4; Sacvan Bercovitch, *Typology and Early American Literature* ([Amherst], 1972) 3-160.

[43]Bampfield, *Seventh-Day Sabbath*, 101 (quoted), 108, 117. In 1681 Edward Pearse attacked advocates of the Saturday sabbath as "the Judaizing Seventh-day-Sabbath Sect. . . ." *The Conformists Plea for the Nonconformists* (London, 1681) 31.

During the storm of concern that swept England with the news of the Popish Plot, Bampfield became associated with a prophetess named Elizabeth Hooker. At her behest he sent a warning from her to the king, announcing that "the Land doth tremble, it is broken, it shaketh: the right Way, and proper Method to heal its Breaches is plain and evident." Charles, she said, had seen the Lord's hand at work in the unfolding of the plot, and now he must declare to the next session of Parliament that he is resolved "to set up the Laws of Christ in the Scriptures of Truth, as the one, and the only Rule of . . . Government. . . ." Only then, she promised, would the king's name be recorded in the *English Chronicle* "with a Crown Royal upon it. . . ." According to Bampfield the same woman had submitted comparable admonitions to the king and to the Lord Mayor of London on the occasion of a comet sighting. Bampfield does not indicate whether he forwarded this warning to the recipients as well, but the link to Hooker indicates that Bampfield was as prone as most other religious persons in his day to see the working of providence in spectacular events, and to use such occurrences to advance his own views. [44]

By 1681 Bampfield claimed to have established churches in two or three counties, though he did not identify them. Certainly his own congregation had grown to the point that it had to find larger accommodations. Three possibilities were considered: Great Moorfields (where Bampfield had moved from Bethnal Green), Spitalfields (to which he would shortly move), and Pinners' Hall in Broad Street. Because there was division within the congregation over the most suitable site, after considerable debate it was determined to leave the choice to God, as revealed by the use of lots. A fourth lot was included, "we not being [willing] to limit the All-free Agent. . . ." But the lot that was drawn was for Pinners' Hall—the Old Glass House—which Thomas Hollis rented to Bampfield's church as well as to Richard Wavel's open-communion congregation. As a result of the move, Bampfield claimed that his church became especially successful in attracting young men and women to its meetings. [45]

---

[44]Bampfield, *A Name*, 26.

[45]Ibid., 21; Bampfield, *The Lords Free Prisoner*, 1-2 (quoted); W. T. Whitley, *The Baptists of London* (London, [1928]) 117. During Bampfield's pastorate, his congregation never owned its own building.

The move to Pinners' Hall was part of a major new program launched by Bampfield about this time. Another facet of the program was his plan to organize an association of sabbatarian churches that would meet annually (or more frequently) and would include churches in New England and the Netherlands. He sent an invitation to the London sabbatarian churches announcing his plan about 1681. Such an association, he promised, would promote unity and lead to "a more exact bringing of all the Ordinances of Christ's New Spiritual House to the Laws and Orders of the Prophetical Pattern according to Scripture-Institution. . . ." The association would be concerned with training ministers, sponsoring a more accurate translation of the Bible, improving the education of children in families and schools, relieving the poor, and studying means to convert the Jews. Nothing seems to have come of Bampfield's proposal to found an association of sabbatarian Baptists.[46]

Bampfield's planned association was intended in part to oversee the education of ministers. In this connection he also urged the founding of a school to train "the Sons of the Prophets" in "useful Arts and Sciences in the Book of Books. . . ." Details of this plan were set forth in בית חכמות. *The House of Wisdom* (London, 1681). There are schools and villages, he complained, to train young people in classical philosophy and pagan religion, but none where the Bible is the only authority, Christ the principal subject of study, and Hebrew "the Tongue of Tongues." Arts and sciences should be included in the curriculum only if they are lawful (according to Scripture) and useful "in Church, or in State, in Commonwealth, City, or Family." Bampfield's proposed academy would be staffed only by instructors who were humble and godly, whereas students must be sober, modest, meek, studious, healthy, teachable, and already "well educated." In their hands would be placed the "Scripture weapons" of learning. Each student moreover would learn according to his abilities and inclination. Among the subjects included in the curriculum were religion, law, medicine, such sciences as astronomy and geography, geometry, husbandry, seamanship, the military arts, crafts, and training for the magistracy and ministry. Bampfield would not, however, allow the

[46]Bampfield, *A Name*, 25.

study of cabalistic Pythagorean numerical systems. His interest in the academy extended even to the students' diet, which he carefully pre-scribed: "Proper wholsom diet, as it doth make much for the health of young Students, so also doth it much promote their Learning. . . ."[47]

Bampfield's attack on the traditional, classical curriculum was a reflection of the earlier calls for reform by such critics as John Web-ster, William Dell, William Sprigge, and Gerrard Winstanley.[48] Bampfield's program was unique, however, in the role it gave to He-brew. Once again he argued that it was the mother tongue, with which all other languages were in harmony, and "which cognation of Consanguinity, and Affinity should be preserved and propagated." The best way to do this, he suggested, was for the Christian princes of the world to make the Hebrew alphabet the universal character. Even better, Hebrew should become the universal language. "Were this once thoroughly effected, it would carry the Self Evidence of its own Excellency and commendations along with it, before the Eyes of every Spiritual discerner." The benefits, he averred, would be enor-mous in matters as diverse as diplomatic relations, the conduct of war, maritime matters, and trade.[49]

Bampfield's enthusiasm for Hebrew led him in *The House of Wisdom* to call for its use in working with the deaf. Because the Hebrew letters were divinely created and were thus more natural than the letters of other alphabets, they could be more easily learned "by the motion of the Mouth and Tongue, and other Organs . . .; by observation whereof, those who are born Deaf, may yet be taught the knowledge, and use of Speaking, Writing, and Printing."[50] Others in Stuart En-gland were also interested in helping the deaf, but Bampfield appears to have been unique in approaching this problem through the use of Hebrew. John Bulmer, for example, examined the possibilities of com-municating with the hands and in 1654 called for the founding of an

---

[47]Ibid., 20 (quoted); Bampfield, בית חכמות. *The House of Wisdom* (London, 1681) 7, 9.

[48]Richard L. Greaves, *The Puritan Revolution and Educational Thought: Background for Reform* (New Brunswick NJ, 1969) passim.

[49]Bampfield, *House of Wisdom*, 7-8.

[50]Ibid., 8.

academy to aid the mute. Francis Bacon, John Wilkins, and John Wallis were also concerned with the deaf.[51]

Like the proposed association of sabbatarian churches, Bampfield's vision of a major academy oriented toward the study of Hebrew and with a curriculum governed by Scripture never materialized. Perhaps sensing the difficulties that lay ahead, he offered in a postscript to *The House of Wisdom* to establish his own small academy, where boys could learn free of charge. Classes would be held three times a week, the first to explain the meaning and significance of Hebrew words and phrases, the second to study biblically oriented philosophy, and the third to discuss "Textual Sermons: To which may be added a Specimen or Example of some particular Art or Science."[52]

Bampfield's autobiography appeared in the same year as *The House of Wisdom*. Its bizarre title reflects both his devotion to Hebrew and his apocalyptic expectations: שם אחר. *A Name, an After-one; or* Ὄνομα Καῷὸν. *A Name, a New One, in the Later-Day-Glory: or, an Historical Declaration of the Life of Shem Acher* (London, 1681). The book was written, he said, to refute various accusations made against him, particularly in the preceding six years. Among them, of course, was the charge that he had married beneath his social station. In a particularly revealing statement, he depicted himself as a special servant of God, especially in the previous two decades. Writing as usual in the third person, he "declared against his being staked or teddered down to any one Place or People, he being Christ's Servant, at his Masters dispose, to do what publick work his LORD shall call him unto. . . ." Most Nonconformists, he asserted, erroneously repudiated the legitimacy of this concept of an extraordinary calling. Appealing to history, he buttressed his argument with the contention that "the Lord has not been wanting to his Church and People . . . as to his gifting, gracing, calling and sending extraordinary Officers . . . when the ordinary ones have been corrupted or negligent, ignorant or unfaithful, or upon

---

[51] J. R. Knowlson, "The Idea of Gesture as a Universal Language in the XVIIth and XVIIIth Centuries," *Journal of the History of Ideas* 26 (1965): 500-501; W. H. G. Armytage, *Four Hundred Years of English Education* (Cambridge, 1964) 19-20.

[52] Bampfield, *House of Wisdom*, 26.

some other special Occasions." Bampfield, of course, envisaged his own ministry in precisely these extraordinary terms.[53]

In his autobiography Bampfield made a special point of discussing the conversion of the Jews, an event fraught with millennial significance for Protestants of this era. Referring to 1 Corinthians 1:22, Bampfield contended that God would send a special prophet, bearing a sign, as his special agent to convert the Jews. He had met, he claimed, five or six persons who falsely claimed that role. The revival of the Saturday sabbath, however, was in itself a millennial sign, for it "doth make way for the later-day-Glory-Conversions, and Ingatherings of the Outcasts of Israel. . . ."[54]

One further topic deserves mention concerning the autobiography. Bampfield opposed the prevailing system of land tenure based on the principle of primogeniture, though he stopped short of calling for gavelkind as William Sprigge did. A system of primogeniture, he argued, not only had ruined many ancient and honorable families but was unscriptural. Referring to Deuteronomy 21:17, he advocated instead that an estate be divided equally, but with the eldest receiving a double portion. He made it clear, however, that he was personally satisfied with his own annuity of £80 p.a. because it left him free of material concerns.[55]

Bampfield's last difficulties with the law commenced on 17 February 1682 as he was preaching in Pinners' Hall on Isaiah 63:4. Accompanied by halberd-bearing men, a constable stopped the service and ordered Bampfield from the pulpit. To this Bampfield retorted that he was discharging his office in the name of the King of kings. Unimpressed, the constable warned that he possessed a warrant from the Lord Mayor, but Bampfield shot back that his own warrant was from Christ, the Lord Maximus. As he resumed preaching with the

---

[53]Bampfield, A Name, 11, 19 (quoted), 20.

[54]Ibid., 18. For interest in the conversion of the Jews, see Capp, FMM, 190-91, 213-14; Peter Toon, ed., Puritans, the Millennium and the Future of Israel: Puritan Eschatology 1600 to 1660 (Cambridge, 1970), especially ch. 7.

[55]Bampfield, A Name, 23. For Sprigge's view of gavelkind, see Richard L. Greaves, "William Sprigg and the Cromwellian Revolution," Huntington Library Quarterly 34 (February 1971): 103.

warning that God would "pull down his Enemies," Bampfield was
hauled from the pulpit and taken with about six others to appear
before the Lord Mayor, who accused them of preparing the ground for
popery. To this Bampfield responded that his zeal against Catholicism
exceeded the Lord Mayor's, and that the open doors of his church
were proof against surreptitious plotting. Charged with breaking the
king's law by worshiping on Saturday, Bampfield claimed adherence to
Christ's law. After the mayor imposed fines of £10 on some of them,
they were released. The congregation was again forced out of Pinners'
Hall the same afternoon, but they finished their service in Bampfield's
house.[56]

One week later, on 24 February, a constable again disrupted
Bampfield's service. As he was taken through the streets, Bampfield
proclaimed to any who would listen that he suffered for the cause of
Christ. "I went along with my Bible, as one of the old Martyrs . . .,"
but some called him a Christian Jew while others threw stones and
dirt on the constable. In Bampfield's appearance before the sessions,
one of the three magistrates denounced his praying as mere prating.
The following day Bampfield appeared before the bar for an examination and was remitted to Newgate prison.[57]

On 17 March Bampfield was taken to the Old Bailey for his trial.
Insisting that Christ was his judge, he refused to take the oaths of supremacy and allegiance tendered by the recorder. He claimed he had
been unlawfully deprived of his liberty, and would do nothing until
this issue was settled. Nor was he persuaded by the recorder's argument that he had taken oaths while at Oxford. Even as the oaths were
read to him, he refused to remove his gloves or place his hand on the
Bible. At the judge's direction, the jury found him guilty. On the 28th
he and the others tried with him were sentenced: "That they were out
of the protection of the king's majesty; that all their goods and chat-
tels were forfeited; and they were to remain in jail during their lives,
or during the king's pleasure." As Bampfield tried to speak, there were
cries of "away with them." He managed, however, to call out that "the

---

[56]Bampfield, *The Lords Free Prisoner*, 2.

[57]Ibid., 3-4; Calamy, *Non. Mem.*, 2: 152.

righteous Lord loveth righteousness: the Lord be judge in this case."
Bampfield was returned to Newgate.[58]

On 18 April Bampfield was taken again to the Old Bailey, where
the oaths were tendered to him as well as to the General Baptist John
Griffith. Lord Chief Justice Saunders presided with three other
judges, the Lord Mayor, the recorder, and several aldermen present.
After Bampfield refused to take the oaths, Griffith stood before the
bench and was informed that taking the oaths would bind him to conform to the requirements of the Church of England, including the use
of the Book of Common Prayer. Neither man could accept such conditions, and both were therefore returned to Newgate.[59]

Bampfield and Griffith took up their pens to record their legal
misfortunes, the latter in *The Case of Mr. John Griffith* (1683). Bampfield
told his story in *A Just Appeal from Lower Courts on Earth to the Highest Court
in Heaven* (London, 1683), *A Continuation of a Former Just Appeal* (London,
1683), and *The Lords Free Prisoner* (London, 1683), the latter contained
in a single printer's sheet. He was very careful to explain that his refusal to take the oaths was not a repudiation of the monarchy. In
prison with Bampfield and Griffith were Thomas Delaune, the Baptist
schoolmaster and printer; Hercules Collins, pastor of the Baptist
church at Wapping; Jeremiah Marsden, a Congregationalist minister
and suspected plotter; and Laurence Wise, a Baptist minister with ties
to John Simpson at Allhallows the Great in 1661.[60]

While in prison Bampfield became associated with a circle of radical printers. On 30 May 1683 Roger L'Estrange informed Secretary
of State Sir Leoline Jenkins that he had interrogated the printer Brad-
dyl. From him L'Estrange learned that Francis Smith, who published
various works of John Bunyan, had sent a letter to Bampfield in
Newgate, which the latter was to forward to a Mr. Culliford. Bampfield gave it to Jane Curtis, wife of the printer Langley Curtis. She had
been arrested early that year on suspicion of publishing the treasonous

---

[58]Bampfield, *The Lords Free Prisoner*, 4; Calamy, *Non. Mem.*, 2: 152 (quoted);
Crosby, 2: 360.

[59]Crosby, 2: 361; *Calamy Revised*, 559.

[60]Bampfield, *A Just Appeal*, 8; Whitley, *A History of British Baptists*, 147; Wilson,
HADC, 2: 178; *Calamy Revised*, *s.vv.*

book, *The Perplext Prince*, by one S. T. The contents of the letter had a suspicious ring: "Have a good heart, for, when the business comes [to] a push, I'll do you no hurt." The allusion may be to Culliford's suspected association with the publication of Robert Ferguson's *The Second Part of No Protestant Plot* (London, 1682) and Edward Whitaker's *The Ignoramus Justices* (London, 1681). Culliford, in fact, was tried at the Old Bailey in the summer of 1683 for publishing these works. Found guilty, he was sentenced to the pillory, fined two hundred marks, and imprisoned, and the books were burned by the common hangman. It is impossible to ascertain whether Bampfield was any more than an interested outside party to this underground network of radical printers.[61]

The rigors of prison life were too much for the elderly Bampfield, who died in Newgate on 16 February 1684. His final illness may have started during his last trial when he was kept ten hours in the bail dock, "a cold and loathsome place." He was buried on the 19th in a new graveyard purchased by Baptists in Glasshouse Yard, near Aldersgate Street. According to Anthony Wood his corpse was accompanied by "a very great company of factious and schismatical people. . . ." This is corroborated by the account of a contemporary newsletter, which sarcastically observed that Bampfield "had as many followers to his grave as ever he had to his conventicle, the whole rabble of Dissenters being mustered together to show yet their readiness to appear upon the least occasion." The divisiveness occasioned in life by Bampfield's espousal of sabbatarian views was overlooked by many who saw him in death as another illustrious martyr of Stuart persecution. An elegy was published by Joseph Stennet, and Hercules Collins wrote *Counsel for the Living Occasioned from the Dead* (1684), a discourse on the deaths of Bampfield and Jeremiah Marsden.[62]

Bampfield's final work, published in the year of his death, was מקרא קדוש. *The Holy Scripture* (London, 1684). In it he returned to the exegetical treatment of Old Testament passages in the manner of his 1677 tomes. The proper study of Hebrew remained, in his judgment,

[61]*CSPD, 1683 (I)*, 278; *CSPD, 1683 (II)*, 352, 374.

[62]*Ath. Oxon.*, 4: 128; Crosby, 2: 361; Calamy, *Non. Mem.*, 2: 153; HMC 36, *Ormonde*, n.s., 7: 198 (quoted); *BQ*, 1: 254.

the key to understanding and the proper basis for an educational system. Consequently he renewed his call for the founding of "Schools of learning, and Houses of Wisdom . . ., especially for the education of the Sons of the Prophets, where skill in the Hebrew-Tongue, and in Scripture-arts and Sciences, are principally to be taught. . . ."[63]

In his will Bampfield bequeathed his books and manuscripts to his congregation "to be employed & Used (as far as might be) to promote a Design of Training up Young Men in Scripture-Learning," particularly as outlined in *The House of Wisdom*. There was, however, a proviso permitting his widow Damaris to sell the books if necessary for her maintenance. The issue was not immediately settled because the congregation disbanded at Bampfield's death. Not until 14 October 1686 was it reconstituted by Edward Stennet of Wallingford (1686-1689) and his son Joseph, who was pastor of the church from 1689 to 1713. In December 1686 representatives of the church spoke with Mrs. Bampfield about the will and also sought the advice of her brother-in-law, Thomas Bampfield. The latter had been converted to Seventh-Day Baptist views by Francis, and was now sympathetic to his deceased brother's wishes. In fact he defended sabbatarian tenets in *An Enquiry Whether the Lord Jesus Christ Made the World* (1692) and *A Reply to Doctor Wallis* (1693). Jehudah Stennet, Edward's son, assured him that the congregation did not intend "to Leave any thing in their Power, Unattempted, to accomplish the Will of their late Honored Friend." Thomas Bampfield informed them of his desire to see Francis's library divided among the three sabbatarian Baptist congregations of Stennet, John Belcher, Jr., and Henry Soursby, contingent only upon these churches providing Damaris Bampfield with a life annuity. Belcher's and Soursby's churches, however, refused.[64]

When Damaris Bampfield died on 6 February 1694, she bequeathed what was left of her husband's library to Stennet's church, to be used as his will had instructed. The books, however, were in the control of Joseph Davis, one of Mrs. Bampfield's executors, who refused to give them to Stennet's congregation for fear that they would

---

[63]Bampfield, מקרא קדוש. *The Holy Scripture* (London, 1684) preface.

[64]"Bampfield's Plan for an Educated Ministry," *TBHS* 3: 10-11, 15; Wilson, *HADC*, 2: 585.

not use the library to establish an academy. Davis's co-executor, Belcher, Jr., was in Rhode Island, hence Stennet's group decided to postpone action until his return. The fate of Bampfield's library had not been resolved by the time the church minutes ceased in January 1703.[65]

Bampfield was, in Anthony Wood's judgment, "strangely fickle and unsteady in his judgment" because he left the Church of England to become a Presbyterian and ultimately a Seventh Day Baptist. There was, however, nothing unusual about such a spiritual pilgrimage in seventeenth-century England. The quest for spiritual certainty and inner peace led many through a series of religious groups until they found their elusive goals. In Bampfield's case that quest culminated only when he established his own sabbatarian congregation, and even then he died well before realizing his dream of a new school devoted to the discovery of all knowledge in the pages of Scripture.[66]

Wood castigates Bampfield for being "so enthusiastical and cant-ing that he did almost craze and distract many of his disciples by his amazing and frightful discourses." But this spiritual enthusiasm was again typical of that which pervaded the radical religious groups. In intensity and appeal it was akin to that manifested by the Quakers, but it was different too in that it was closely controlled by the boundaries of Scripture. Bampfield's spiritual zeal was perhaps most closely akin to that of persons such as John Bunyan, who proclaimed that "I preached what I felt, what I smartingly did feel, even that under which my poor Soul did groan and tremble to astonishment."[67]

It was this strongly personal and experiential appeal that made Bunyan and Bampfield attractive to those who found little solace in the more formal, liturgical worship of the established church. It was also this pronounced sense of spiritual piety that made Bampfield and his fellow Nonconformists the heirs of a broad Puritan tradition that extended back into the Elizabethan period. Differences in polity and

---

[65]*TBHS*, 3: 15-17.

[66]*Ath. Oxon.*, 4: 126.

[67]Ibid., 4: 126-27; Bunyan, *Grace Abounding*, §276 (p. 85).

worship notwithstanding, they shared an intensely personal piety and a commitment to practical Christianity that are the hallmarks of the Puritan tradition.

Index

London, 193-94; ideas on educational reform, 194-97, 201-203, 207-208; views on the covenants, 198-99; and the Popish Plot, 200; moves congregation to Pinners' Hall, 200-201; plan for association of sabbatarian churches, 201; views on land tenure, 204; death, 207; library, 208-209
Bampfield, John, 180, 182
Bampfield, Joseph, 60
Bampfield, Sir Coplestone, 180
Bampfield, Thomas, 180, 187-88, 194, 208
Banger, Josiah, 187-88
Baptism, Conflict about, 22, 125, 135-36, 157, 169-72
Baptists, 1, 4, 6, 21-22, 29, 36, 41-42, 88, 91, 94-95, 99, 101-102, 106, 108-109, 118, 121-22, 128, 138, 147, 164, 167-72, 206-207; General, 1, 4, 29, 110, 146, 157, 161, 172, 206; Open-Communion, 4, 102-103, 110, 139, 200; Particular, 4, 101-103, 107, 110, 119, 129, chap. 5 passim, 157, 165, 172; Seventh-Day, 4, chap. 7 passim
Barber, Edward, 29
Barebones, Praisegod, 116, 122
Barker, Matthew, 86, 89-90, 95
Barnard, John, 45
Barrington, Sir Thomas, 16
Bates, William, 42, 51n, 52-53, 56, 59, 60n, 91-92, 94, 95n, 96
Baxter, Richard, 7, 9-10, 37, 42, 45-56, 59, 81, 88, 90, 93-95, 136, 147, 157, 170-72, 182, 185, 188, 191
Beale, Bartholomew, 37, 126
Beaumont, Richard, 137
Bedfordshire: Bedford, 93, 127
Beke, Richard, 40
Belcher, John, 193
Belcher, John, Jr., 208-209
Bell, Richard, 161
Belvoir Castle, 159
Benn, William, 190-91, 198
Bennet, Sir Henry, 90, 153, 168

Berkshire, 194; Maidenhead, 85; Wallingford, 208, 194
Berry, James, 119
Best, Paul, 148
Biddle, John, 36, 135, 148
Birch, Thomas, 52
Blague, Thomas, 161
Blake, Robert, 110
Blinman, Richard, 170-71
Blood, Thomas, 150, 167-68, 173
Bolton, Robert, 25
Bolton, Samuel, 29, 34-35
Bond, John, 33
Book of Common Prayer, 11, 15, 45-46, 48-51, 56, 70, 101, 108, 181, 186, 206
Book of Sports, 11, 23, 64, 68
Booth, Sir George, 41
Boys, Edward (of Betteshanger), 67, 69
Boys, Edward (of Bonnington), 64
Boys, Sir Edward, 69-70, 74
Boys, John, 67, 69n
Bradford, John, 16
Bradshaw, Richard, 112
Bragge, Robert, 105, 129n
Brent, Sir Nathaniel, 64
Bridge, William, 17, 80-81, 87, 97, 131
Bristol, 84, 136, 138, 154, 161
Broghill, Lord, 120
Brooke, Joshua, 191
Brooks, Thomas, 86, 89-91, 97, 102, 106
Broughton, Sir Edward, 130
Buckingham, Duke of, see Villiers, George
Buckinghamshire, 5, 134; Newport Pagnell, 136-37
Bulmer, John, 202
Bunce, James, 41
Bunyan, John, 7, 93, 96, 100, 127, 148, 157-58, 169-70, 183-84, 189, 206, 209
Burgess, Anthony, 24, 28
Burgess, Cornelius, 12, 14, 17, 21, 27, 32, 101
Burgess, Daniel, 95n

MUP *Saints and Rebels*

Designed by Alesa Jones

Composition by MUP Composition Department

Production specifications:
    text paper—60 pound Warren's Olde Style
    endpapers—Gainsboro Silver Text
    cover—(on .088 boards) Holliston Roxite Crown Linen #13449
    dust jacket—Gainsboro Silver Text, printed PMS 539

Printing (offset lithography) by Omnipress of Macon, Inc., Macon, Georgia

Binding by John H. Dekker and Sons, Inc., Grand Rapids, Michigan